I0812730

IMAGES
of America

TECUMSEH
THE FIRST CENTURY

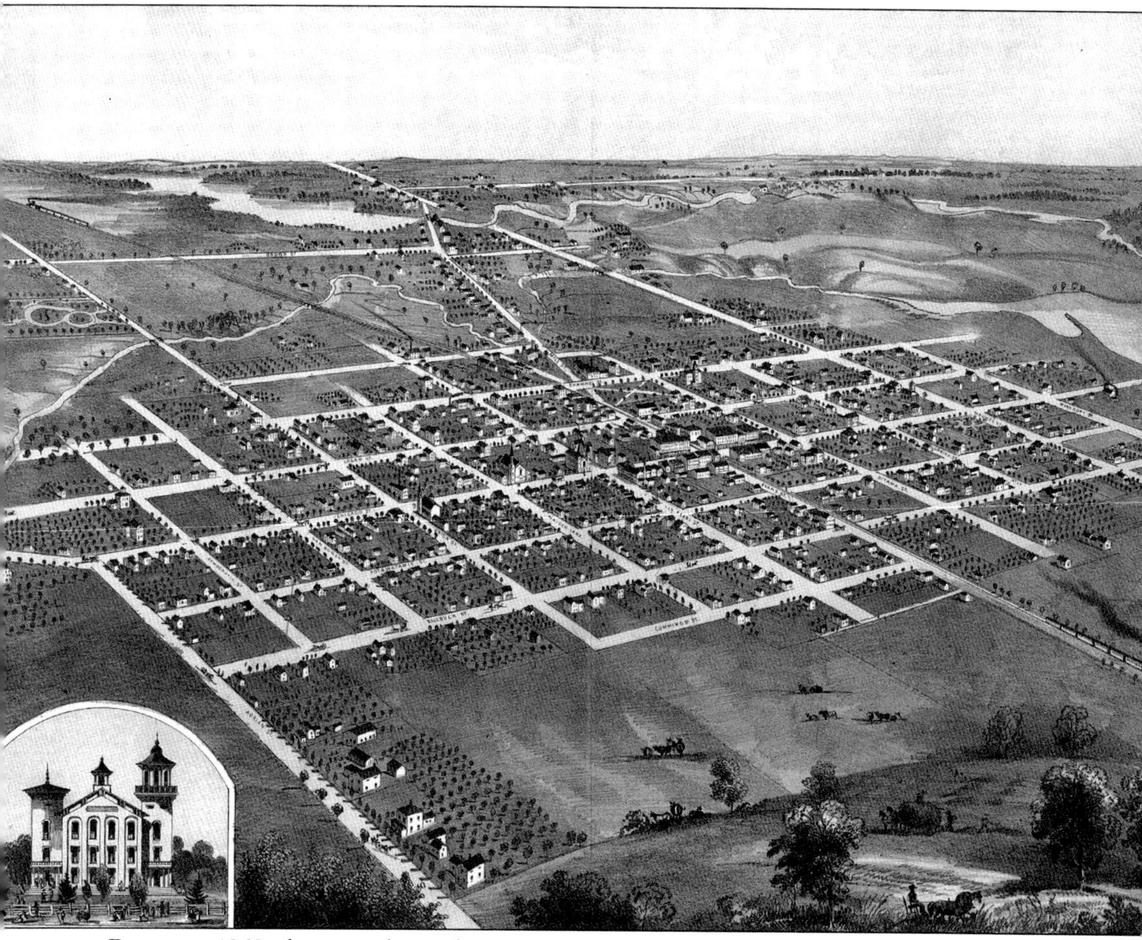

Drawn in 1868, this map shows the source of Tecumseh's early prosperity and power; the Red Mill Pond north of town and the Globe Mill Pond east of town. The inset drawing is of the Union School, which was built in 1856 but was still a source of civic pride 12 years hence.

On the cover: This early car show, "the M. F. Bonisteel Display of International Auto Buggies," which was quite likely composed of only the four cars shown here, was held in Tecumseh on June 15, 1909, with L. C. Hayden as agent. This was a very early automobile show, as Henry Ford had produced his first car in 1903 and cars were not mass-produced until 1913. (Photograph courtesy of the Tecumseh Historical Society Museum.)

IMAGES
of America

TECUMSEH
THE FIRST CENTURY

Kern Kuipers and Amanda Payeur

ARCADIA
PUBLISHING

ISBN 978-0-7385-4077-1

Published by Arcadia Publishing
Charleston, South Carolina

Printed in the United States of America

Library of Congress Catalog Card Number: 2006924920

For all general information contact Arcadia Publishing at:
Telephone 843-853-2070
Fax 843-853-0044
E-mail sales@arcadiapublishing.com
For customer service and orders:
Toll-Free 1-888-313-2665

Visit us on the Internet at www.arcadiapublishing.com

Contents

Acknowledgments

We would like to thank the Tecumseh Area Historical Society, the Lenawee County Historical Society, and the staff of the Tecumseh Public Library for all of their assistance, patience, time, talents, and resources, without which this book would not have been possible. Thank you to Christopher Grove for his friendship and his portable scanner. We would also like to offer our special thanks and appreciation to George Elliott for sharing his personal and family stories, Ed Hodges for sharing his knowledge of Tecumseh history and especially his knowledge of the railroads, and Robert Elliott for his assistance in finding hidden resources and his expertise in matters of military history. Last on our list but first in our appreciation is Ashley E. Chase, whose seemingly limitless resources and historical background have made this book infinitely better then it would have been without his kind and patient assistance.

I would like to thank my wife Diane, who has allowed this book to consume all of my free time over the last few months. Without her understanding and willingness to personally take over or allow me to put off those many things that a partner must do to maintain a home and a family, I could not have taken on, much less have completed, a project of this magnitude.

—Kern Kuipers

I would like to thank my family, especially my mom, whose love and support meant the world to me during this project. Mom, thank you for all your insights and allowing me to talk to you nonstop about this project and not hang up the phone! I would also like to thank Kern's wife Diane for always making sure I was fed!

—Amanda Payeur

Photographs used in this book were collected from the following sources: the Tecumseh Area Historical Society and Museum; the Tecumseh District Library, Clara Waldron Room; the Lenawee County Historical Museum; the private collection of Ashley E. Chase; and the Tecumseh Herald.

INTRODUCTION

Tecumseh's first settlers arrived as a group in March 1824. Although there are no momentous events to speak of, the town's past is fascinating in its depiction of "normal" people overcoming adversity with hard work and perseverance to establish a community in the wilderness and nurture its growth and progress. Tecumseh's early claim to fame was perhaps that it was the first settlement in the interior of Michigan intended from its very conception to become a town.

Musgrove Evans and Gen. Joseph Brown founded the town in partnership with Austin Wing. Evans had made a trip west from New York State to look for work as a surveyor. In Monroe, he met with a relative by marriage, Austin Wing, who suggested that Evans not just look for work, but consider creating a new settlement. These three men (Evans, Wing, and Brown) formed the Tecumseh Company for the express purpose of holding properties that they would purchase in order to establish a new town. Evans, being a surveyor, laid out the first streets of the town early on, and the company donated land for public use even before there was a public to use it. Evans and Brown also knew that the government intended to open a military road across Michigan from Detroit to Chicago and would capitalize on its construction and traffic—Evans by being its surveyor and Brown by starting an inn and coach line to promote travel along the new road. It did not hurt that their cousin Jacob Brown was army chief of staff in Washington, D.C., and would have some control over the awarding of contracts for the building of this road.

Some of Tecumseh's very early past still exists, including the location of the original mill pond created by the first settlers, the layout and names of many of Tecumseh's streets, the house of Musgrove Evans, and present day roads that still run along the Sauk Trail, the Native American path that became the military road to Chicago.

The land was excellent, although not always easy to clear for farming. The town prospered as agricultural goods were sold in the east and an ever-increasing number of settlers headed west. Many beautiful homes and buildings were built with this new wealth, and most of them remain to this day. Agriculture has always played an important part in the economics of Tecumseh, readily available and easily harnessed water from the River Raisin was used to power sawmills, gristmills, woolen mills, furniture factories, and paper mills; thus manufacturing also played a prominent part in the diverse economy of the town. Even tourism—if you can call it that—played a roll in the early history of Tecumseh, as people traveling west from the ports of Monroe and Detroit passed through the town and found it convenient to stay over for the night or even a few days.

Those who came to stay would build a town that was quaint yet hardworking, esthetically pleasing, yet rugged enough that most of its historic structures have withstood the elements as well as the pressures of change and progress. Today Tecumseh remains strongly tied to its history but not inhibited by it. It has found a way to embrace technology, growth, and progress without sacrificing small town atmosphere, historic neighborhoods, and friendly folks who are always willing to stop and chat.

One

Downtown Tecumseh

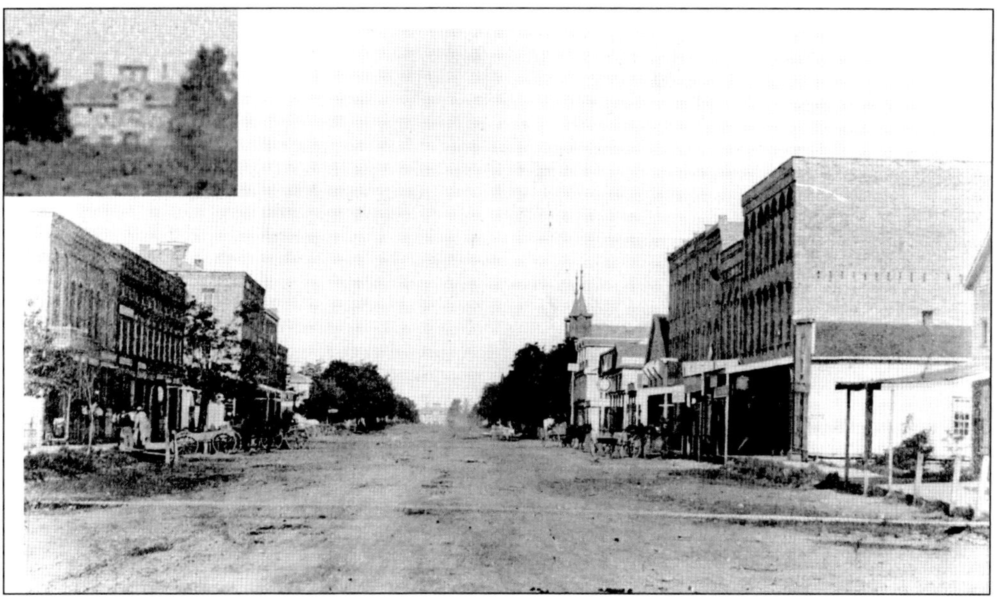

Taken in 1864, this photograph is perhaps the oldest image of downtown Tecumseh. The Snell Mansion House Hotel can be seen on the corner of Chicago Boulevard and what is now Evans Street. The twin steeples of the Methodist church grace the skyline, but the elegant steeple of the Presbyterian church is missing, as it had not yet been built. In the background of the photograph (pictured in the insert), the Stacy Mansion dominates the street west of town.

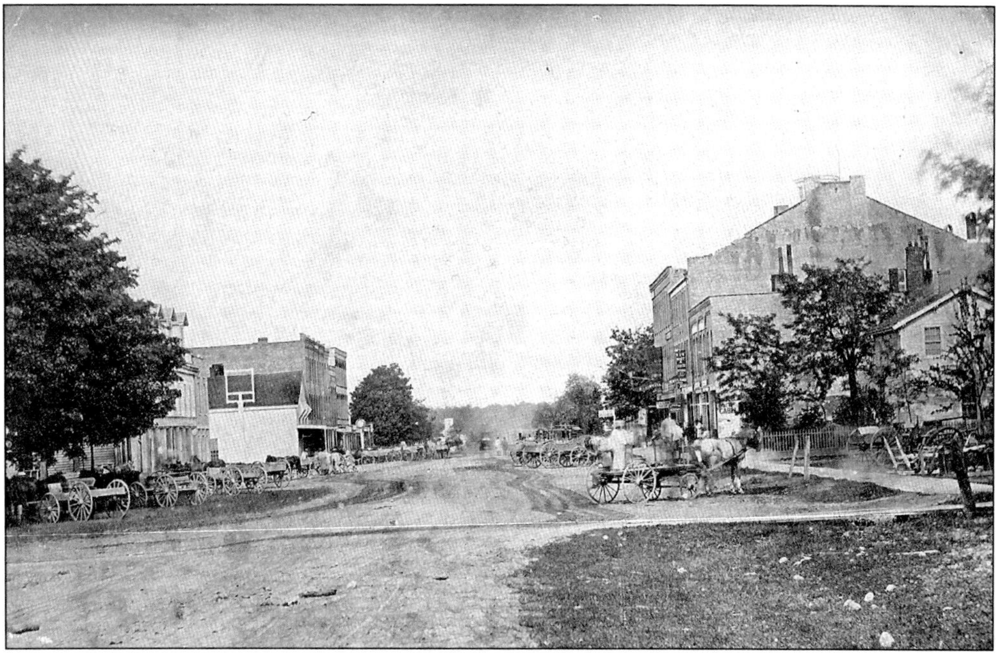

This view of downtown Tecumseh looks east, around 1865. The Union Building, dominating the right (south) side of the street, was the town's first brick block, built in 1849 by C. A. Stacy and Perley Bills. The large boot sign on the Union Building advertises the location of proprietor H. Nyland's shoe store. The house in the right foreground belonged to Eunice Henry, who owned the property and lived there on and off from the 1850s until her death in 1886.

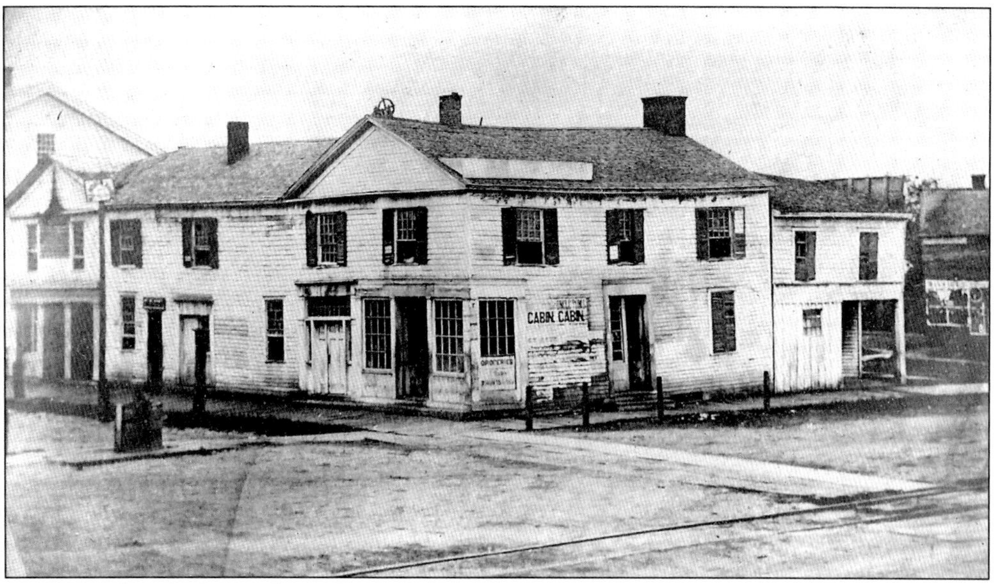

Hiram Snell built the Snell Hotel, photographed here around 1860, and also called the Mansion House Hotel, in 1835 on the northwest corner of Chicago Boulevard and Evans Street. The dark spot directly in front of the building was the Tecumseh community well. In 1865, Snell sold the corner property to the Merchants Association and the building was moved to Logan Street.

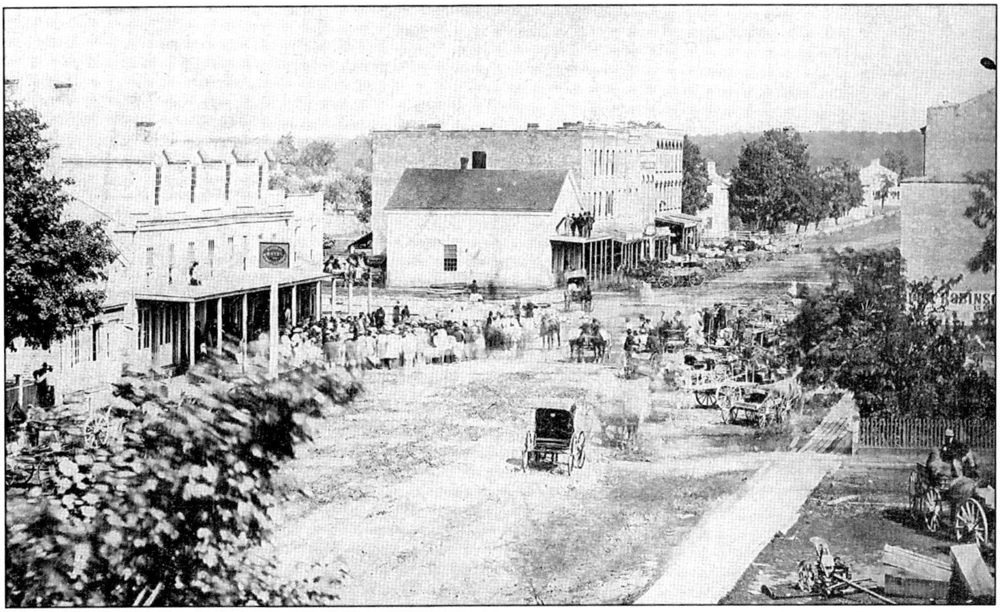

This view of downtown Tecumseh, around 1866, was taken from an upper floor or the roof of the Tecumseh Furnace Foundry. The National Hotel is the large gabled building in the foreground. The Snell Mansion House Hotel is missing, having been moved to make way for the Merchants Block. At the northeast corner of Chicago Boulevard and Ottawa Street, the Musgrove Evans house can be seen in its original location.

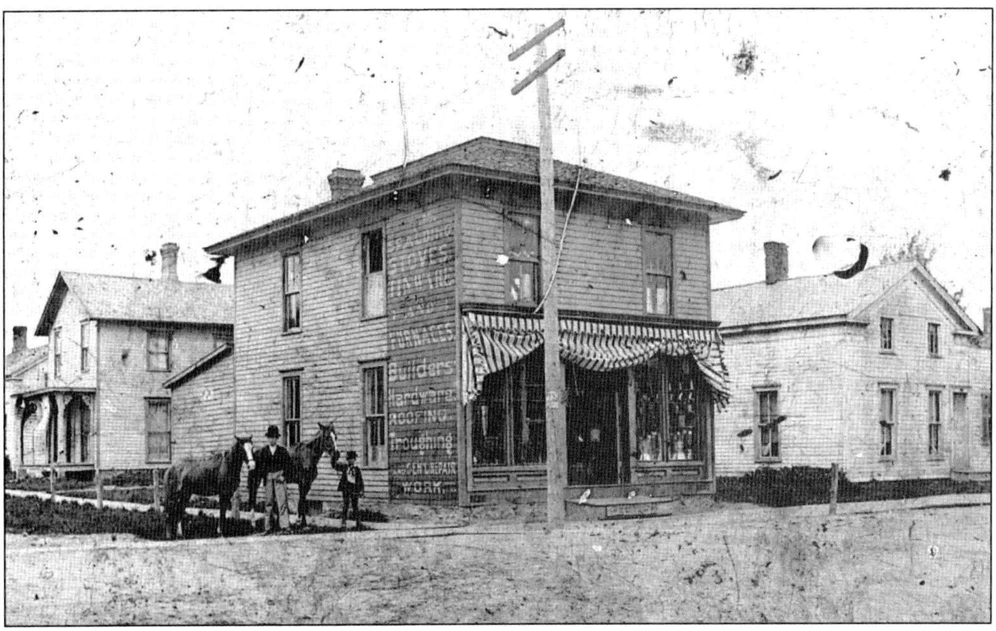

When the Snell Hotel was moved to make room for the Merchants Building, part of it landed here on the northwest corner of Logan and Evans Streets. Some accounts say that other portions of the former Mansion House Hotel were used as parts of houses, perhaps the two in this picture. This was taken some time not long after 1895. The building was then Spalding Hardware. All these buildings would eventually be torn down to make room for a gas station.

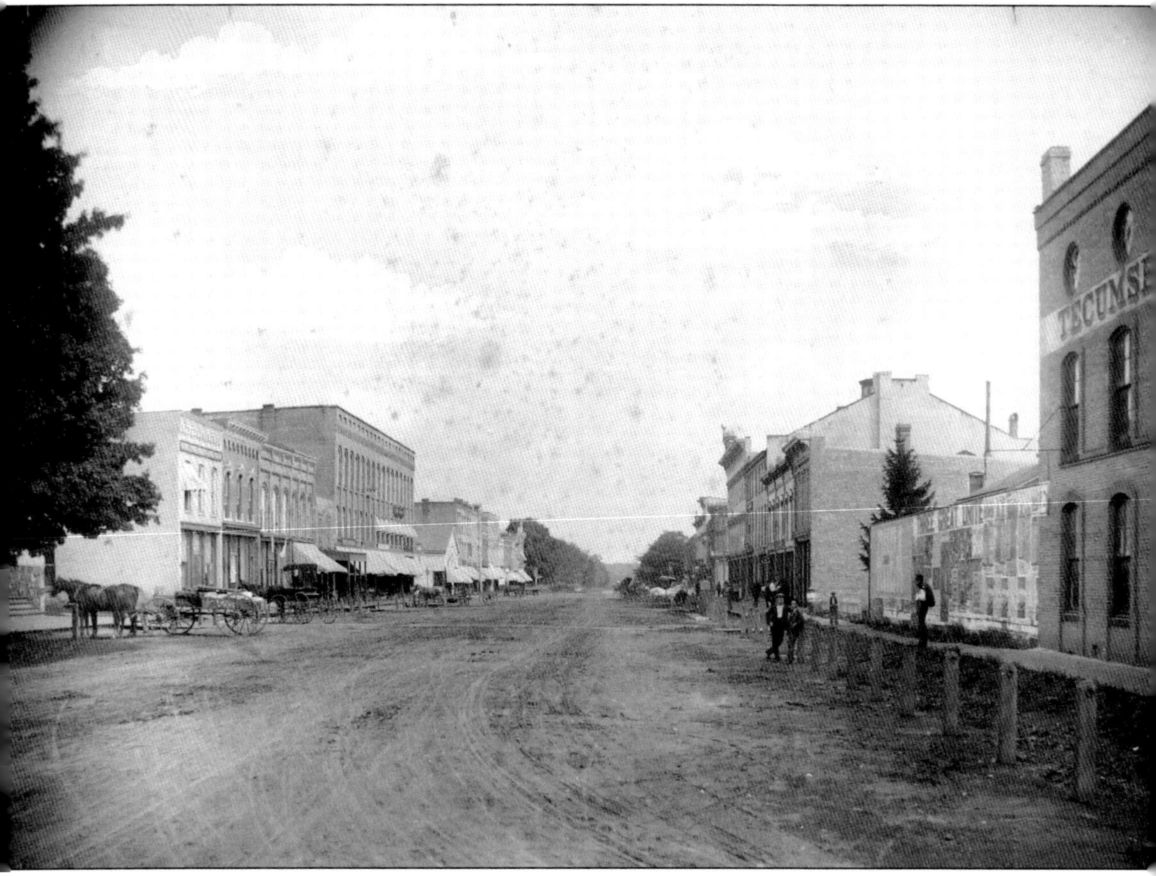

By the time this picture was taken on Sept 4, 1884, downtown was starting to look much as it does today. Alfred James's wood-frame store is still on the corner of Chicago Boulevard and Evans Street, instead of the prominent Masonic temple building. The Merchants Block has been standing for 17 years, and in 1884, the Lilley House Hotel occupied the top two floors of the east side of the building, the decorative cornice and window hoods have been added to the Bidwell Block, and many of the brick storefronts that still grace downtown have been built, including the elegant Mills Block on the northwest corner of Chicago Boulevard and Ottawa Street.

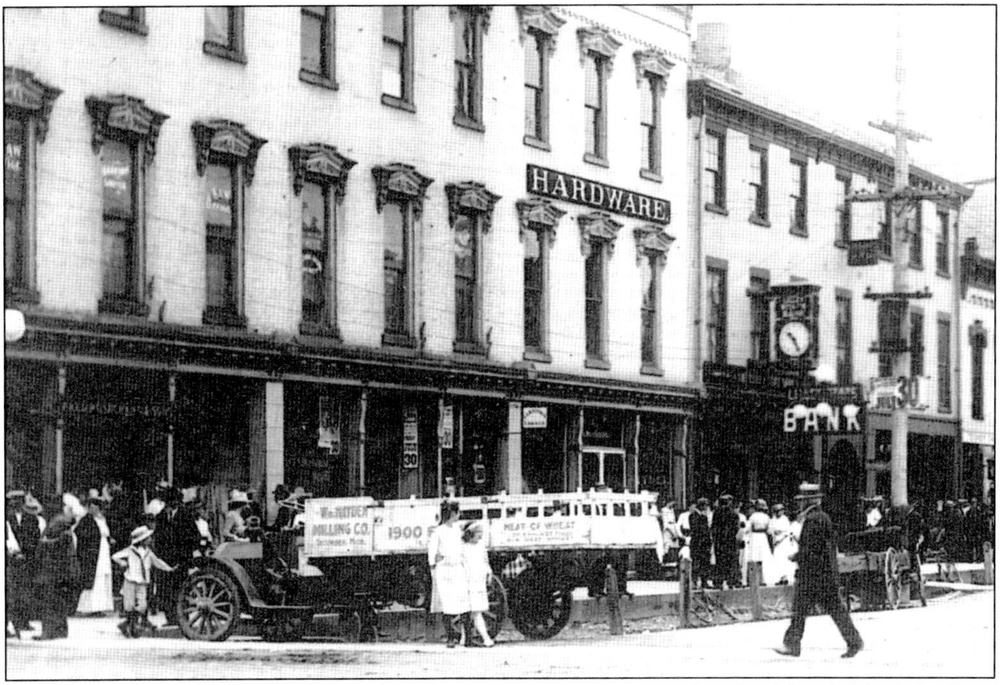

The Bidwell Building, built by Birdsley J. Bidwell in 1852, was the third brick block built in downtown Tecumseh. Bidwell named his new building the Metropolitan Block, but the name never stuck. The decorative cornice and window hoods were not original to the building; however, the cast corner and post decorations were original and made in Tecumseh at the Anderson-Brewer foundry. (Photograph courtesy of Ashley E. Chase.)

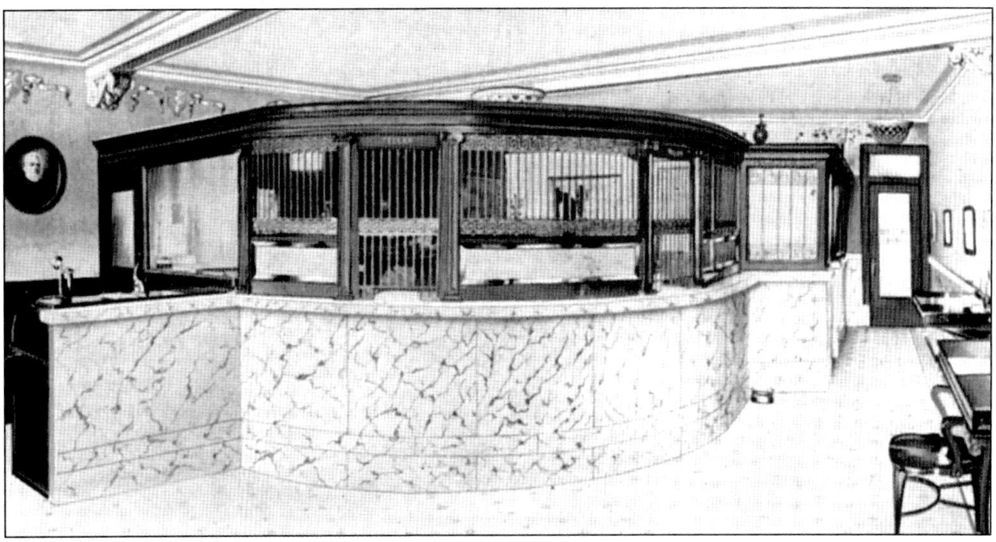

The interior of the Lilley State Bank is shown around 1919. This handsome lobby takes up the entire east half of the Union Block ground floor. In 1931, the Lilley State Bank and the Tecumseh State Savings Bank joined to form the United Savings Bank of Tecumseh, which is still in business today. Even though the bank no longer inhabits the Union Block, this lobby has been beautifully restored, and today, looking much as it did then, it serves as an ice-cream parlor and soda fountain.

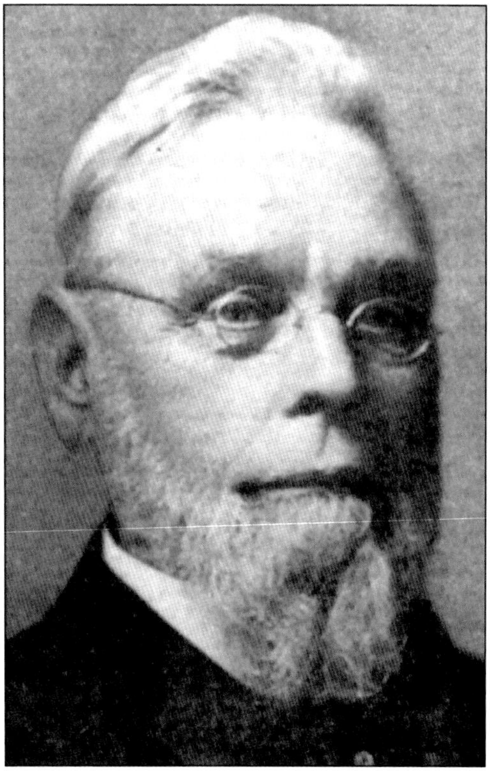

In 1855, at age 32, Lucius Lilley came to Tecumseh having already had a successful career in business. He arrived to take the position of assistant cashier at the Bank of Tecumseh, which eventually failed. Undaunted, Lilley helped found a new bank with Perley Bills that would eventually be called the Lilley State Bank. Lilley had a hand in many other Tecumseh enterprises including a creamery, an electric company, the Lilley House Hotel, and the Tiffany Iron Works to name just a few. (Photograph courtesy of The Tecumseh Herald.)

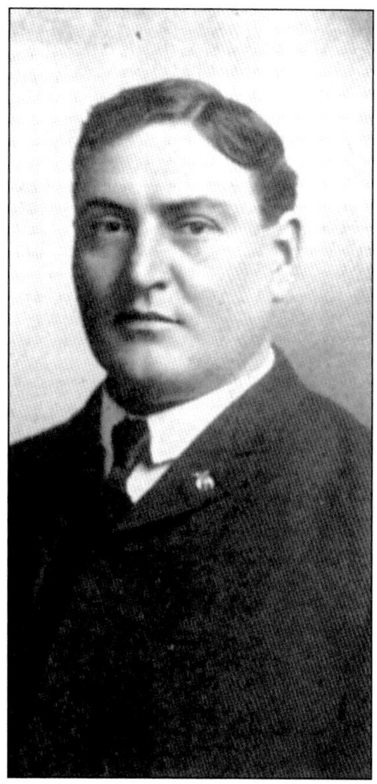

Rudolph "R. A." Heesen is pictured here in 1919, when he was president of the Lilley State Bank. Rudolph was the son of successful retailer and manufacturer George Heesen. He took over the Heesen foundry in 1898, and was village president for two terms in the 1920s. He was among the business consortium that helped establish the first railroad to Tecumseh in 1896, and he and his wife built two beautiful homes that still grace Tecumseh today.

Herbert S. Temple was a cashier of the Lilley State Bank at the time of this photograph in 1919. Herbert graduated from Tecumseh High School, class of 1900. There is no indication that Herbert was any relation to the extremely successful S. W. Temple. Herbert was a thriving businessman in his own right, being a prominent banker and, among other things, one of the owners of the Tecumseh Indians baseball team.

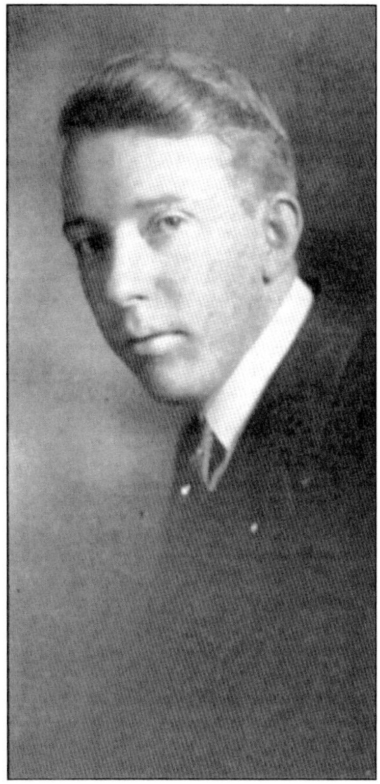

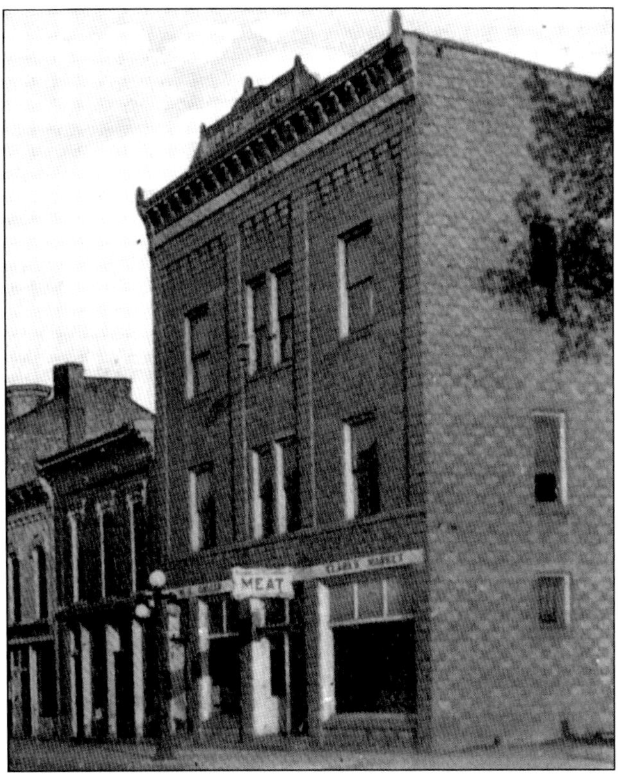

William Witherell built Witherell Hall in 1904. Witherell Hall was not built of brick but of formed concrete blocks, a new technique for downtown Tecumseh. The name "hall" may have come from the fact that one of the upper floors was a dedicated dance hall and the other upper floor was the International Order of Odd Fellows hall. Witherell Hall stood at 132 West Chicago Boulevard until it succumbed to fire in the 1960s.

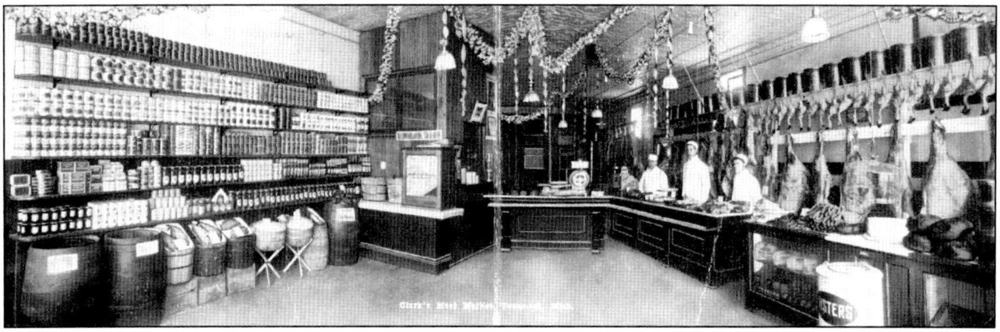

Clark's Meat Market is pictured around 1915. From left to right are Albert Clark, Glen Tansley, and unidentified. For many years, Clark's was in the storefront of Witherell Hall. If the c. 1908 date found on a copy of this photograph is accurate, it would have been taken shortly after they took residence at the Witherell location.

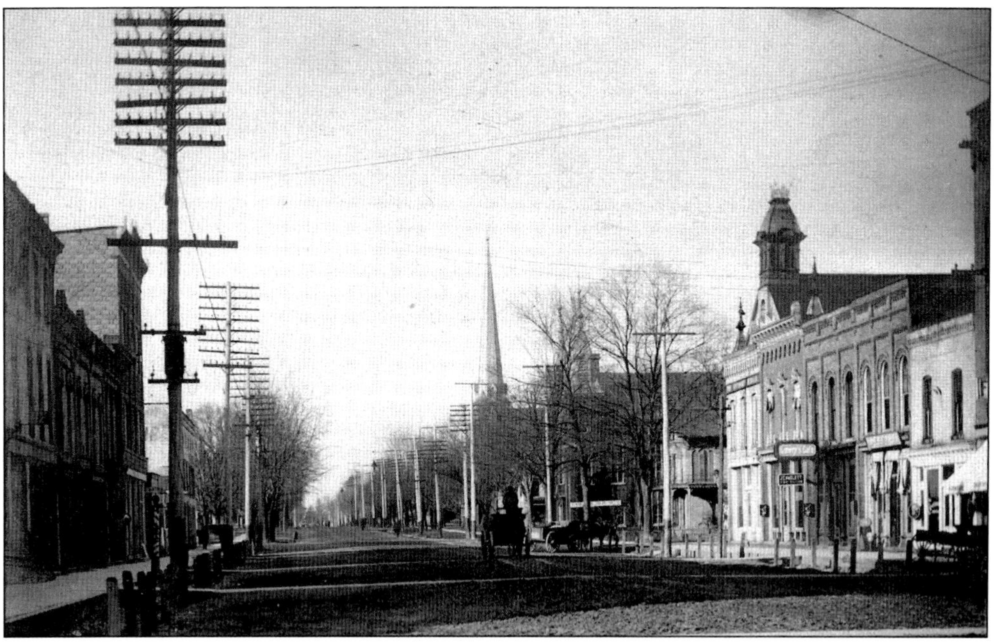

This view looks west down Chicago Boulevard in 1906. Visible are the steeple of the Presbyterian church, the twin bell towers of the Methodist church, and the intricate cupola of the opera house. The elegant house of B. J. Bidwell—by this time the Coller House Hotel—can be seen on the corner of Chicago Boulevard and Pearl Street. It was torn down in 1921. In 1878, Benjamin J. Swan built the white two-story brick building east of the opera house, and in 1882, the Tecumseh Herald moved in. Two storefronts east of the Swan Building, one could get a bite to eat at Lowry's Café. (Photograph courtesy of Lenawee Historical Museum.)

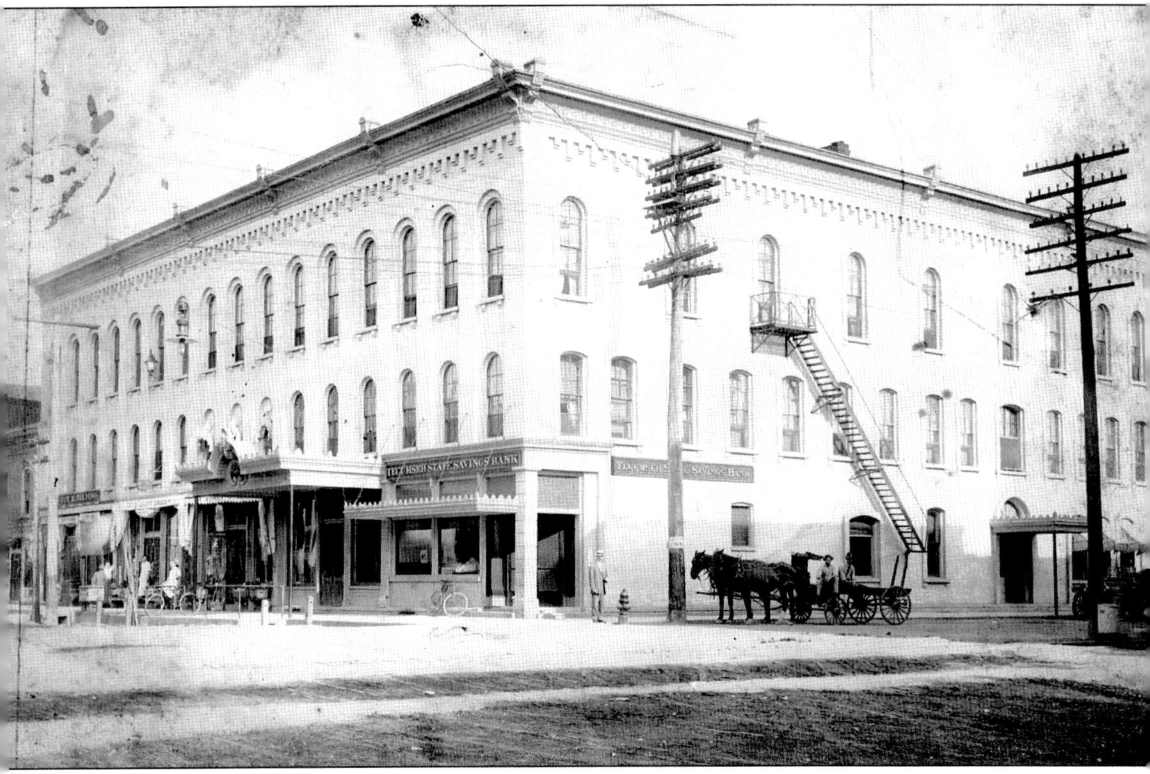

Shown here around 1910, the imposing and elegant Merchants Block was built in 1867 by the Merchants Association, which was comprised of local businessmen B. J. Bidwell, Jarius P. Slayton, and Alfred James—all of whom where already involved in downtown real-estate and retail businesses. The building had a large ballroom on the third floor, hotel rooms on the second, and retail space on the first. In May 1910, the Tecumseh State Savings Bank moved to this location in the Barrett Brothers Hotel Office on the northwest corner of Chicago Boulevard and Evans Street. In a newspaper article of the time they described a new office that boasted marble counters, tile floors, and a ladies parlor with a writing desk and toilet accessories. It also had two safes, one for bank use and one for customer safe-deposit boxes, a service that had not previously been available to Tecumseh residents. However, the Lilley State Bank also offered safe-deposit boxes the same year.

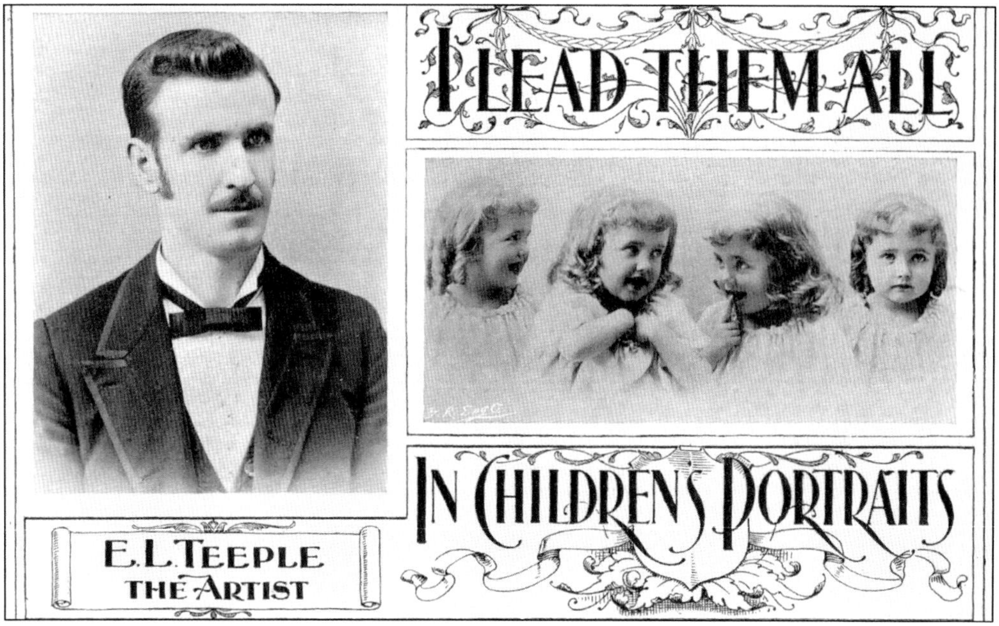

E. L. Teeple had a photography studio on the southwest corner of Evans and Logan Streets (behind the Merchants Block). He was one of many professional photographers that would hang their shingles in Tecumseh, including Cynthia Spofford Bissell, the town's first bride who had returned from adventures in the west to settle again in Tecumseh and become the town's "first business woman" when she set up a professional photography studio. E. L. Teeple will be remembered for supplying all of the photographs for an illustrated booklet about Tecumseh in 1895. Some of those same pictures are reproduced in this book.

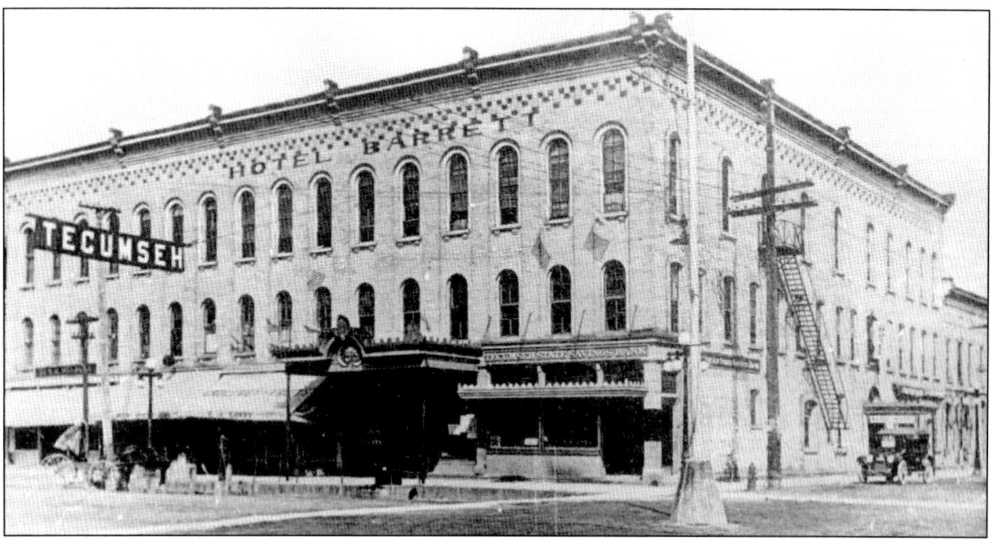

This picture, taken around 1920, shows the Merchants Block housing the Hotel Barrett. At some point around 1900, the Lilley House Hotel had become the Shawnee Hotel. In 1908, the Shawnee was sold to the Barrett brothers, Will and Lavern, and by the 1940s, it was the Hotel Chief. The top two floors of the east half of the building, those which housed the various hotels, were damaged by fire in the 1940s and again in the 1950s, after which the top two floors of the east section of the building were removed.

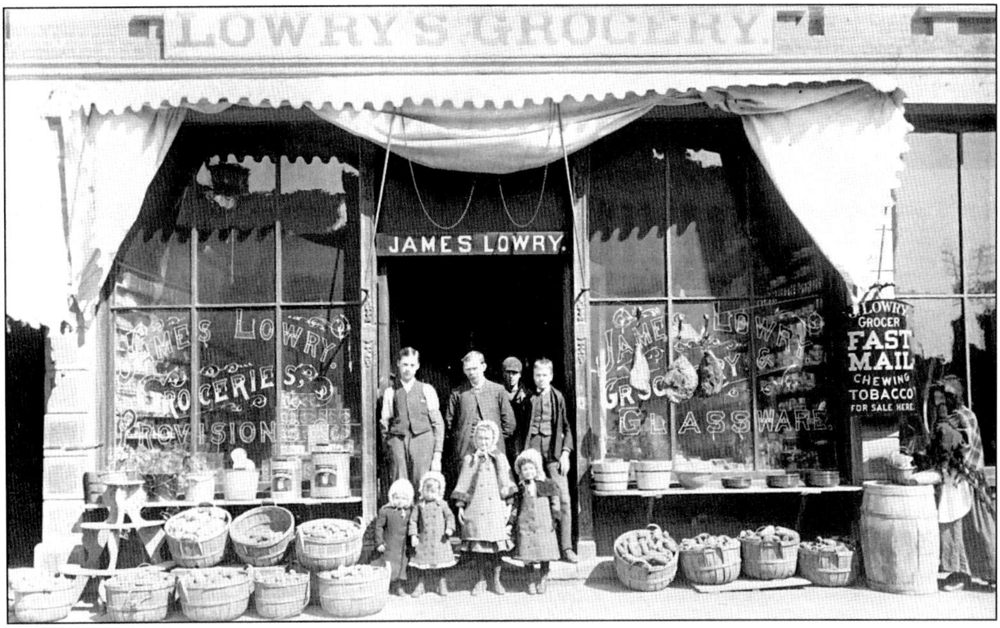

Lowry's Grocery is shown in 1887, ten years after James Lowry first opened the store. Lowry's Grocery eventually occupied a storefront in the Merchants Block directly west of the entrance to the Hotel Barrett. The grocery, one of many located downtown at the time, was still in business 37 years later and can be seen in pictures of the Tecumseh Centennial Parade of 1924. Listed as pictured here, from left to right, are (first row) two unidentified girls, May Lowry Werser, Julia Lowry Temple, and Rosie Young, the lady to the far right; (second row) James Lowry, Will Mobbs, Albery Lowry, and Edwin Lowry.

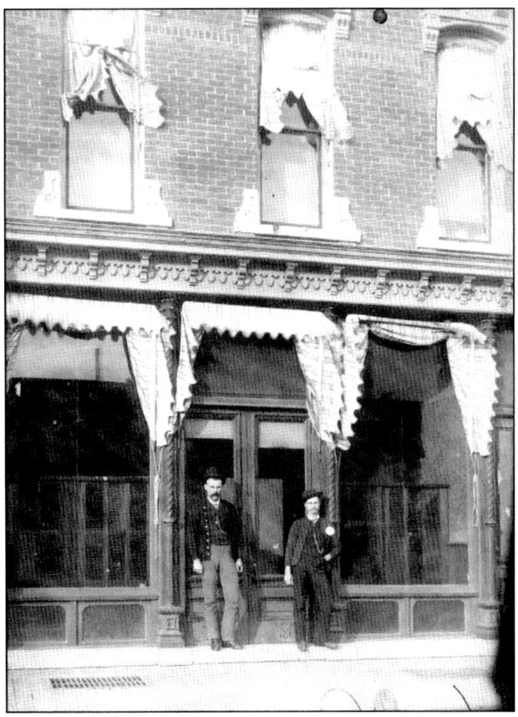

Frederick Kolkloesch and Eugene Service stand in front of what is now 123 West Chicago Boulevard. In 1900, Eugene Service was the proprietor of a saloon at this location. Oddly enough, Frederic Kolkloesch was the proprietor of a saloon just three doors to the east. It appears that being competitors was not a cause for animosity. This building and the wooden building that stood here before it were both known as the Usborne building.

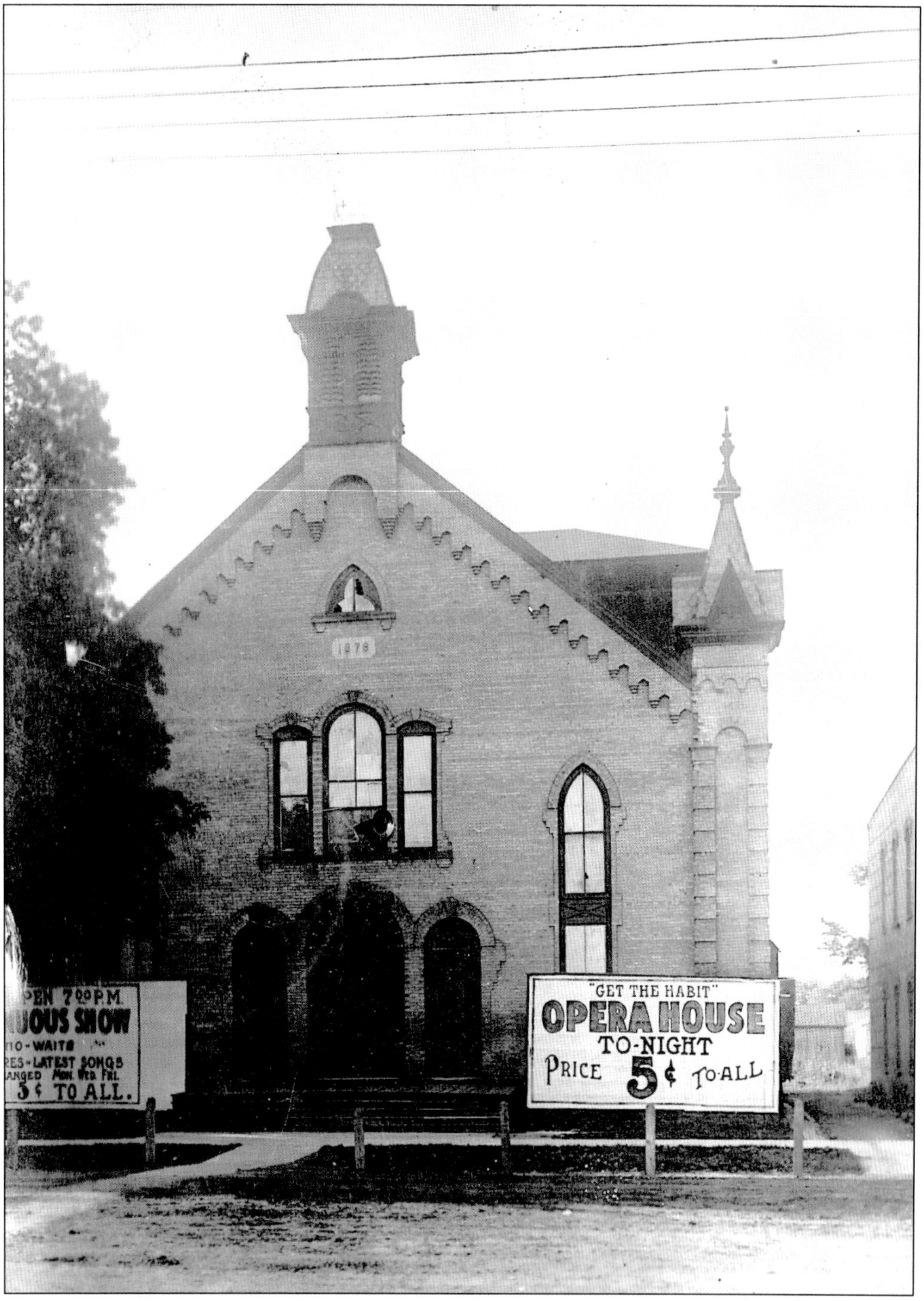

Completed and opened on December 26, 1878, the Tecumseh Opera House, often called Sutton's Opera House, had seating to accommodate 1,000, standing room for an additional 200, and was "lighted with Gas." The opera house got electric lights in 1895. Floyd H. Guy, who added a brick front and made it the Strand Movie Theater, purchased it in 1922. The opera house was torn down in the late 1900s. (Photograph courtesy of Ashley E. Chase.)

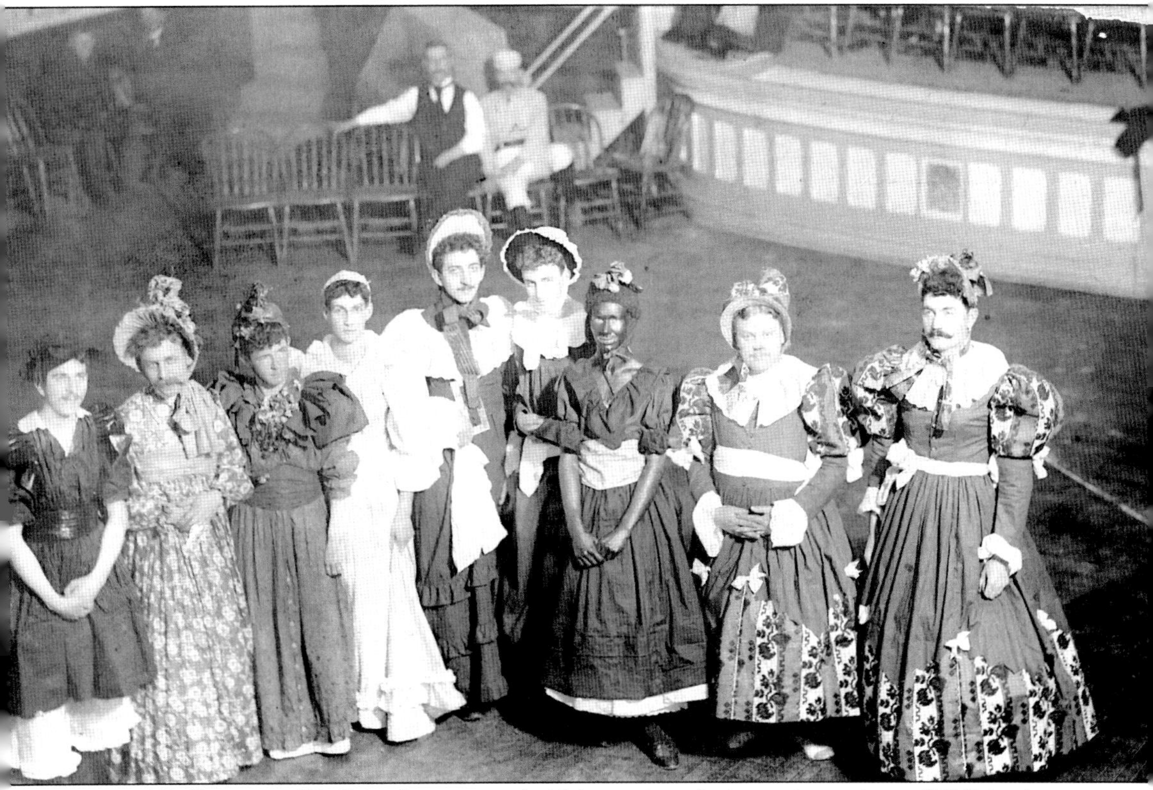

A Grand Ballgame and Ball fund-raiser was held (sometime during or just prior to 1894) in the Tecumseh Opera House to raise money for purchasing an armory for Company C. Just before the ball, an exhibition baseball game was held between the Annie Rooneys and the Ta Ra Boom De Ays. The Annie Rooneys are shown here, wearing their official game uniforms to boot. The Rooneys team roster was Maggie Murphy Ross (catcher), Little Eva Harris (pitcher), Nancy Lee Hosmer (first base), Lydia Pinkham Hayden (second base), Annie Rooney Hayden (third base), Mother Hubbard Garlinghouse (shortstop), Betsy Bobbet Burlinggame (right field), Dr. Mary Walker Bowen (center field), and Annie Laurie Tiffany (left field). A distinguished list of Tecumseh professionals and businessmen, the Rooneys, although quite stylish, lost the game 51 to 48.

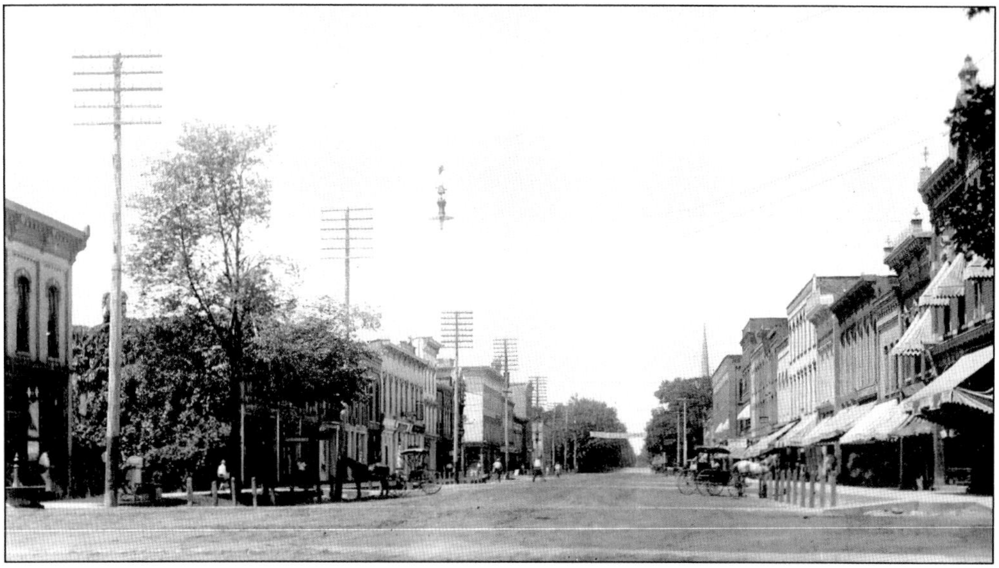

This view of the downtown looks west from Ottawa Street around 1904. The sign hanging across Chicago Boulevard at Pearl Street reads, "BASE BALL TO DAY." The 50-year-old Patterson block, a long two-story, three-storefront brick building can be seen on the south (left) side of the street. It was built around 1850 by Dr. Michael A. Patterson and still stands today. Dr. Patterson came to Tecumseh as a pioneer in 1827, just three years after the town was founded, and practiced medicine until retiring in 1876. (Photograph courtesy of Lenawee Historical Museum.)

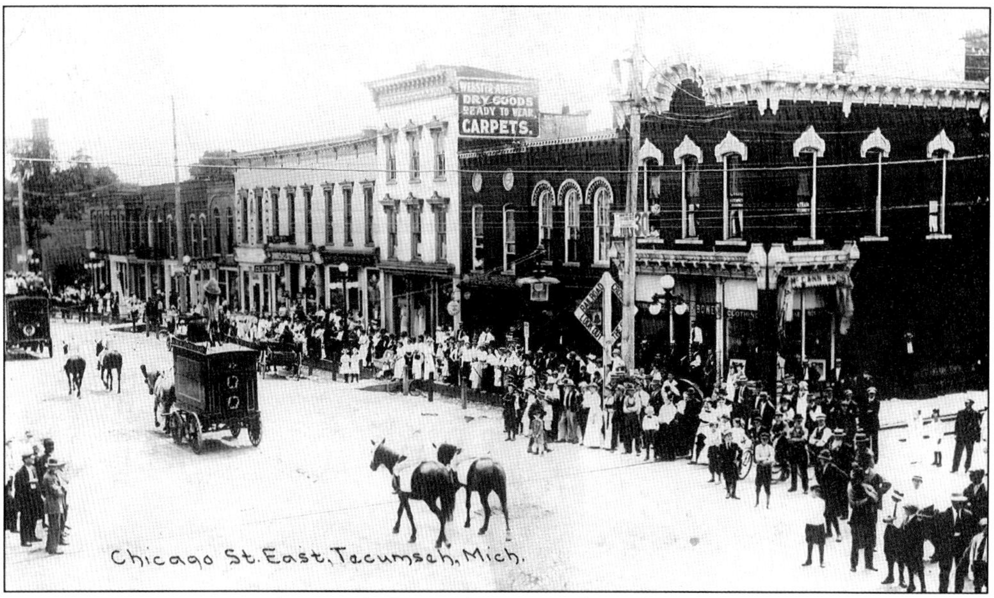

A circus comes to town with a parade down Chicago Boulevard around 1900. Dr. M. A. Patterson developed the majority of the buildings shown here (the southeast section of downtown looking west). The Lilley-Wright building, one exception, is on the corner of Evans Street and Chicago Boulevard. This photograph shows it with its original, striking decorative window hoods. Dr. Patterson built the next building east in 1868 and the next in 1864. The long two-story building was the second brick block downtown, built by Patterson around 1850, and still stands today, as do most of the buildings on this block.

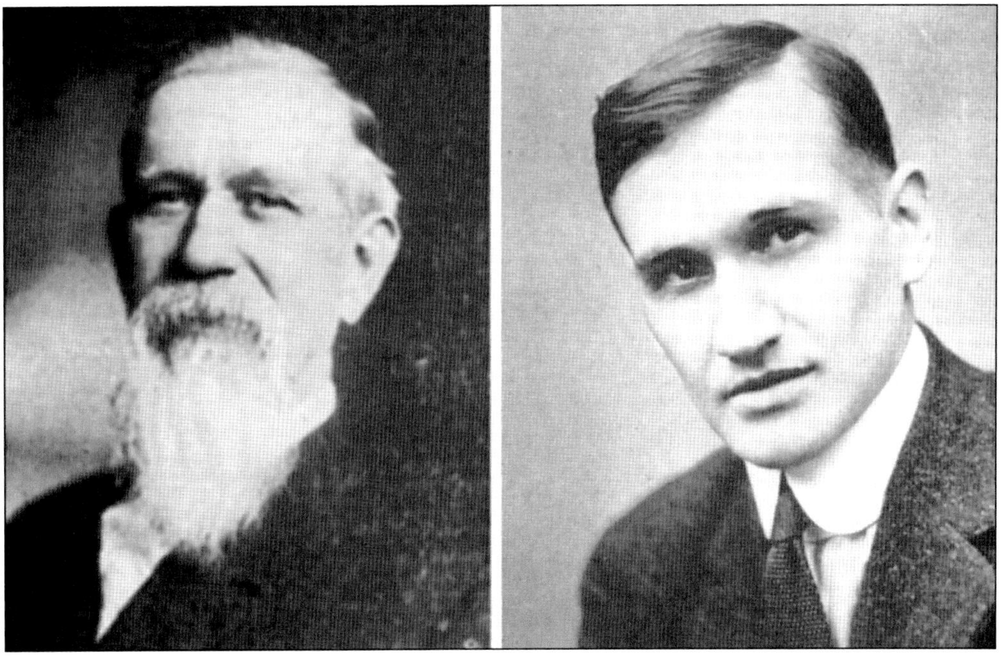

In the 1880s, William Gaston (left) established a meat market at 110 East Chicago Boulevard. Later his younger son John (right) joined the business, and they switched from meat to jewelry. Perhaps not the most predictable change, but one that seems to have worked, as the business lasted well into the next century. For a time, the store also sold railroad tickets to passengers who boarded when the train stopped in the middle of downtown.

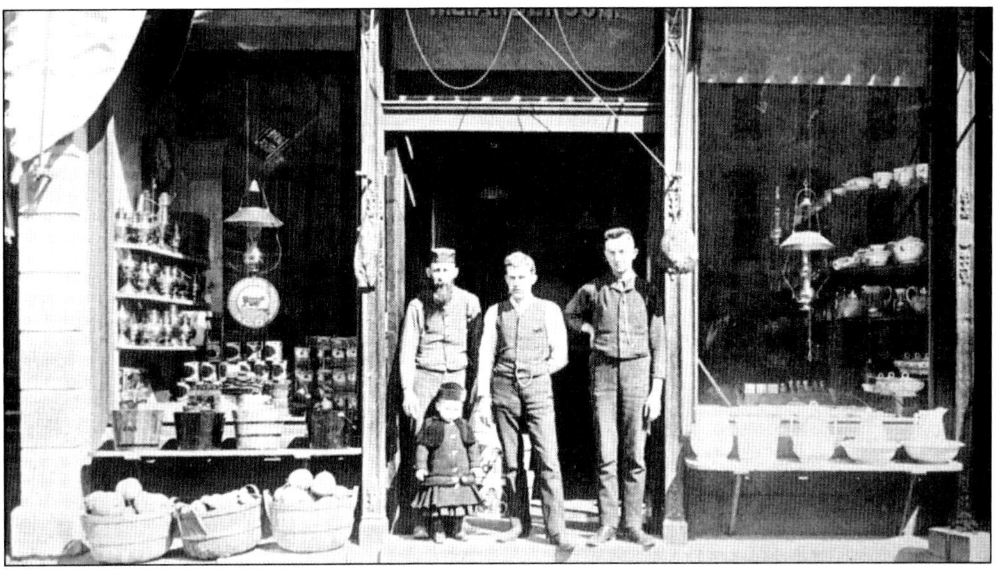

Anderson Dry Goods store (not to be confused with Anderson Grocery) was located on the south side of the street in two storefronts of the Patterson Building. The Andersons had part interest in the Patterson Building, as well as the three-story brick building to the west, which they purchased in 1872. Anderson Dry Goods was so successful in the 1890s that they had their own mail-order business. Unfortunately no date is given for this photograph and no record of the persons pictured.

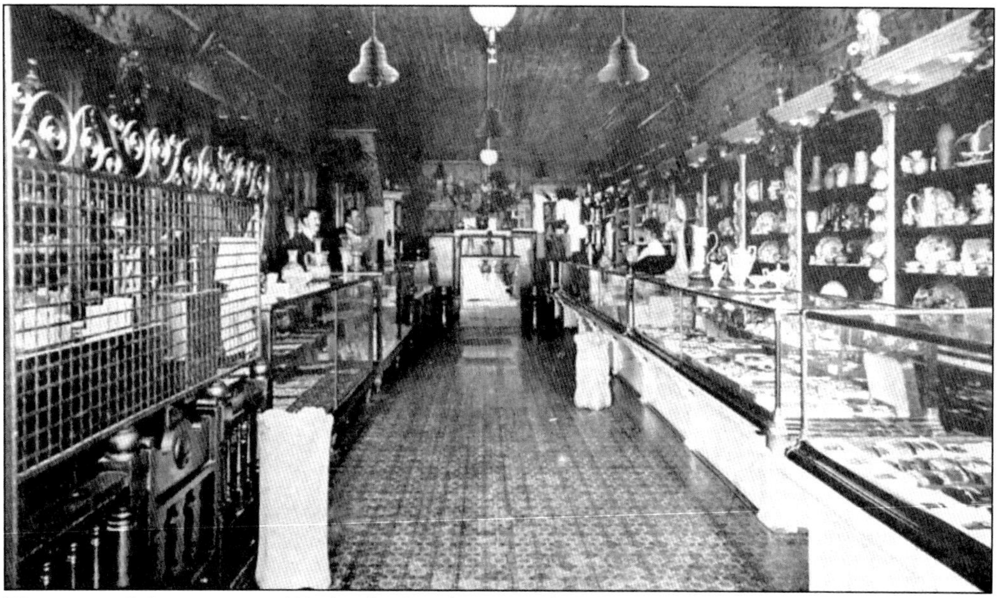

This view of the interior of Hicks the Jeweler was taken around 1910. Hicks was in the Hewitt Block, a brick storefront built in 1871 by Charles Hewitt on the lots just west of his home. Sometime in 1904 or January 1905, Hicks the Jeweler assumed the stock and location of Adamson Brothers jewelers. Adamson Brothers had been in this same downtown location since the 1870s.

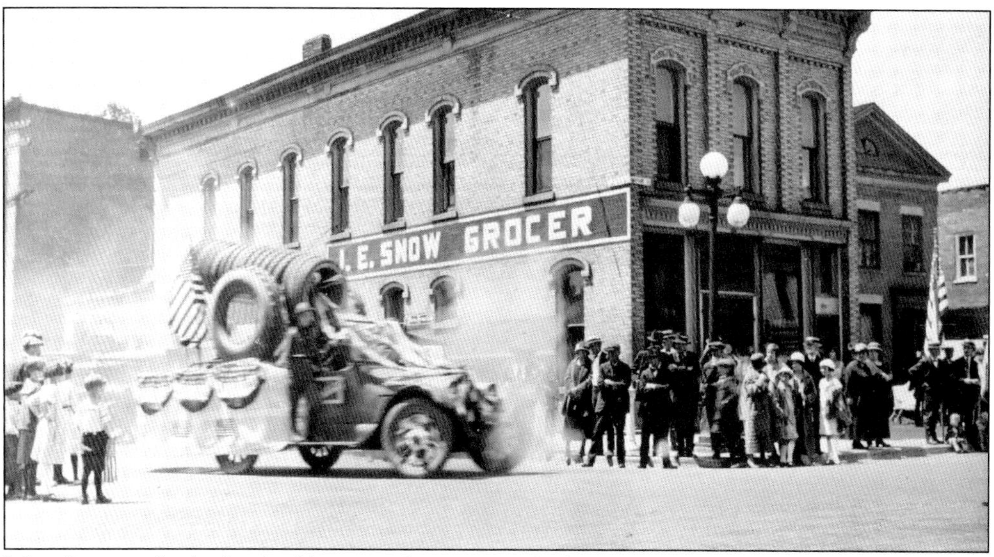

John Bauman built this building on the corner of Chicago Boulevard and Ottawa Street in 1877–1878. It is shown here in 1924 during Tecumseh's centennial parade when it was the Snow Grocery. The house shown behind the building on the right was the Charles Hewitt house. In 1929, the Hewitt house was torn down and the Bauman building was moved one lot west to make room for gas pumps. The Bauman Building then became a gas station, and a large hole was opened in the east side so cars could be driven inside for repair. Today the gas station is gone, and the building has been reclaimed as a retail space.

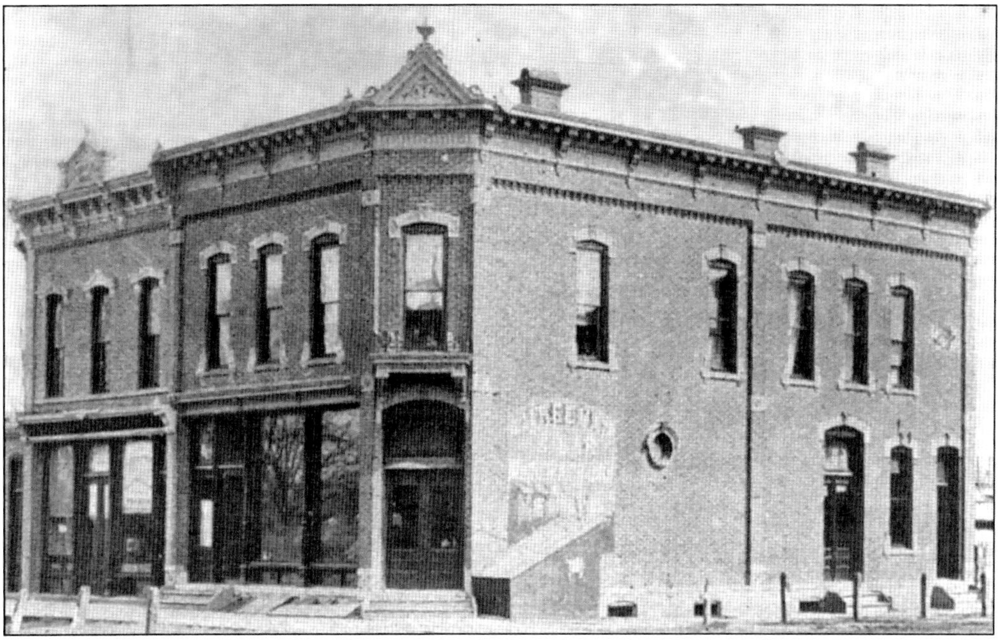

In 1895, about the time of this photograph, this handsome building on the southeast corner of Chicago Boulevard and Ottawa Street was John J. Freeman's cigar manufactory, which had been in business since 1873. It was one of at least two cigar manufacturers in town at the time. By 1900, this was the residence and business of George H. Tansley, "Funeral Director and Embalmer." The building was eventually lost to the march of progress.

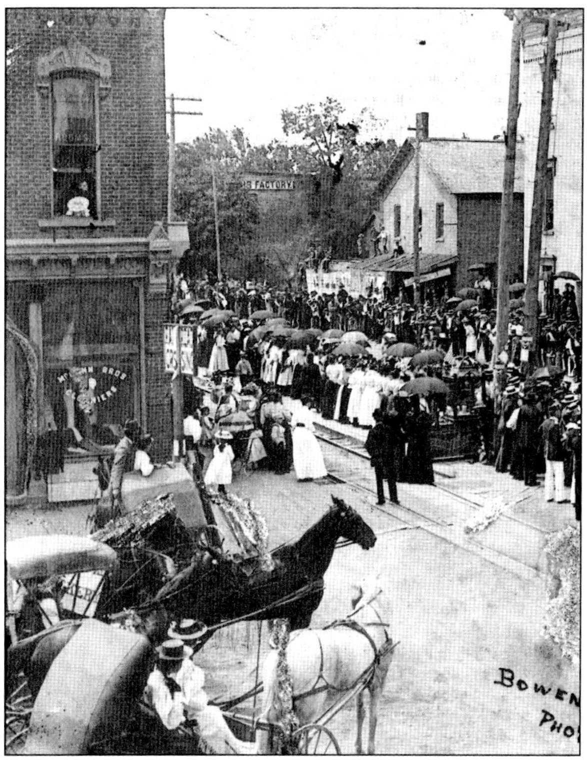

Looking south down Evans Street around 1900, residents of Tecumseh await an unknown entertainment, a bicycle race, a military review, or perhaps another circus parade. The Lilley-Wright building, built by Moses Wright and Lucius Lilley in 1879, dominates the photograph on the left. The sign that reads "Factory" in the center of the photograph is on the Chic (or Chick) Cigar Factory. In 1876, John J. Freeman founded this cigar factory, the second to be established in Tecumseh.

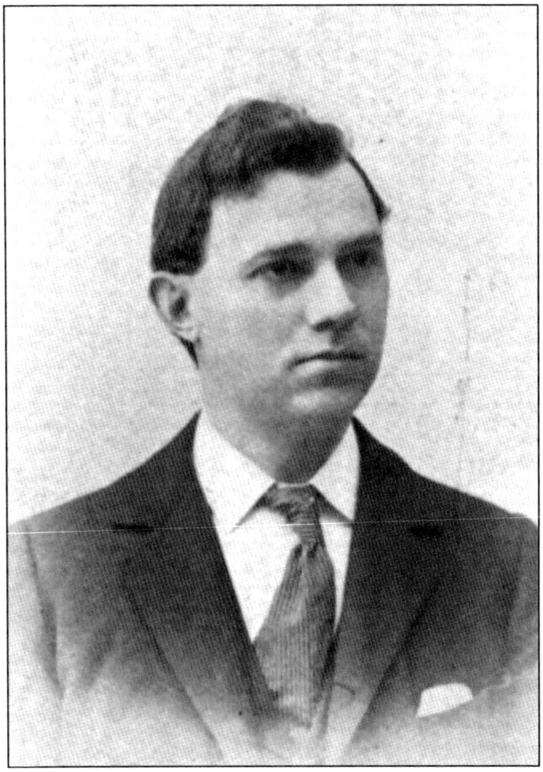

In 1895, the approximate date of this photograph, W. W. Whiting was the proprietor of the Chic Cigar Factory. The factory near the corner of South Evans Street and Pottawatamie Street manufactured both Estrella and Chick or Chic (advertisements of the time have spelled it both ways) brand name cigars. Today the building is the home of the Eagles Hall, 125 South Evans Street.

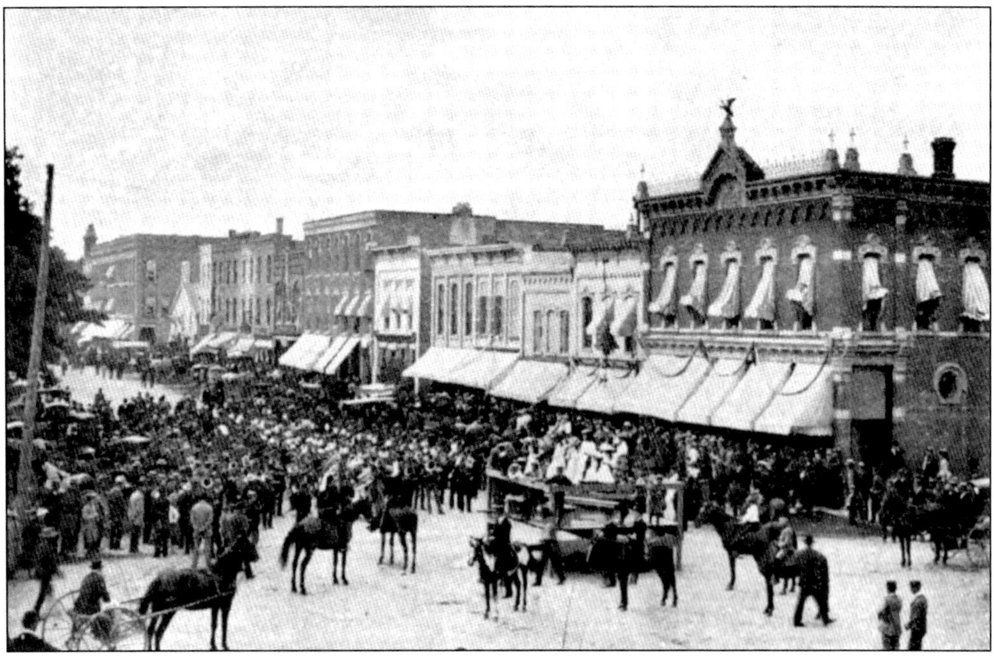

This view of the northeast block of downtown was taken between 1881 and 1893. In 1853, a large portion of the northeast block burned and temporary wooden buildings were built in place of the burned out ones. Eventually the solid brick structures shown in this photograph replaced the temporary wooden structures.

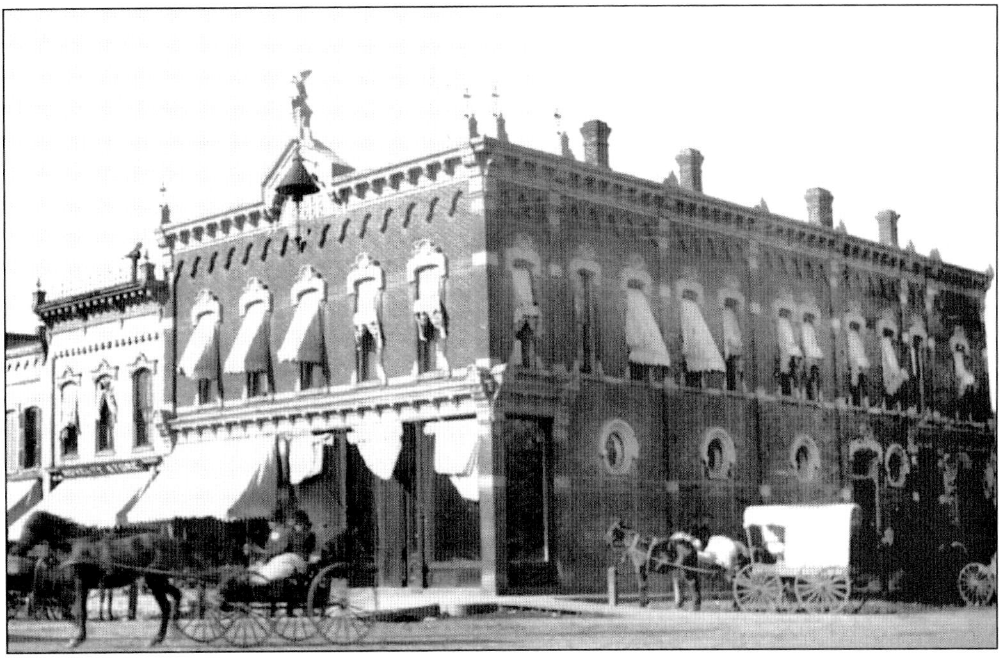

A very successful publishing agent, farmer, businessman, and entrepreneur, Adelbert W. Mills built the Mills Block in 1879 or 1881. He also used the results of his success to build the classic brick Victorian at 107 South Union Street as a home for his wife Rosa and six children. (Photograph courtesy of Ashley E. Chase.)

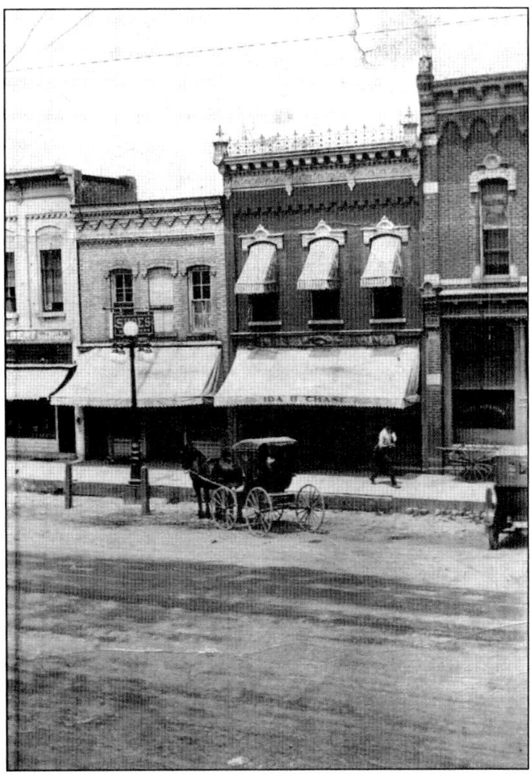

The original buildings on these lots were consumed by the 1853 fire. In 1859, the lots where purchased by Cynthia Bissell (photographer), and in 1865, they were sold to Albert Anderson (merchant/developer). In 1875, E. S. Bardwell built the small building, center left, and a man named Hopkins built the building in the center right. This photograph was taken some time in the early 1900s when the Hopkins building was occupied by the Ida B. Chase dry goods store. (Photograph courtesy of Ashley E. Chase.)

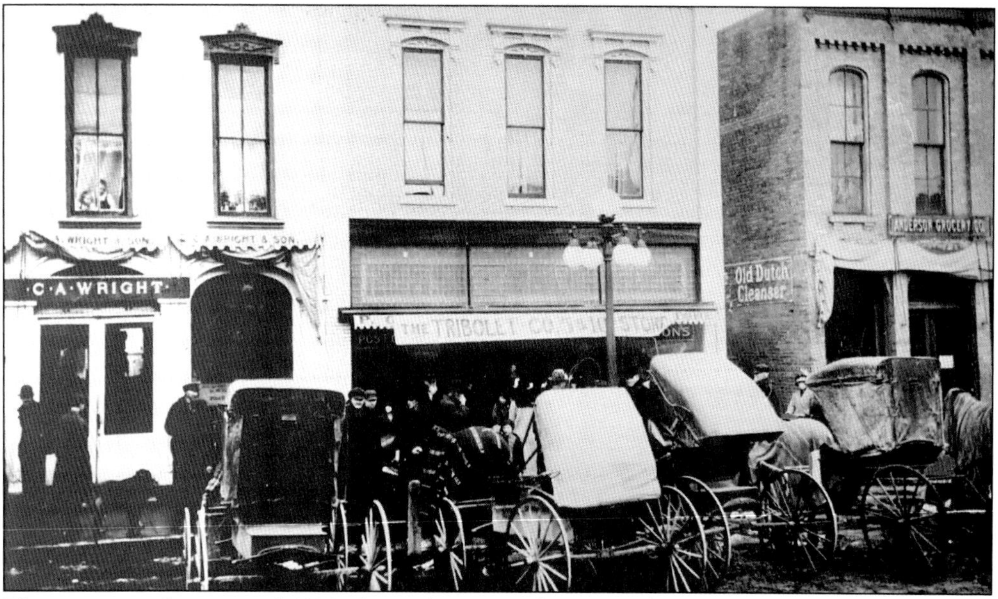

This picture, taken around 1898, shows three storefronts on the northeast block of downtown: on the right, Anderson Grocery Company; in the center, the post office in the Tribolet 5 and 10 Store; and on the left, the C. A. Wright Drugstore. The Wright Drugstore was a family affair, having been established by Moses Wright around 1839. The Wright Drugstore was a fixture of downtown under one name or another and under the guidance of four generations of Wrights. Eventually the store moved across the street to the Lilley-Wright building on the southeast corner of Chicago Boulevard and Evans Street.

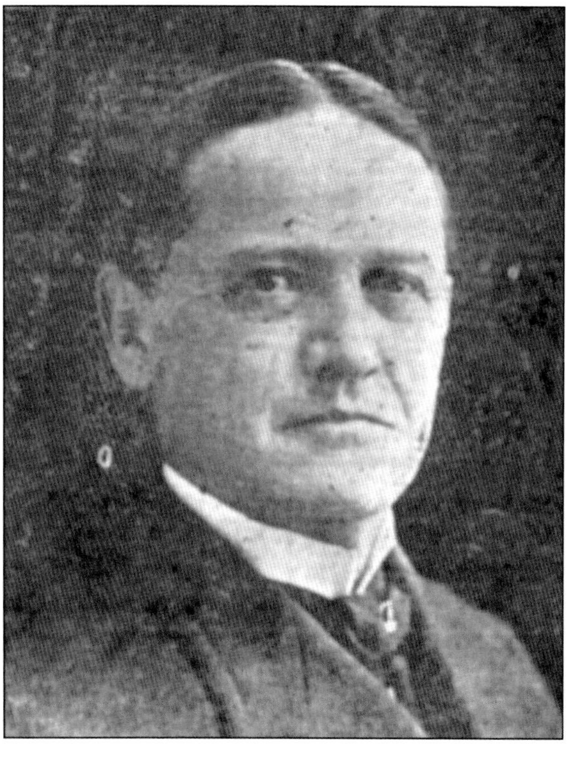

Fredrick B. Wood, the son (one of seven children) of Edwin B. Wood and Harriet Bissell Wood, who was the daughter of Cynthia Spofford and Theodore Bissell who, in 1827, became the first couple to get married in Tecumseh. Fredrick was a prominent lawyer, a businessman with part interest in the first telephone company in Tecumseh, and a civic leader. He built a charming house at 207 North Union Street, just north of his father's stately mansion.

About 1858, Strong and Drew built this stylish two-story brick building to house their hardware store. The Satterthwaite brothers, J. Newton and E. Newbold, worked from a very early age for a different hardware store, Sutton and Swan, located in the Merchants Building. In January 1875, Sutton and Swan Hardware was moved from the Merchants Block to this location. In 1885, it became Swan and Satterthwaite and in 1891, Satterthwaite Brothers Hardware.

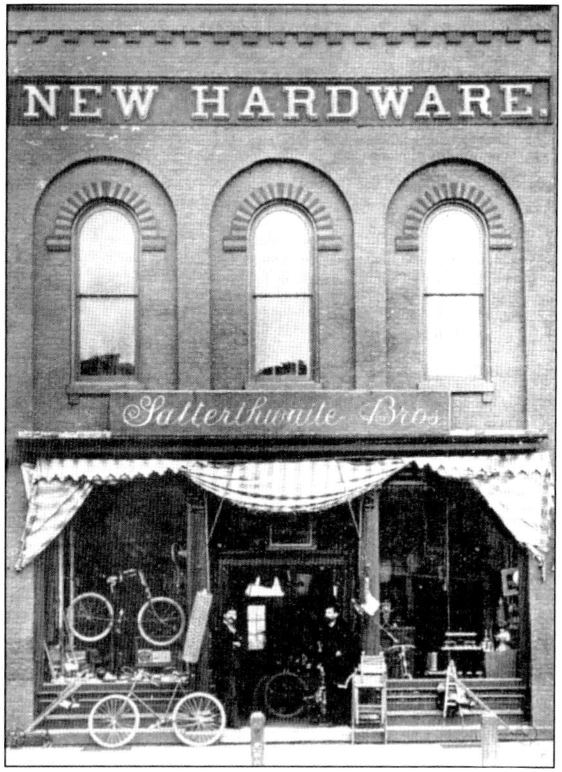

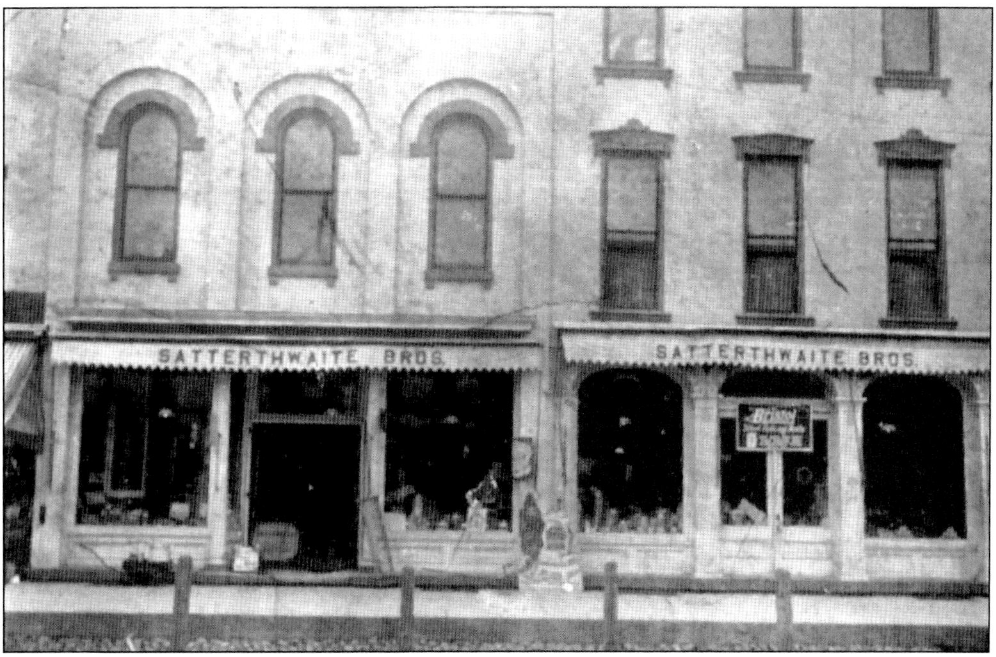

In 1897, the Satterthwaite brothers expanded their hardware store to include what had been the Adams Store—the western half of the large brick building to the east. The storefronts are shown here in October 1911, a number of years after they were painted white, an event important enough to have made the newspaper on August 6, 1891.

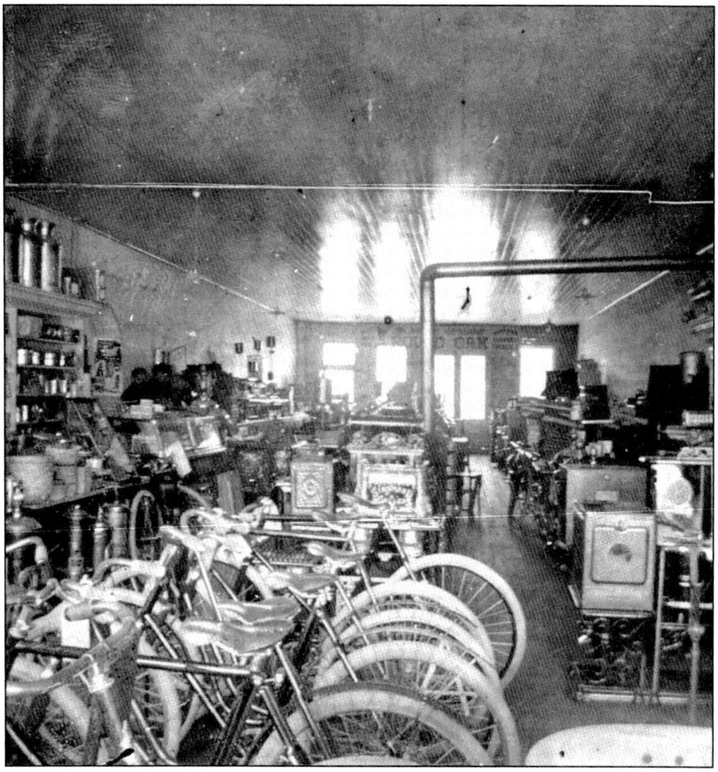

Bicycling was very popular in Tecumseh in the late 1800s and early 1900s, as illustrated in this picture showing the interior of Satterthwaite brothers east store taken in 1899. Satterthwaite Brothers Hardware was a fixture of downtown for over 50 years, selling items as diverse as construction hardware, sporting goods, and wood stoves. The Satterthwaite brothers closed their doors in 1924, and the two buildings that housed their stores were lost to a fire in 1954.

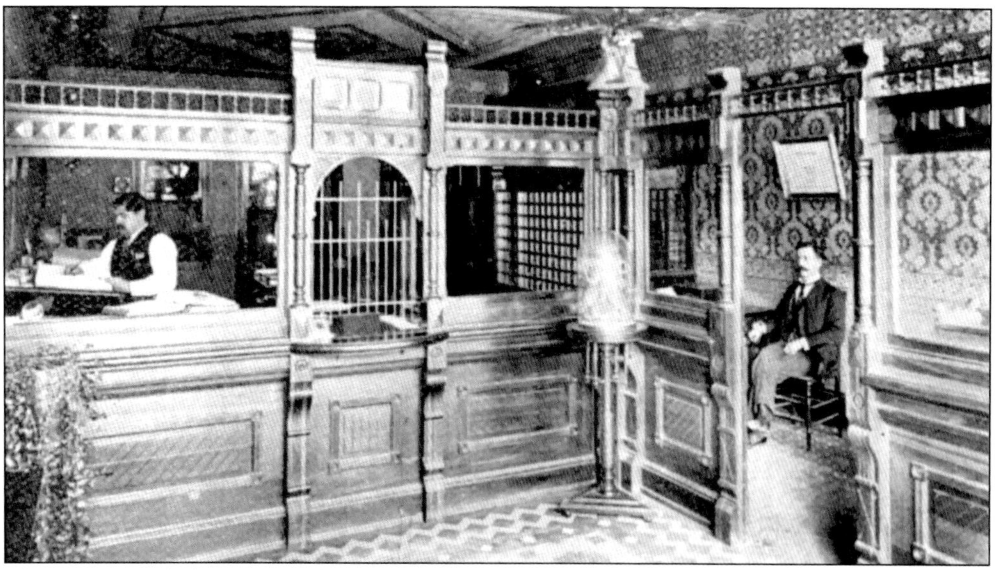

The interior of the Tecumseh State Savings Bank is shown around 1895. The bank was established in 1893 in the building "recently occupied by O. P. Bills & Co.," at 115 East Chicago Boulevard. C. A. Slayton was president and J. H. Smith the cashier. There had been many banks and many bank failures in Tecumseh—the Tecumseh State Bank and the Lilley State Bank, also founded in 1893, being two that survived. As beautiful and ornate as these offices appear, all accounts suggest that the bank was much more impressive after it moved to the lobby of the Barrett Hotel in 1910.

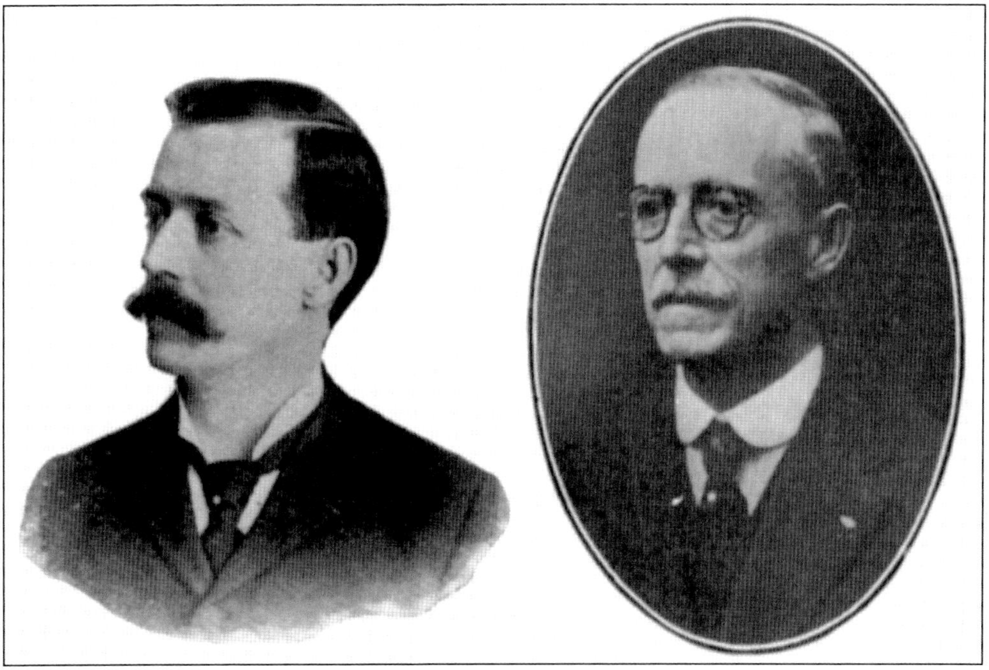

Joseph H. Smith, shown here in 1895 (left) and in 1919, was a prominent member of the community and a tireless promoter of Tecumseh. He had been a carpenter, the manager of Tecumseh Table Company, and in 1895, was the cashier of the Tecumseh State Savings Bank and president of the village council. Smith became president of the bank in the early 1900s and held that position in 1919, when the later picture was taken.

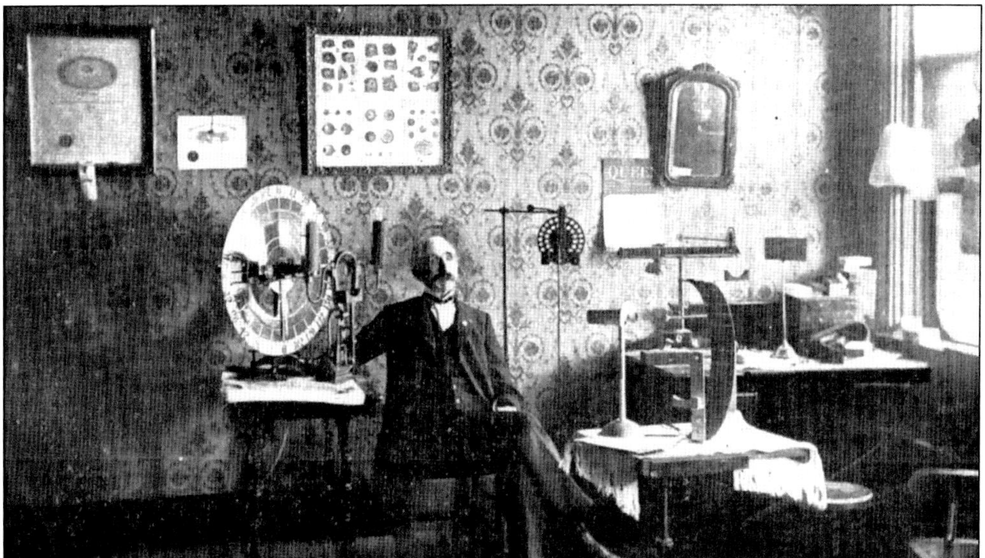

In 1900, Sylvester P. Hosmer, an optician, had offices in what was then known as the U.S. Express building, also holding the offices of the U.S. Express Company and the jewelry store of W. S. Dickinson. The building, at 105 East Chicago Boulevard, was the first structure east of the Masonic temple building and was constructed in 1858 by James L. Gilman. (Photograph courtesy of Lenawee Historical Museum.)

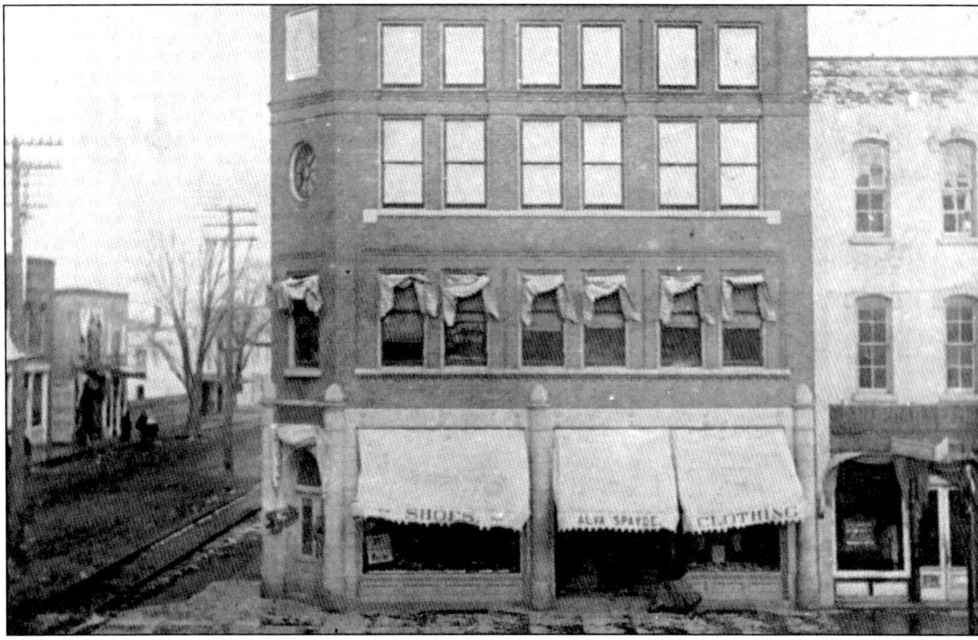

The Masonic temple building is shown around 1900. From 1894 to the present, this majestic building has dominated the northeast corner of Evans Street and Chicago Boulevard. It was built as a cooperative effort between Alfred James and the Tecumseh Masons. James, who would finance the first floor and the front half of the second floor, had owned a grocery in a wood frame building on this same site. The Tecumseh Masonic Lodge would finance the back of the second floor and the story-and-a-half third floor, which was a large auditorium for lodge meetings.

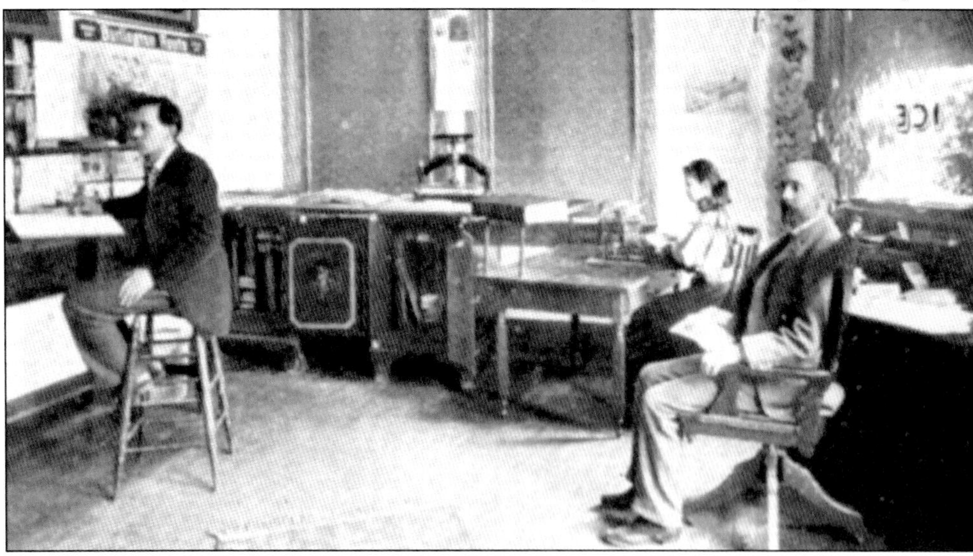

Offices occupied the front of the second floor of the Masonic temple building. The very first tenant of the corner office was A. W. Slayton, a lumber retailer and wholesaler. In a promotional flyer that contained this photograph, Slayton states, "I have been in the lumber business for the last twenty-nine years . . . I make car load lots a specialty, and will deliver to neighboring towns at the lowest possible figures. If you have lumber to sell, I will buy it of you and pay you in cash or shingles."

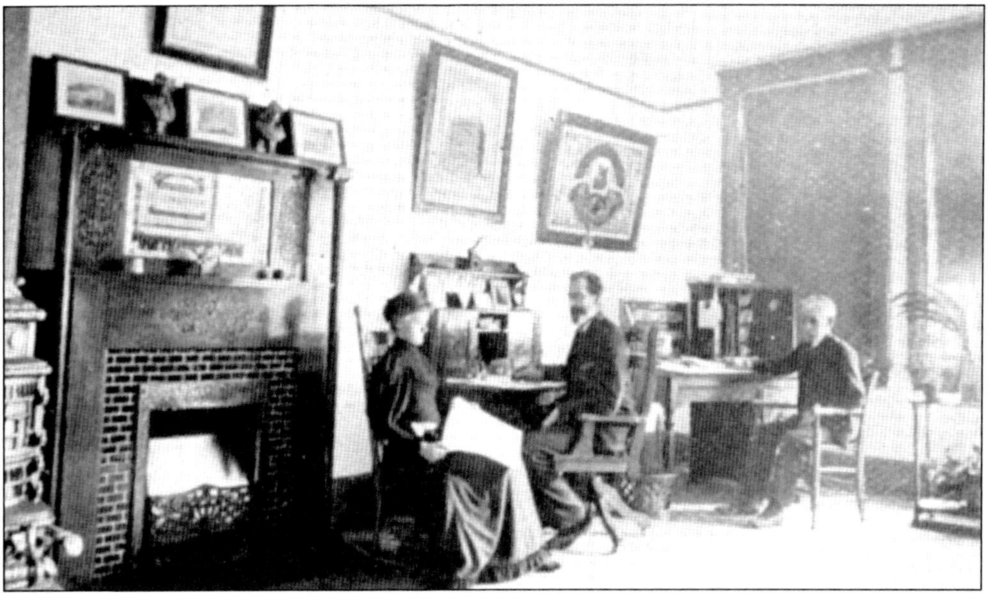

Upon its completion, William DeMott, district agent of the Northwestern Mutual Life Insurance Company, could be found in the southeast office suite of the Masonic temple building—at that time also known as the James Block. DeMott mentions in his advertisement that the office shown here is a part of the Alfred James insurance office. It appears that, after financing half of the Masonic temple building, James had retired from the grocery business and become an insurance agent.

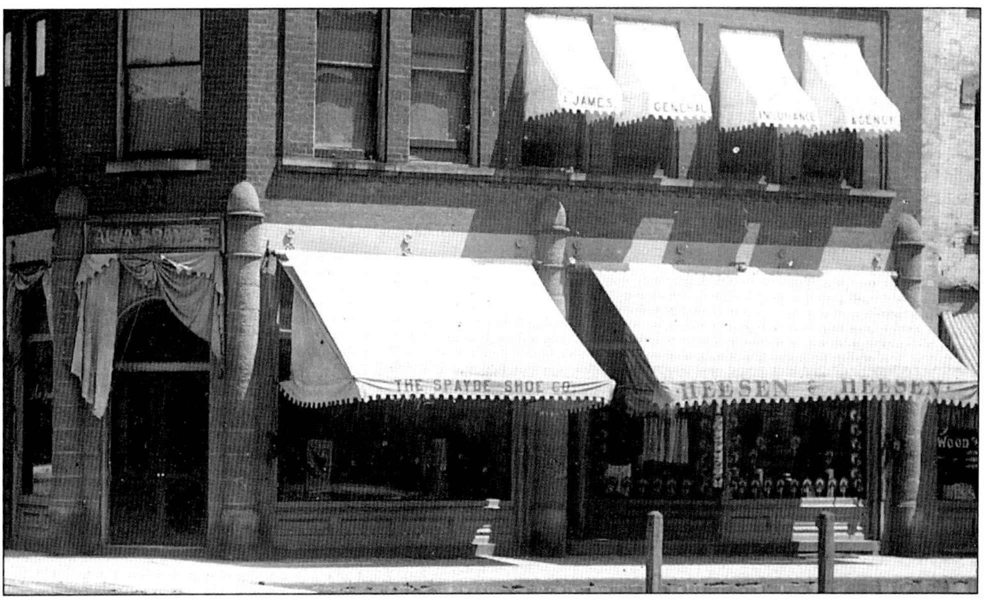

At some point before 1910, when this picture was taken, the retail space in the Masonic temple/James building, which had been only one store operated by Alva Spayde, was divided into two stores. Spayde continued to sell shoes in the corner store while Heesen and Heesen occupied the east storefront, having moved here from their former location in the Union Block. As the awnings suggest, the A. James Central Insurance Company still occupied the eastern offices of the second floor. (Photograph courtesy of Lenawee Historical Museum.)

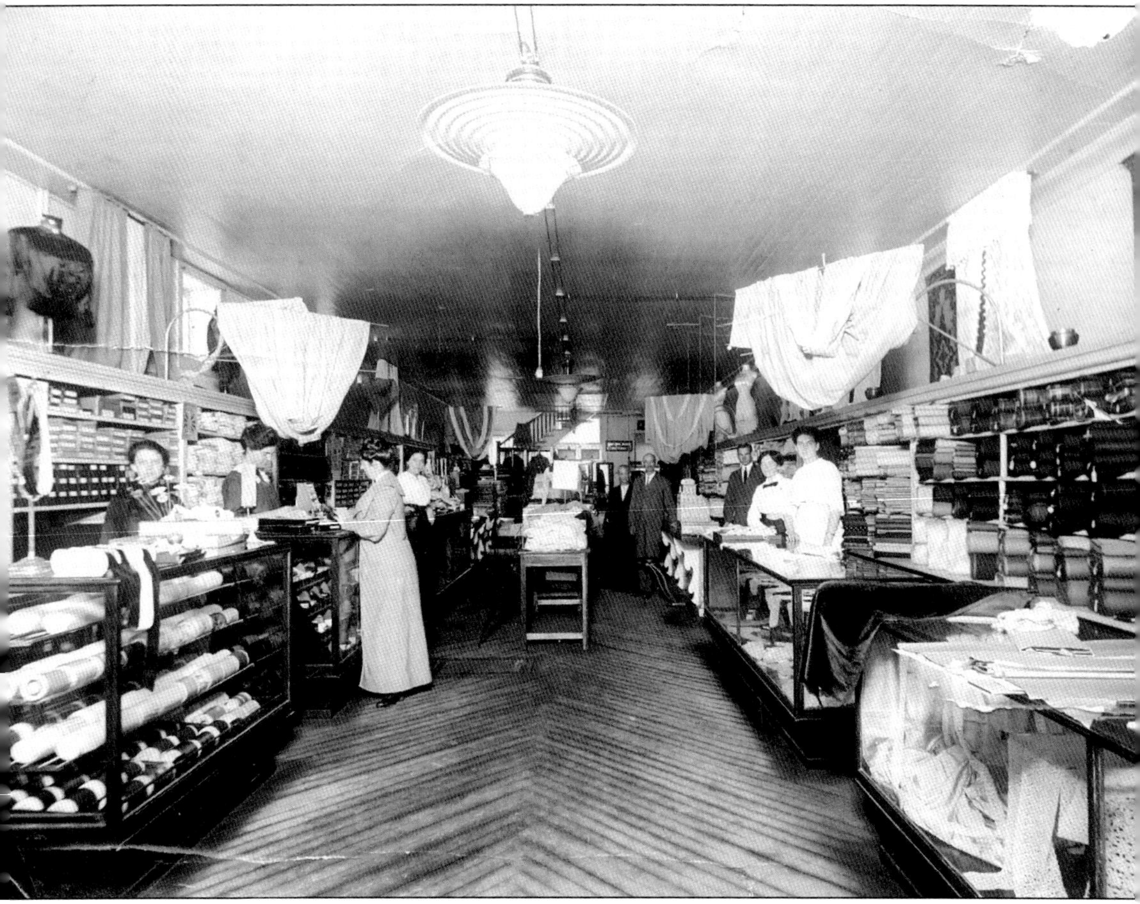

This picture shows the interior of the Fred Rosacrans and Sons dry goods store. The Rosacrans had been in partnership with the Andersons in their dry goods business. Rosacrans and Sons was downtown for 70 years through three generations of Rosacrans. This picture was of their store "on the corner of Chicago and R.R. Tracks," the Masonic temple/James building, sometime after 1910.

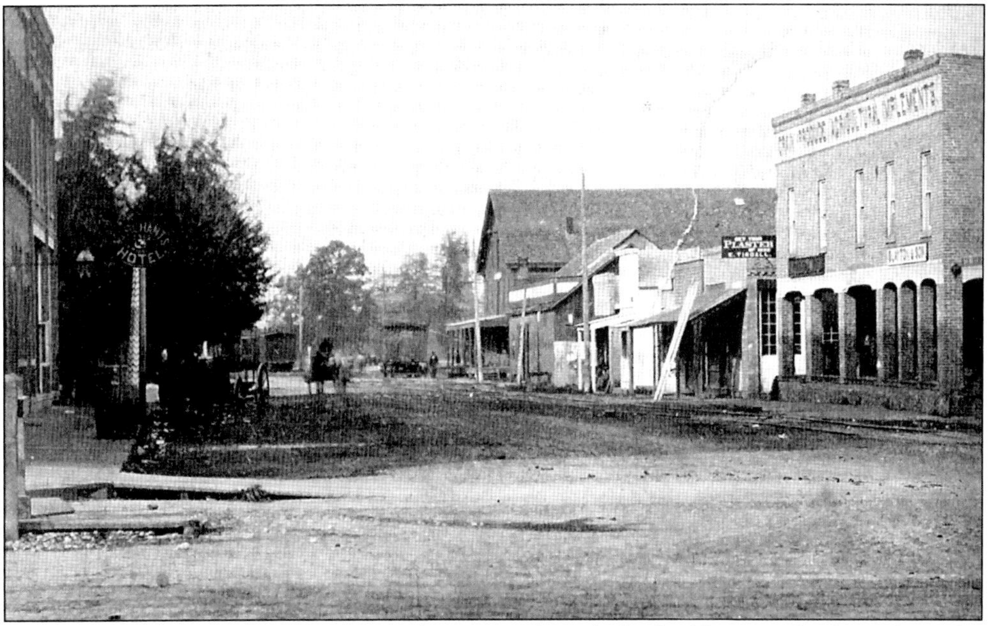

Looking north up Evans Street from Chicago Boulevard, the building on the far right is the C. A. Slayton and Sons and E. Tindall building, which was built in 1883 "next to their wooden warehouse." The wooden warehouse must have been a very early structure as it was enlarged in 1865 with the liberal profits made from selling grain during the war. Still, the wooden warehouse must not have been sufficient for the prosperous Slayton and Sons.

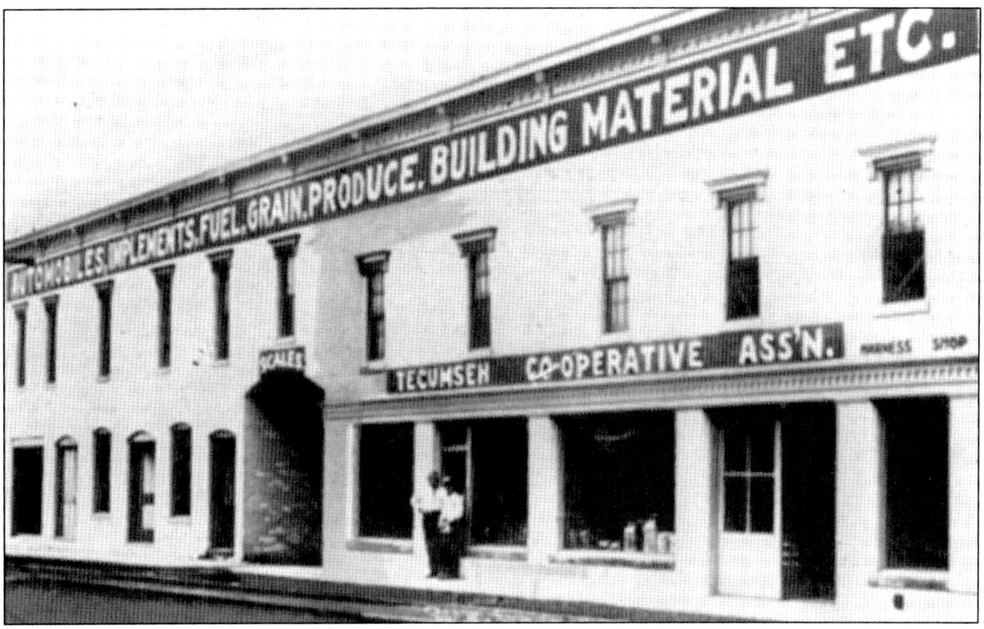

This picture, from around 1919, shows the cooperative association warehouse, quite possibly in its first year of operation. At some point between 1883 and 1919, Slayton and Sons found it necessary to double the size of their "new" brick block on North Evans Street behind the Masonic temple building. It was around 1919 when the building was sold to the Tecumseh Cooperative Association.

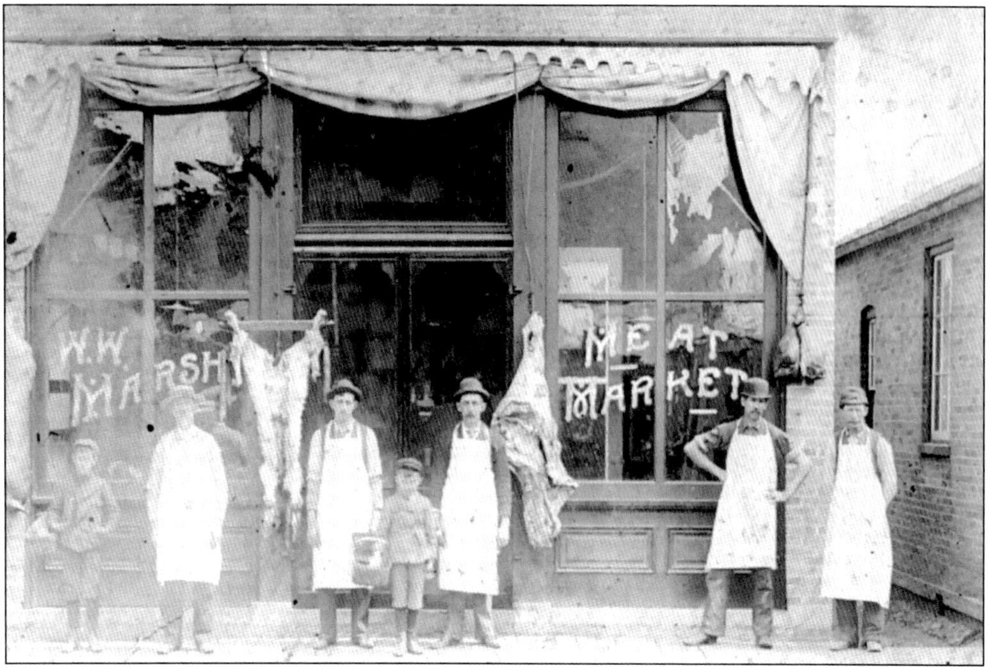

W. W. Marsh's People's Meat Market, shown here in the 1880s, was established on August 18, 1883. The shop was located on the east side of Evans Street along the tracks between Chicago Boulevard and Logan Street.

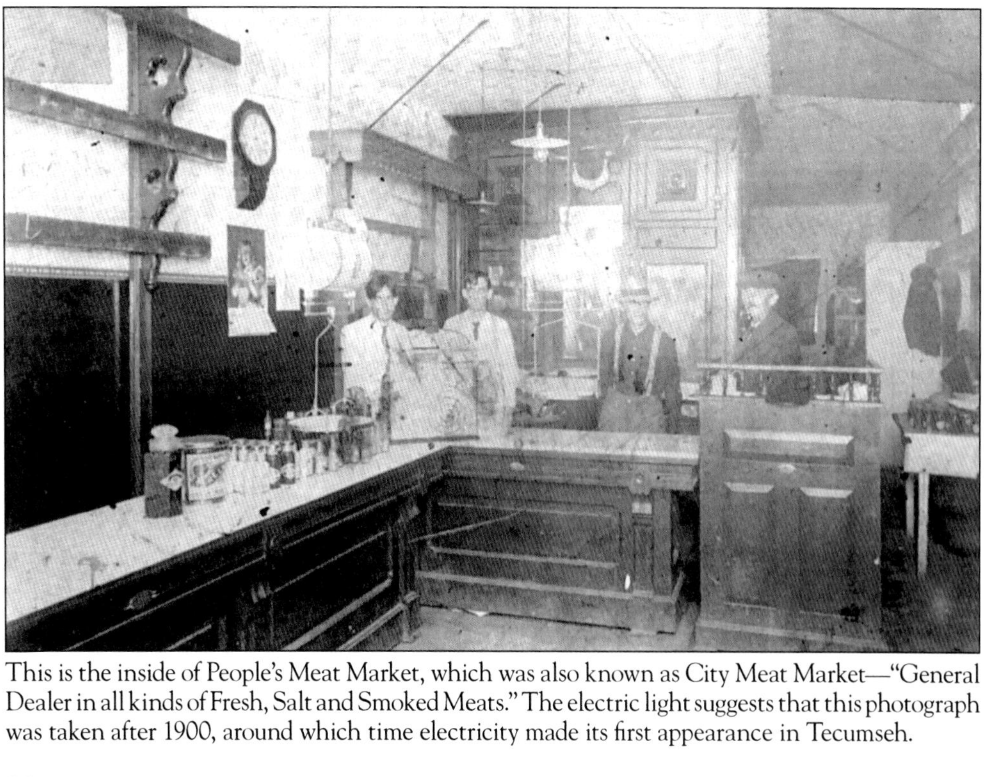

This is the inside of People's Meat Market, which was also known as City Meat Market—"General Dealer in all kinds of Fresh, Salt and Smoked Meats." The electric light suggests that this photograph was taken after 1900, around which time electricity made its first appearance in Tecumseh.

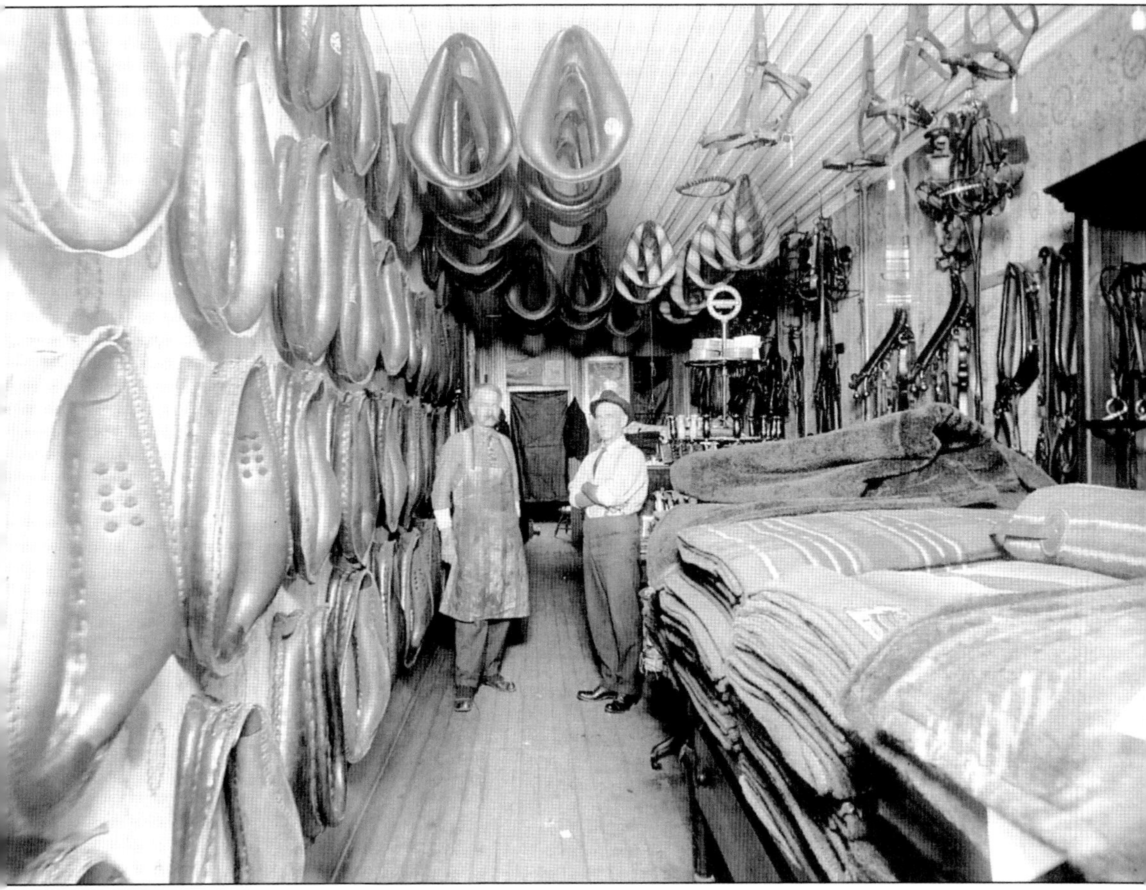

The Vanantwert Harness Shop was on North Evans Street just north of Slayton's and probably south of the Marsh meat market. It was an excellent location, as the Garlinghouse livery was across the street, and, for a time, the stagecoach terminal was on the southeast corner of Evans and Logan Streets. A written note on the back of this photograph said, "Will Vanantwert standing." Not the most helpful of notes.

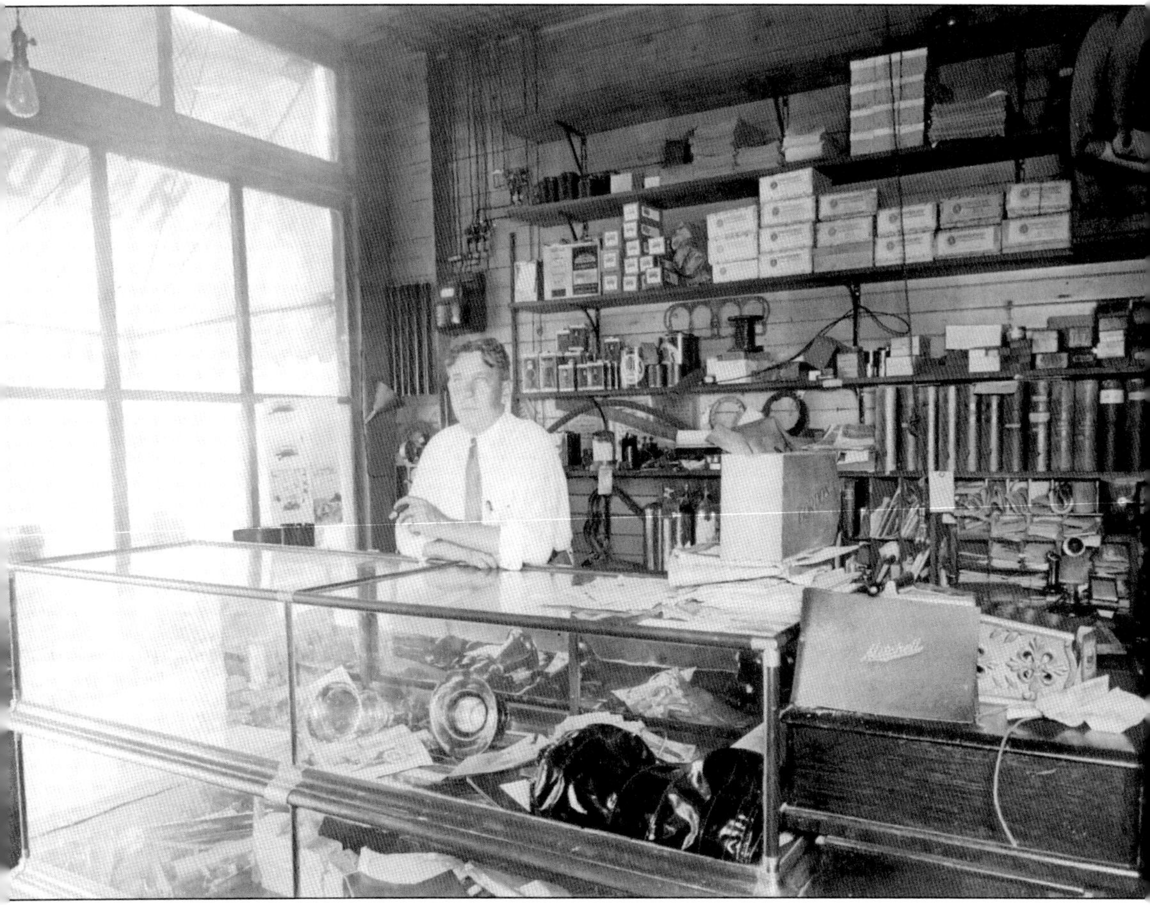

Levi Hayden is seen behind the counter at the Hayden Garage. The garage was on North Evans Street two or three lots behind the Merchants Block, roughly in the middle of the block between Chicago Boulevard and Logan Street. Levi Hayden clearly had more than a passing interest in automobiles, for at this time he was also managing the Hayden Mills, which had become a substantial business in and of itself.

Two

Public Places and Civic Structures

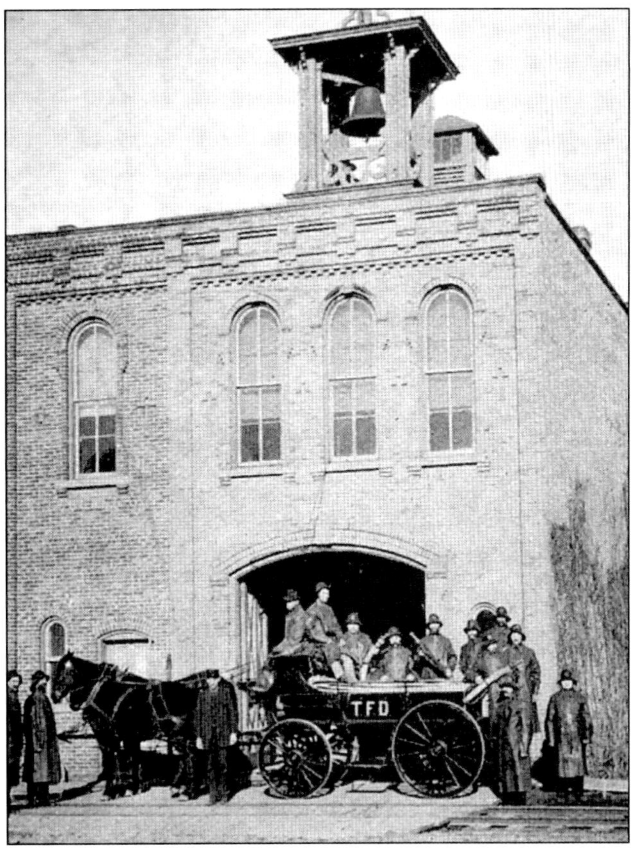

The Tecumseh Village Council building and fire station was contracted in 1871. It was completed in 1873 for a reported cost of $2,000 and stood on South Evans Street in the middle of the block between Chicago Boulevard and Pottawatamie Street. The bell was an additional $140. This photograph shows the building in 1895, ten years after an addition, which included a jail and rooms for full-time firemen, was built on the north side.

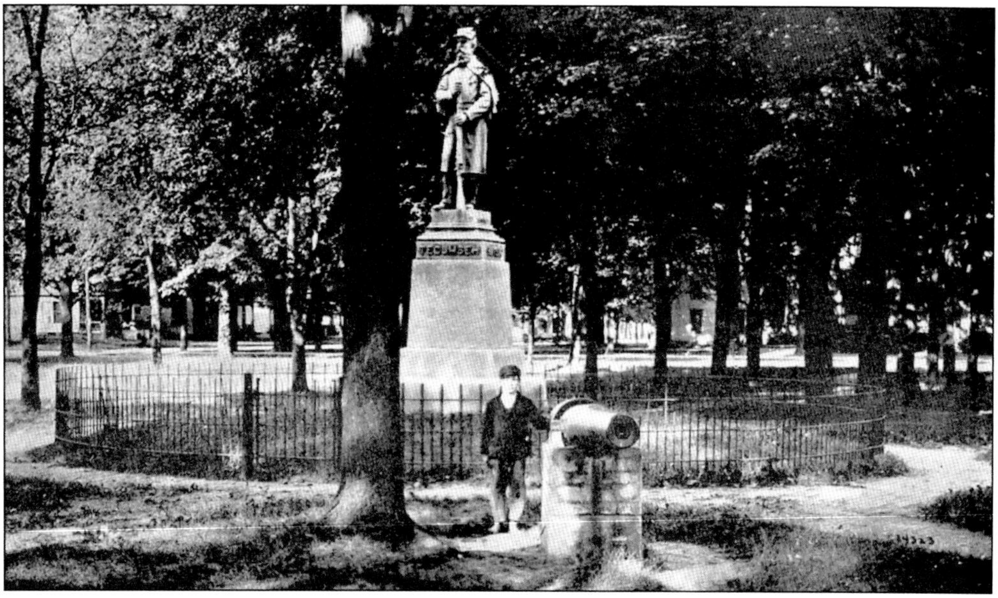

In 1824, the very year Tecumseh was settled, Musgrove Evans registered a plat map laying out the future town. On that map there were four parcels of land that were set aside for public use, one for the court house (now the location of the post office), one as a public cemetery (which became Elliot Park), one as a promenade (now city hall), and one as a military square (now the location of the public library). This picture looks east across Military Square around 1911 before the memorial was moved to Brookside Cemetery. (Photograph courtesy of Lenawee Historical Museum.)

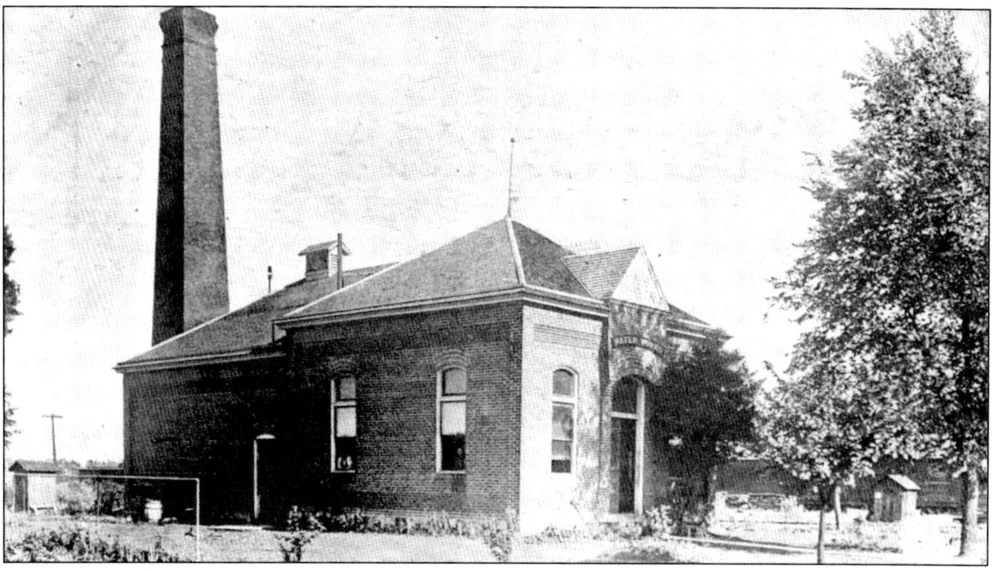

The Tecumseh Waterworks pumping station was built between 1892 and 1893 on South Division Street. It had a coal-fired steam pump and was part of a major reworking of the city's water system that included all new water mains and a standpipe for water pressure. Once the new system was finished, residents and businesses began to rely on it over their wells. A news article from 1893 reads "Garlinghouse Bros. were the first to tap the new mains and put in water connections." A 1928 news clipping states, "New automatic pumping equipment at the waterworks will do away with the need for a night man." (Photograph courtesy of Lenawee Historical Museum.)

Completed in 1893, the standpipe, shown here in 1913, was part of a water delivery modernization project. The city originally had a water delivery system, the primary purpose of which was to supply water to fight fires and water horses. The old system used wooden pipes and windmills for pumping, making it unreliable and inefficient. Built in the old Court House Square, which became known for a time as Adam's Park, the standpipe dominated the east side of downtown for nearly 100 years. Eventually the post office was built in front of it, and in 1984, with a failing foundation, the standpipe was torn down. (Photograph courtesy of Lenawee Historical Museum.)

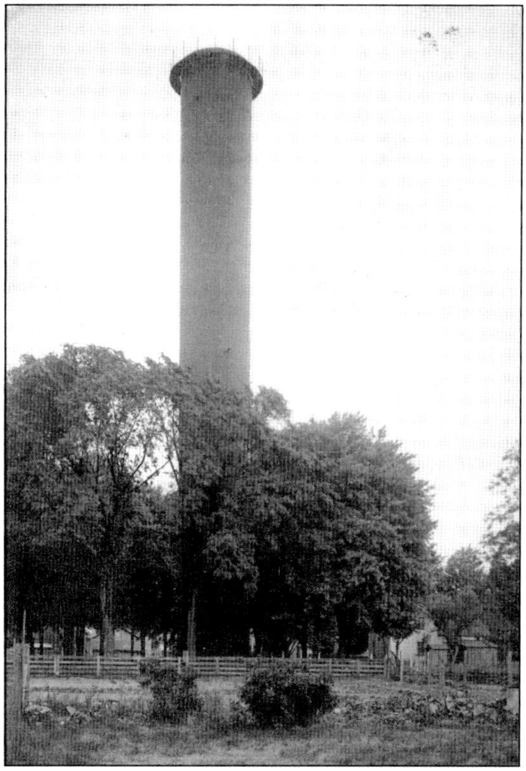

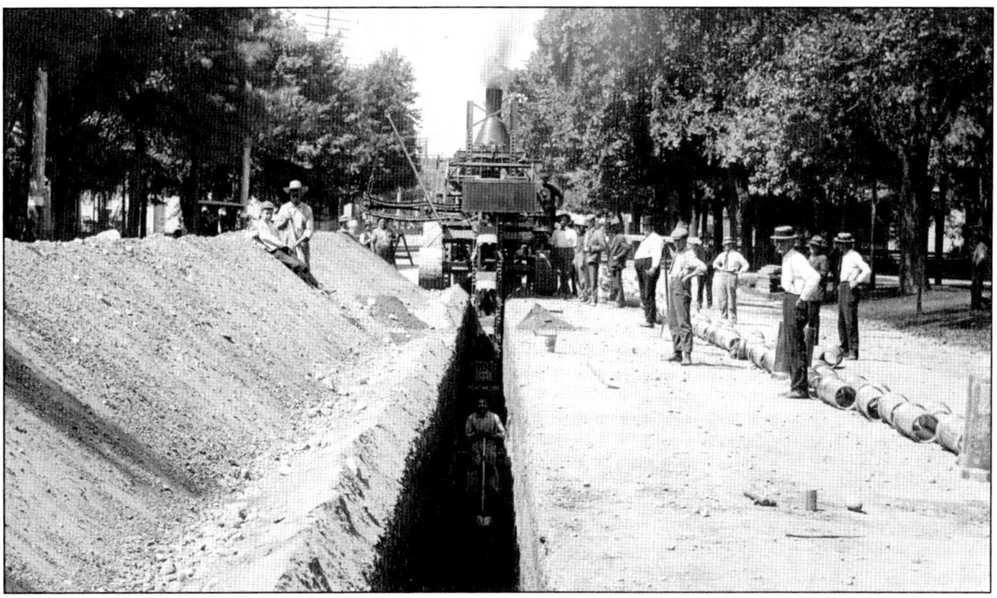

In 1892, eight miles of trenches were dug when the new metal water main was put in. In 1907, fifteen years later, the village voted to add a sewer and the *Tecumseh Herald* editorialized, "Tecumseh only needs a sewer to make it the best kept and most beautiful town in Michigan." Two years later, in 1909, a steam-powered trench digger appeared on the main street of town and was quite the public attraction as it made its way down Chicago Boulevard, prepping the trench for the new sewer tiles.

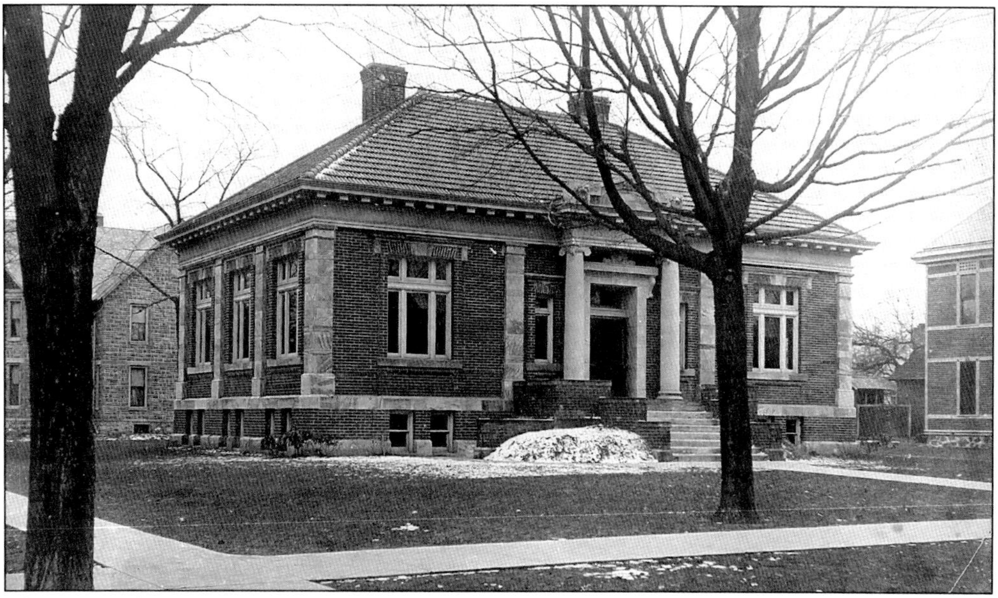

Like many other communities throughout the country, Tecumseh was fortunate to have a library constructed with a grant from Andrew Carnegie. Prior to this building, the "School District Library" was housed on the second floor of the Union Building, over the Lilley State Bank. The handsome brick and marble library was built in 1904 on Chicago Boulevard just west of town. The Carnegie grant of $10,000 covered the majority of the total $12,400 cost, which included the furniture.

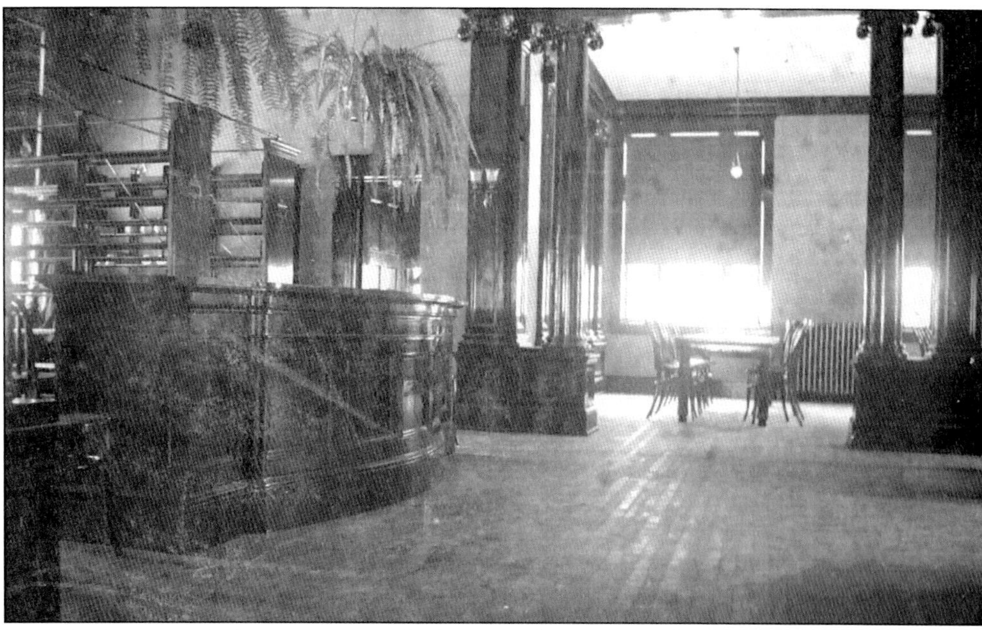

In 1900, four years before moving to the location shown here, the library had 2,200 books in its collection. This photograph shows the interior of the Carnegie Library building in 1904 just after its completion. Eventually the community library outgrew the building, and in 1962 the library was moved to a new building on North Ottawa Street. Until just a few years ago, the old library served as offices for the Tecumseh public schools. Currently it stands empty.

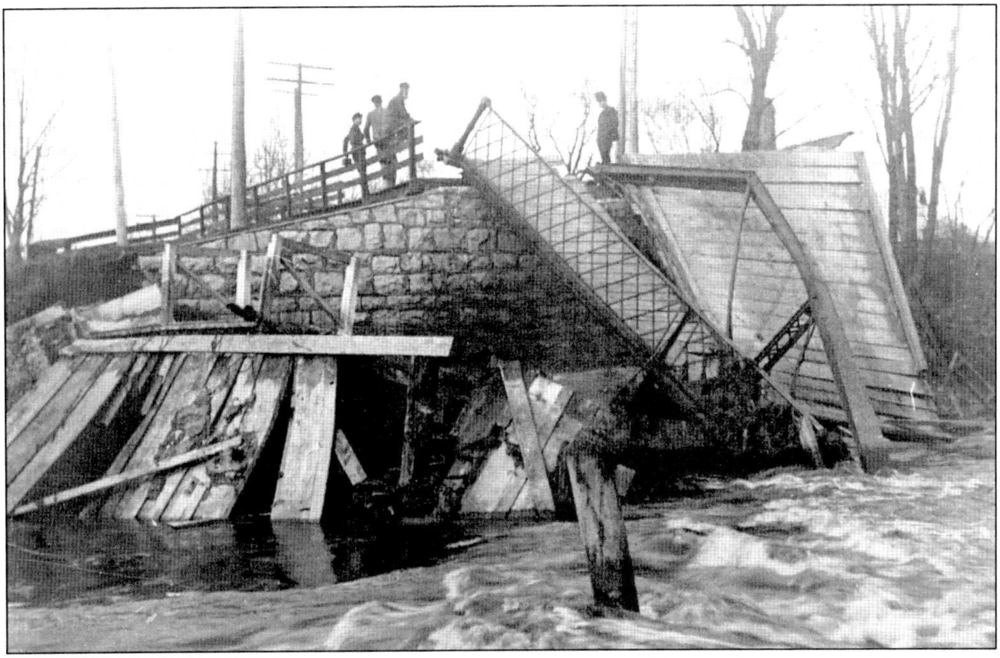

While the river brought prosperity, power, and recreation to Tecumseh, it was not always calm and controlled. This picture shows the Red Mill Dam and bridge destroyed by a spring flood on May 3, 1907. This same flood also knocked out electrical service to the city, at least until they could get the auxiliary steam system running, as the Tecumseh Electric Power Plant used water from the Red Mill Pond to generate the electricity.

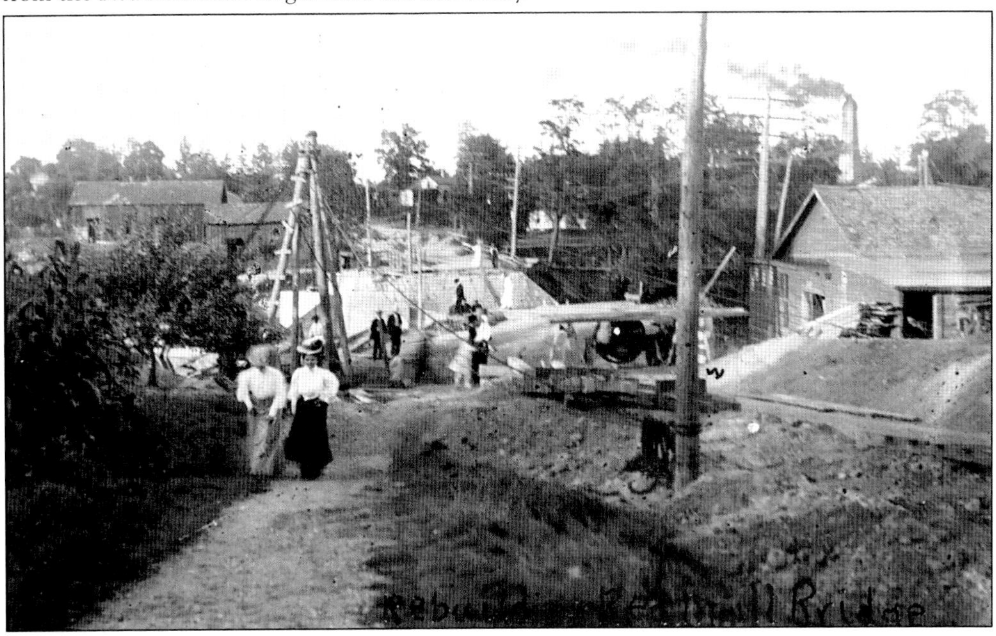

Taken in the spring or early summer of 1907, this picture shows the first stages of rebuilding the washed-out Mill Street (now Evans Street) bridge and Red Mill Dam. The building in the right foreground is a portion of Smith's Paper Mill. Across the river from the paper mill, the smokestack of the Tecumseh Electric Power Plant can be seen.

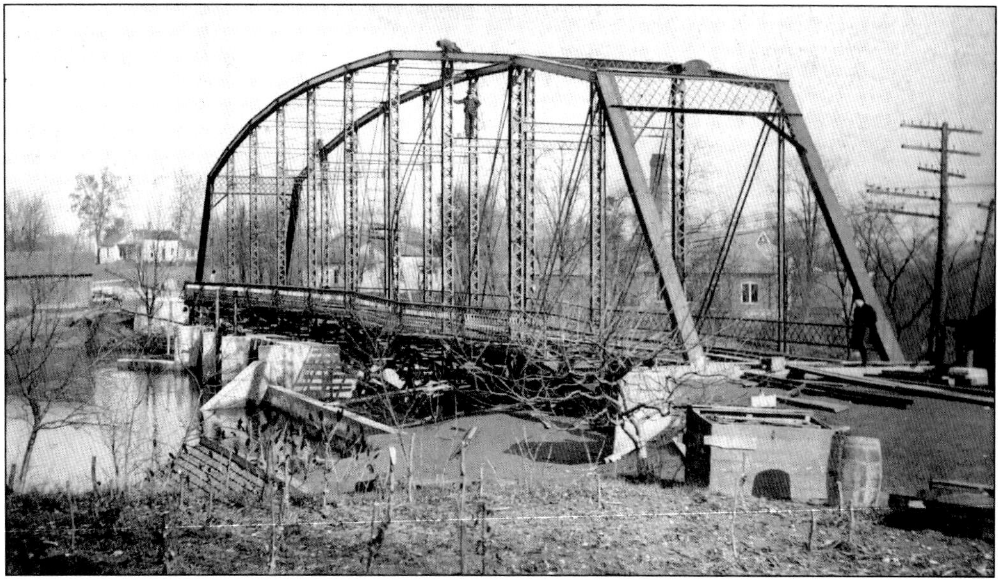

The Red Mill Dam was completed in 1907, and it has not been washed out to this day. Seen here, the Mill Street Bridge, built over the dam, is almost completed, and workmen climb on its superstructure. The power plant can clearly be seen to the right behind the bridge, and since it is not creating any smoke, it can be assumed that the water-powered generators were in use again. (Photograph courtesy of Lenawee Historical Museum.)

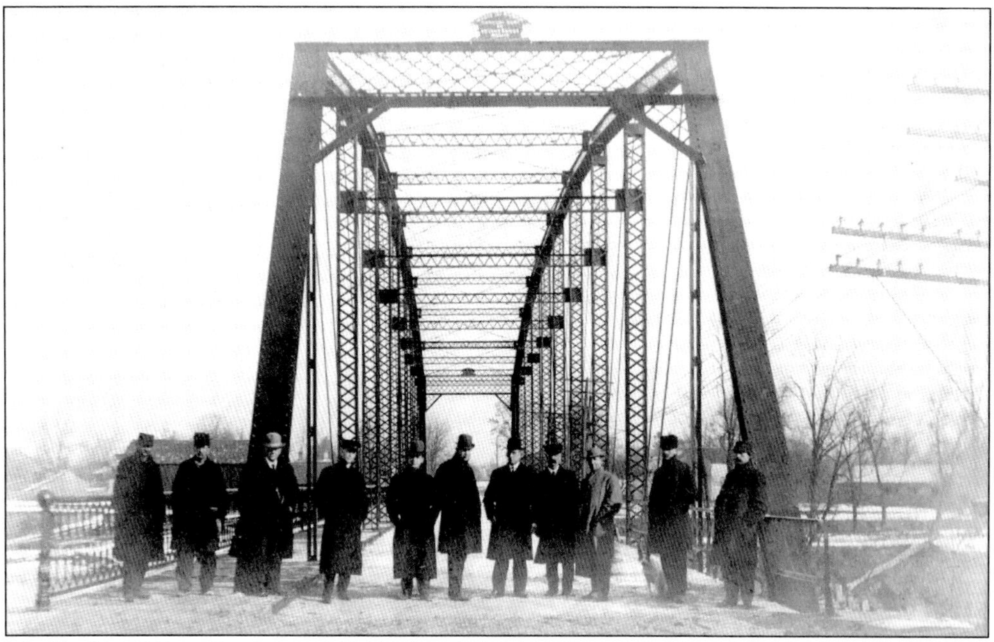

The Red Mill Dam Bridge was finished and dedicated in December 1907. This picture, taken November 2, 1907, shows the township and village boards inspecting the new bridge, which was built in only five months for a total cost of $15,450. A newspaper article written in December 1907 states, "It was made with no idea to save expense but to build a good bridge to last for always." The bridge would serve travelers to and from Tecumseh for 51 years. In 1958, it was torn down to make way for a wider bridge that could handle modern traffic.

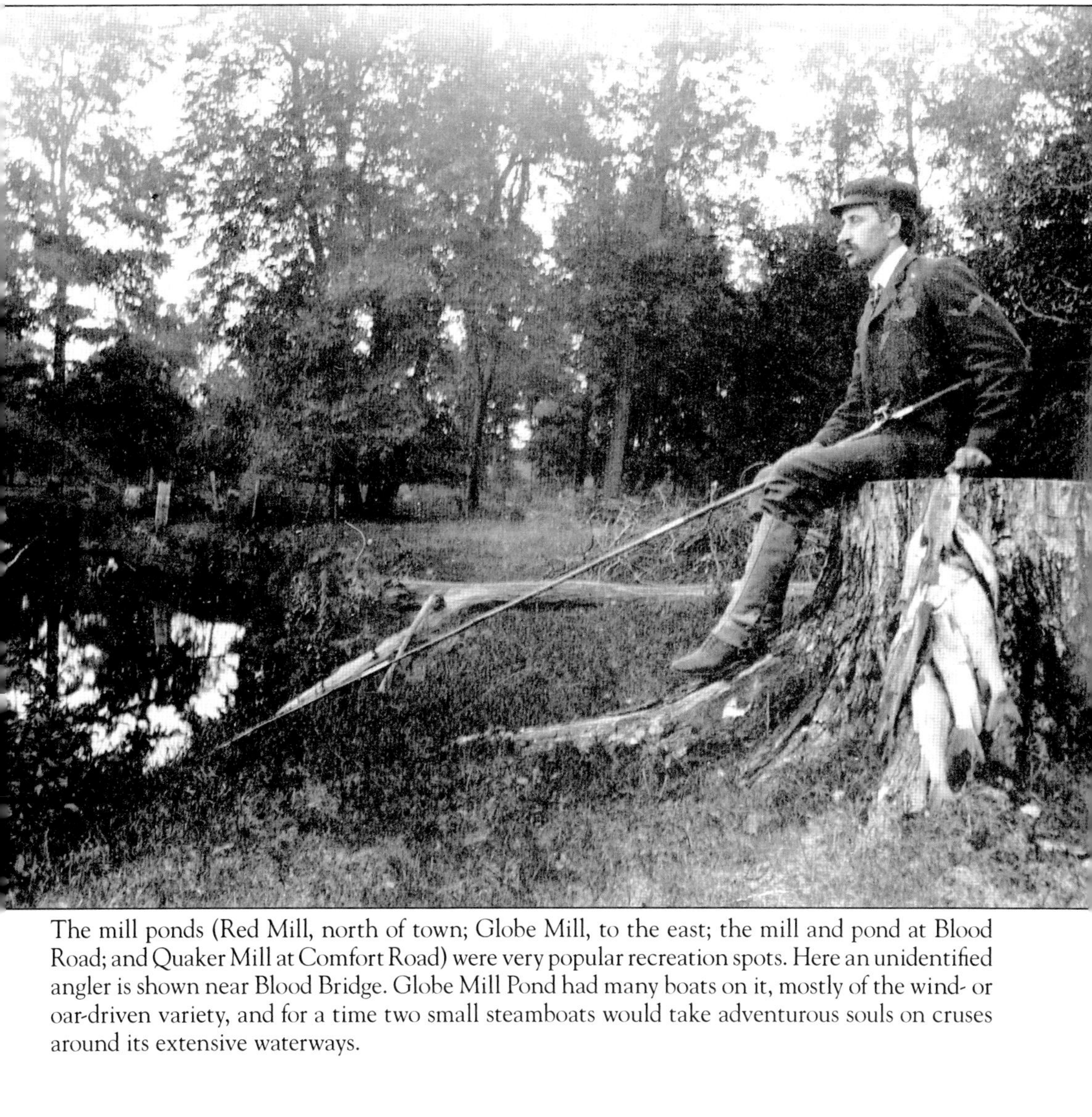

The mill ponds (Red Mill, north of town; Globe Mill, to the east; the mill and pond at Blood Road; and Quaker Mill at Comfort Road) were very popular recreation spots. Here an unidentified angler is shown near Blood Bridge. Globe Mill Pond had many boats on it, mostly of the wind- or oar-driven variety, and for a time two small steamboats would take adventurous souls on cruses around its extensive waterways.

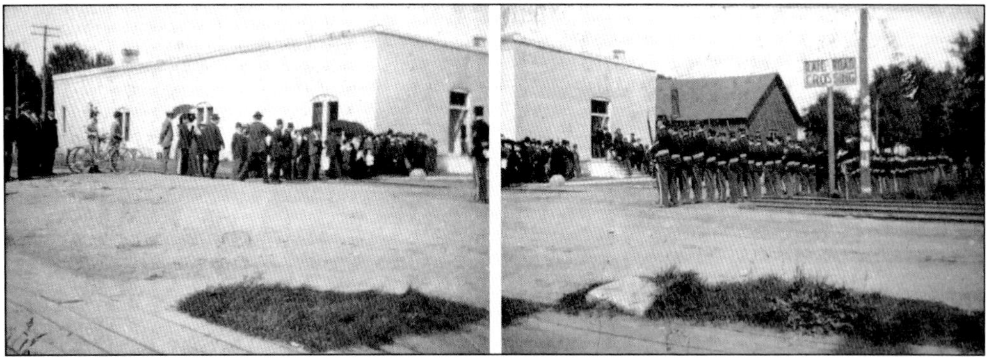

In 1894, the 31st Regiment of the state militia, Company C, which was based in Tecumseh, purchased the Hayden warehouse on the northeast corner of Evans and Logan Streets to be the Tecumseh Armory. These two pictures show the armory and the company, perhaps during the armory's "Grand Opening Ball," which was reported to have been quite the social event. Perhaps during the company's preparations to leave for the Spanish American War, Clara Waldron, in her history of Tecumseh reported that, "at 7:00 a.m., April 26, they marched from the armory to the south depot, all business stopped and 2,000 people lined the streets to watch."

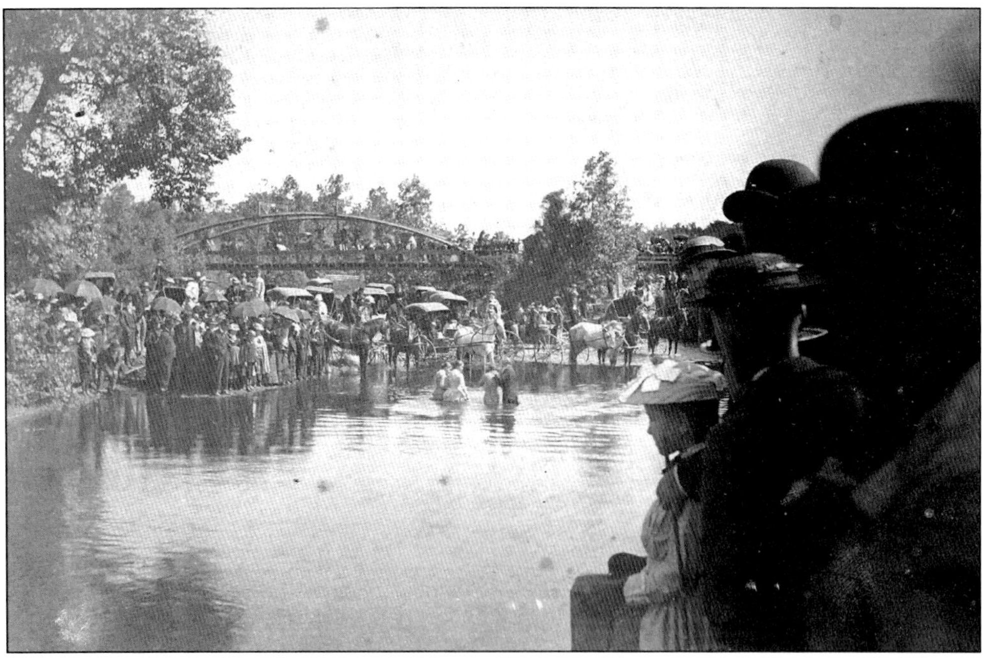

The Reverend B. F. Rapp "baptizes converts" in the River Raisin on June 15, 1884. The location is uncertain, but its bucolic setting would suggest that it was not near the industries on Mill (Evans) Street but was downriver. The shape of the bridge in the background, when compared with other pictures of the era, suggests that it was the bridge that crossed the River Raisin at Blood Road.

St Peter's Episcopal Church was the first church built in Tecumseh. The cornerstone was laid on October 10, 1833, and the building was completed and dedicated on August 2, 1835. General Brown and Musgrove Evans were both instrumental in its establishment, and funds were raised nation wide. Donations for the construction of the church were even received from Andrew Jackson, Daniel Webster, and Henry Clay. The Episcopal congregation outgrew the church, and although there was a strong effort to save the building, it was razed in 1962 to make way for a new church. (Photograph courtesy of Lenawee Historical Museum.)

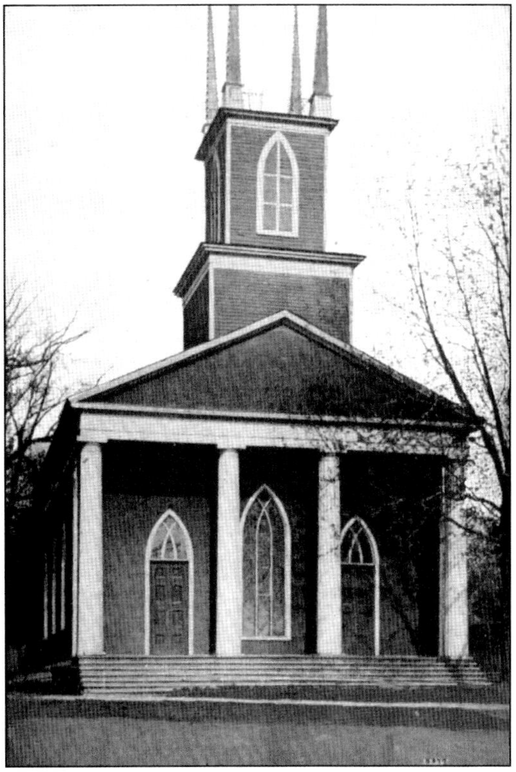

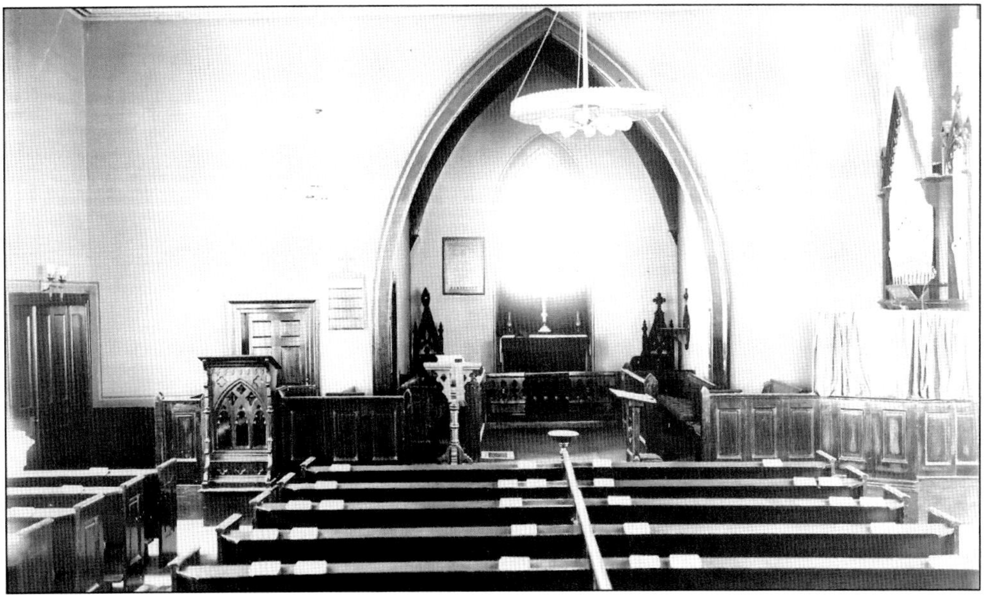

This view shows the inside of the original St. Peters Episcopal Church. The first church in Tecumseh served the community for 129 years when it was scheduled for destruction in 1962 to make way for a larger church. There was a concerted effort to raise the necessary funds to move the building, and although donations were received from far and wide, even from Herbert Hoover, the money could not be raised in time. On December 10, 1962, the building was destroyed, and the new Episcopal church took its place.

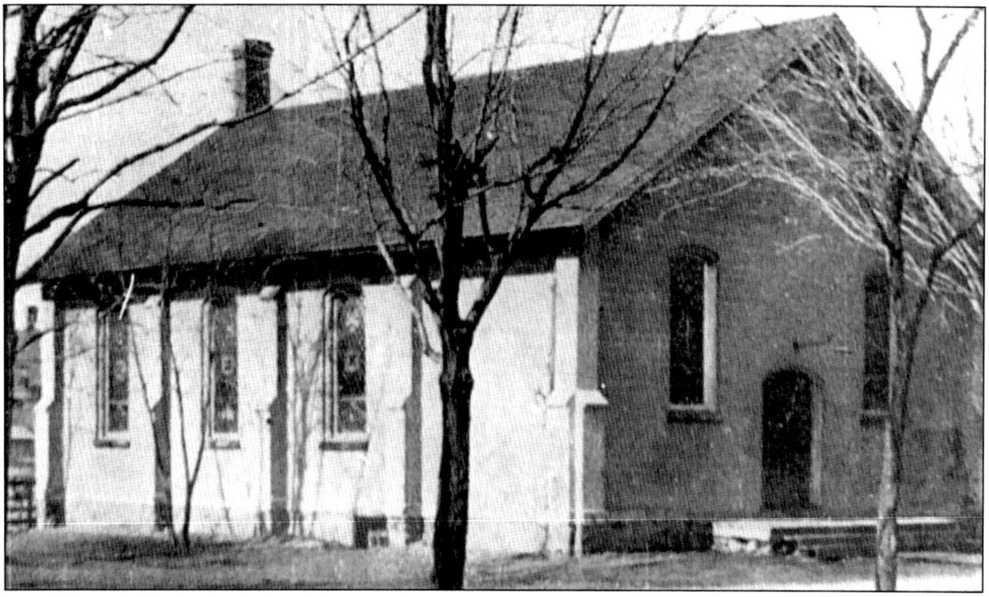

The Universalist church on North Union Street was built in 1859. Judge Consider A. Stacy (responsible for the Union Block downtown and the imposing Stacy Manor) was a member of the congregation and instrumental in making the construction of the building possible. The Universalist congregation was small and never got well established in Tecumseh. The Christian Science Society used the building in the early 1900s. It is now a private residence.

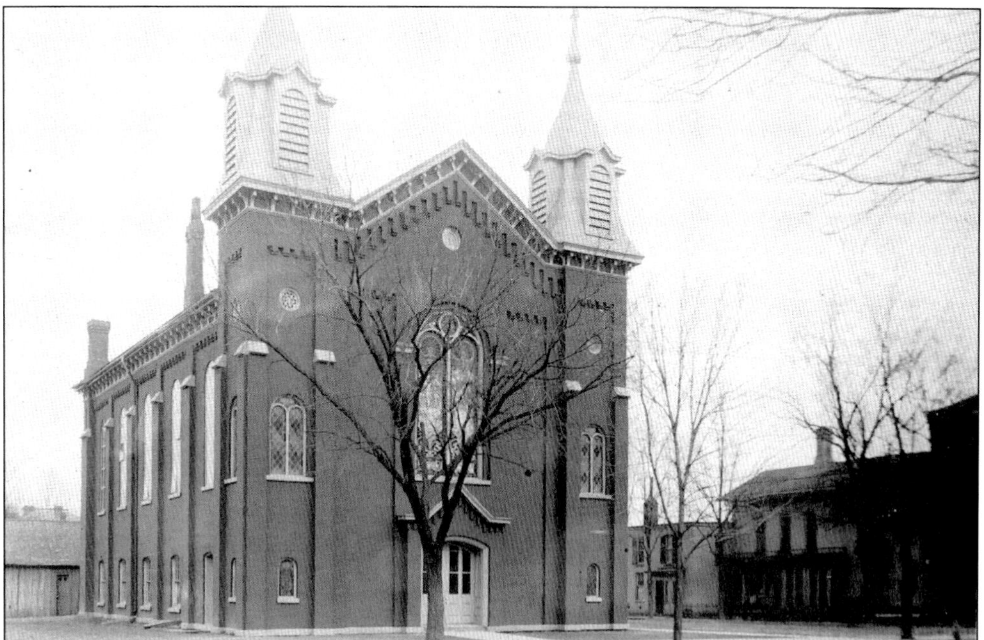

Completed in 1864, the Methodist church stood on the corner of Pearl Street and Chicago Boulevard. It remained until 1967, when it was torn down in favor of a more modern building on Bishop Reed Drive. The building seen to the right of the church in this photograph is B. J. Bidwell's house, which came to be the Coller House Hotel. (Photograph courtesy of Ashley E. Chase.)

The 1860s saw a building boom for churches just west of downtown along Chicago Boulevard. The Baptist church was the second to be built. It was completed in 1865, one year after the Methodist church. It still stands on the corner of Chicago Boulevard and Union Street, although the Baptists have since moved to a new location. (Photograph courtesy of Ashley E. Chase.)

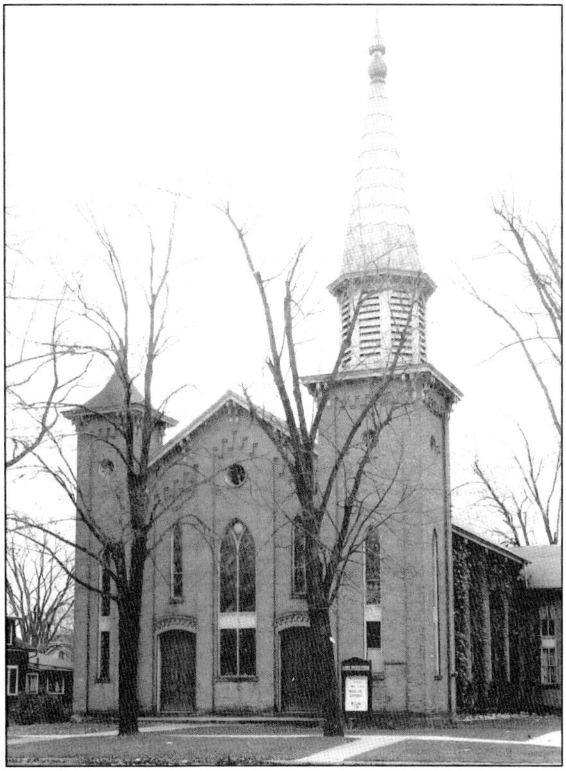

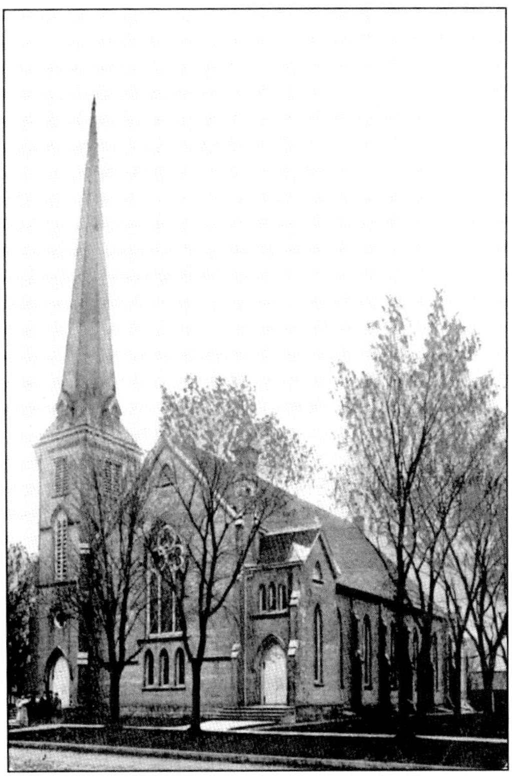

The third church to be completed just west of downtown in the 1860s was that of the Presbyterians. Erected on the corner of Chicago Boulevard and Maiden Lane, it was completed in 1869. The elegant 140-foot steeple of the First Presbyterian Church still graces the Tecumseh skyline, and the building is still occupied by the Presbyterian congregation, which can trace its roots in Tecumseh back to 1828. (Photograph courtesy of Ashley E. Chase.)

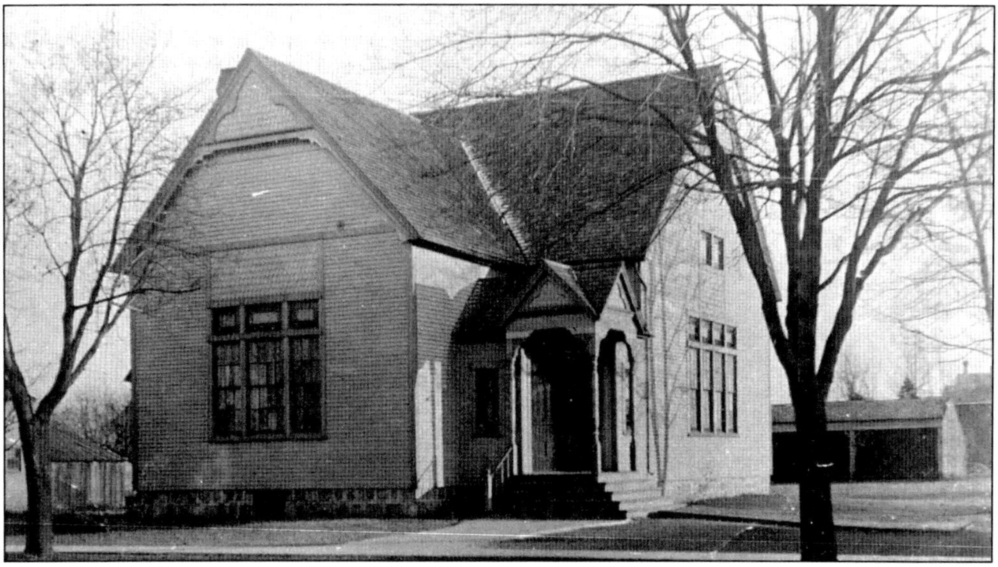

The Society of Friends Church is pictured here around 1910. Originally the Friends met in homes and then in the former Presbyterian session house, after it had been moved. Many of the early settlers were Friends including the Browns, the Evans, the Comforts, and the Satterthwaites. The Friends, or Quakers, built their own church in 1891 on the corner of West Pottawatamie and Van Buren Streets. To make room they tore down the Gridley home. Charles Gridley, who grew up in that home, was in the U.S. Navy, second in command under Admiral Dewy during the Spanish American War.

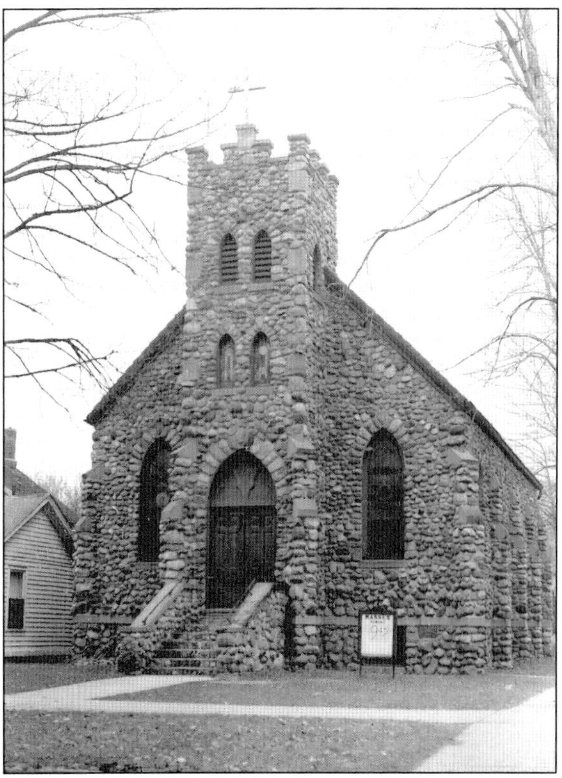

Although its small size and fieldstone construction would suggest that this was one of the oldest churches in town, St. Elizabeth Catholic Church was dedicated on November 27, 1913, decades after other congregations had constructed their places of worship. The Catholic congregation has since moved on, and today the "old stone church" on the corner of Chicago Boulevard and Oneida Street serves as the Tecumseh Area Historical Museum. (Photograph courtesy of Ashley E. Chase.)

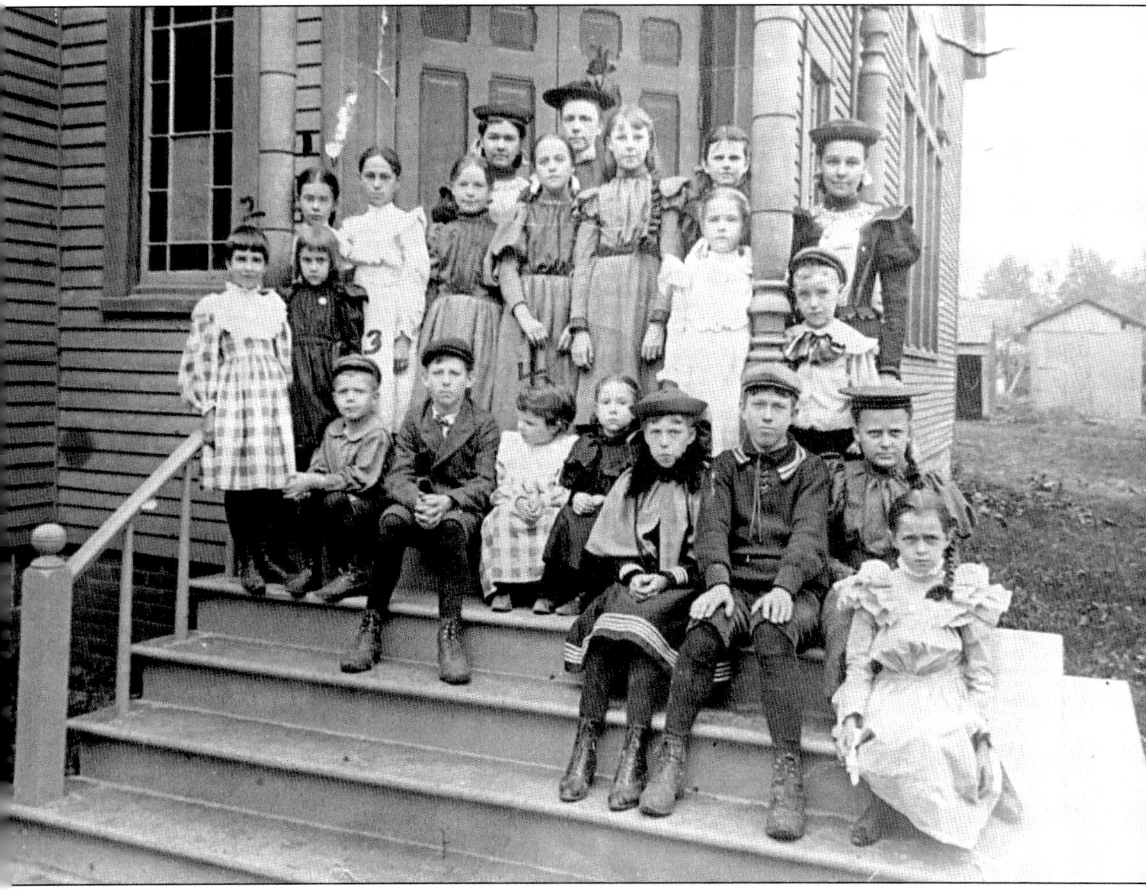

This picture of the Society of Friends Jr. C. E. Society was taken in front of the Friends church in 1897. This picture includes four of the Satterthwaite children shown numbered in the photograph: (1) Alace at age 10, (2) Beth at age eight, (3) Perry at age five, and (4) Eva at age three.

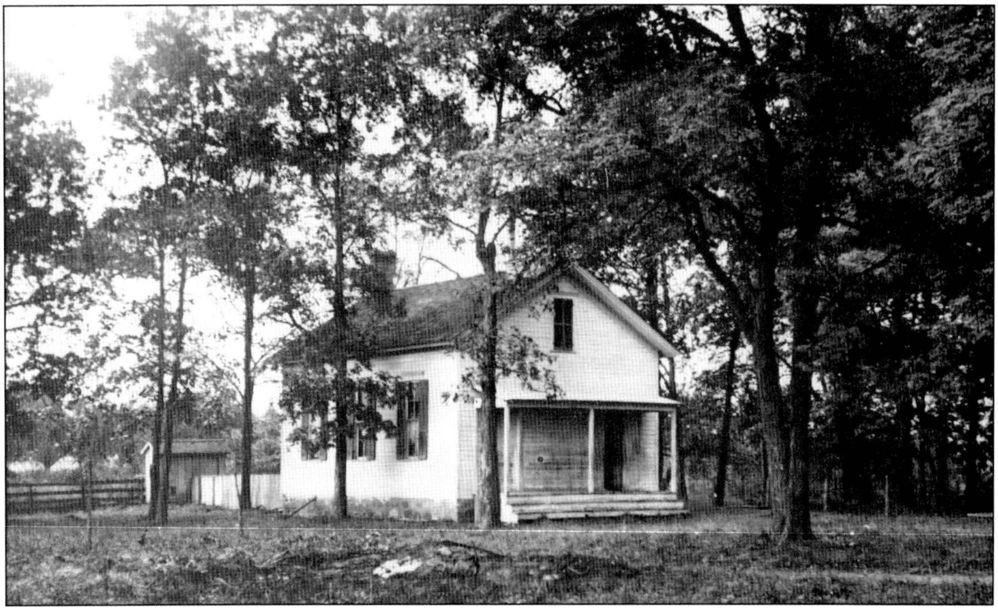

There were a number of one-room schoolhouses in and around Tecumseh. Among them were the Comfort School, south of town, and the Newberg School, north of town. One of the closer one-room schools was the Brownville schoolhouse, built in 1848. The Brownville School stood on a pleasantly wooded lot at the corner of Brown and Mill (Evans) Streets. In the 1930s, Henry Ford's Edison Institute Schools ran the Brownville School, and in 1957, it became the Gloria Dei Lutheran Church. It remains the north wing of their church building to this day.

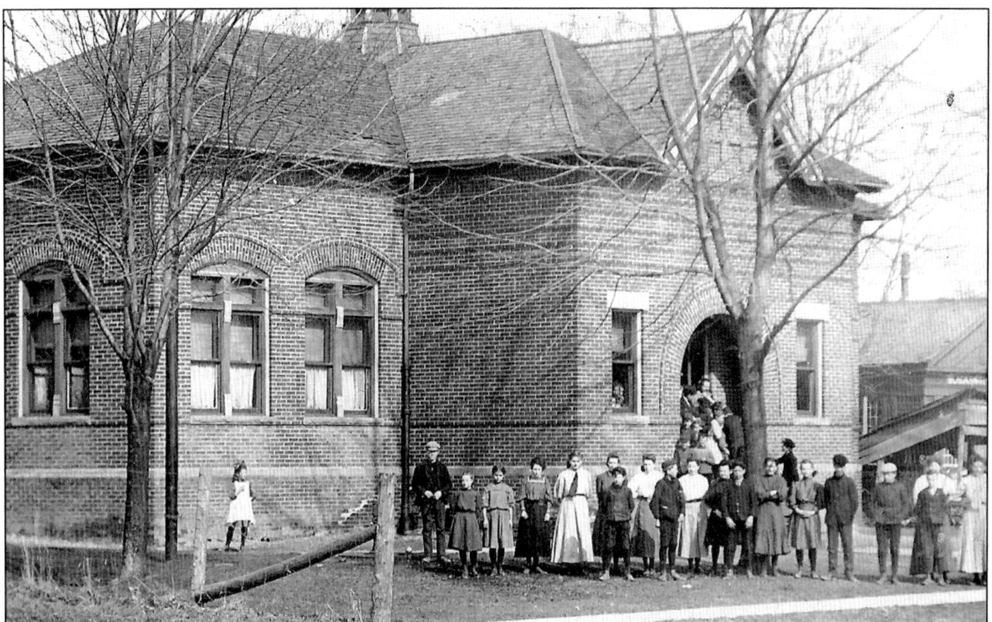

The original East Branch School, built in the 1840s, was located on East Kilbuck Street near the end of Oneida Street. It was abandoned in 1869, when the new East Branch School was built. Notice the blacksmith shop to the right of the school.

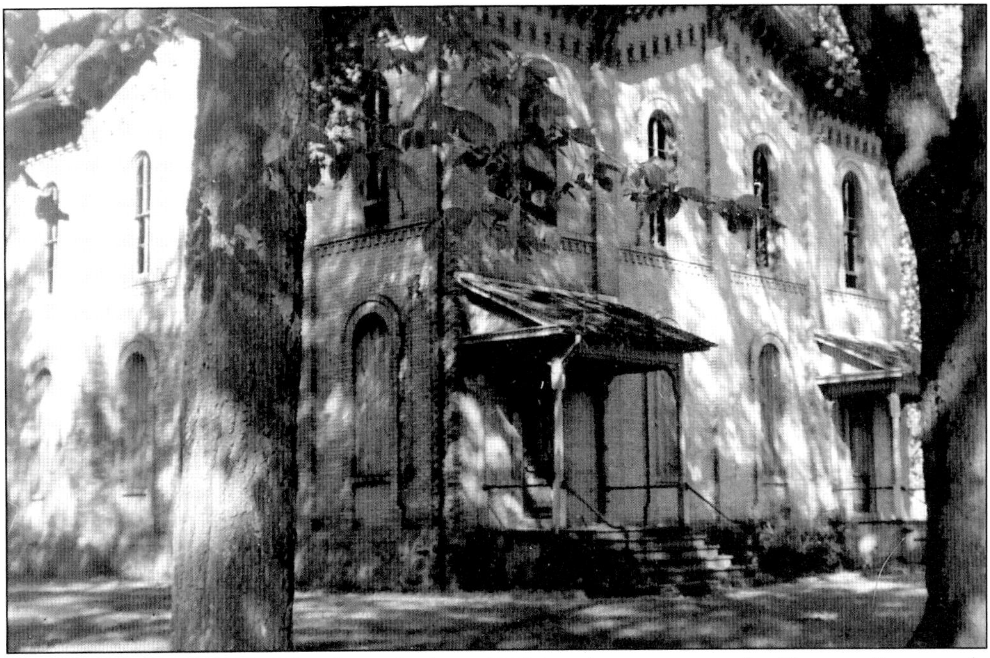

The "New" East Branch School was built in 1869 in what was once the Pleasure Promenade public park on the northwest corner of Chicago Boulevard and Maumee Street. It remained in use as a school in one form or another into the mid-20th century. Students in its later days remember being told by the custodian not to jump up and down when they were on the second floor because it was not safe to do so. Finally the East Branch School was razed to make way for the current city hall. (Photograph courtesy of Lenawee Historical Museum.)

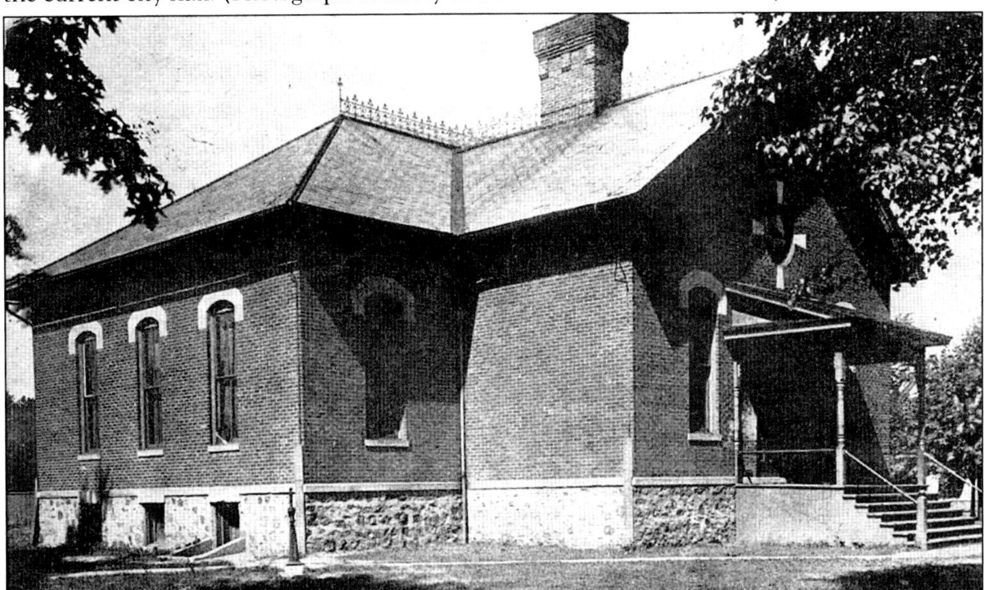

West Branch School, built in 1886, replaced the old one-room West Branch School of the 1840s. The West Branch School served the educational needs of the west side of Tecumseh into the 1970s. The building still stands today on the corner of Kilbuck Street and Maiden Lane, although it is no longer a public building.

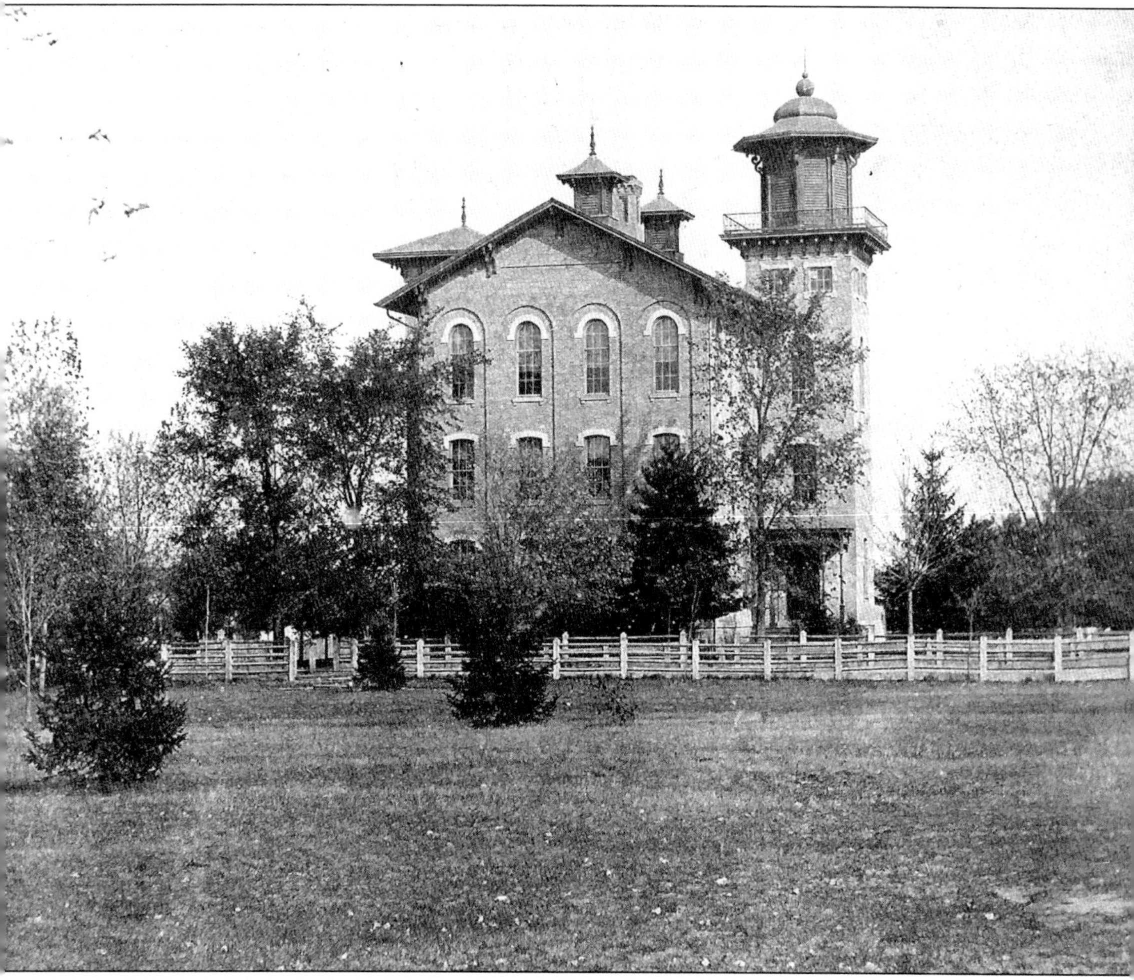

This beautiful view of Union School was taken from Military Square in the 1860s. Built in 1856 for a whopping $16,000, this majestic building was a source of great local pride, and detailed drawings of it appeared on many maps and atlases in the later 1800s as a testament to Tecumseh's beautiful architecture and civic prosperity.

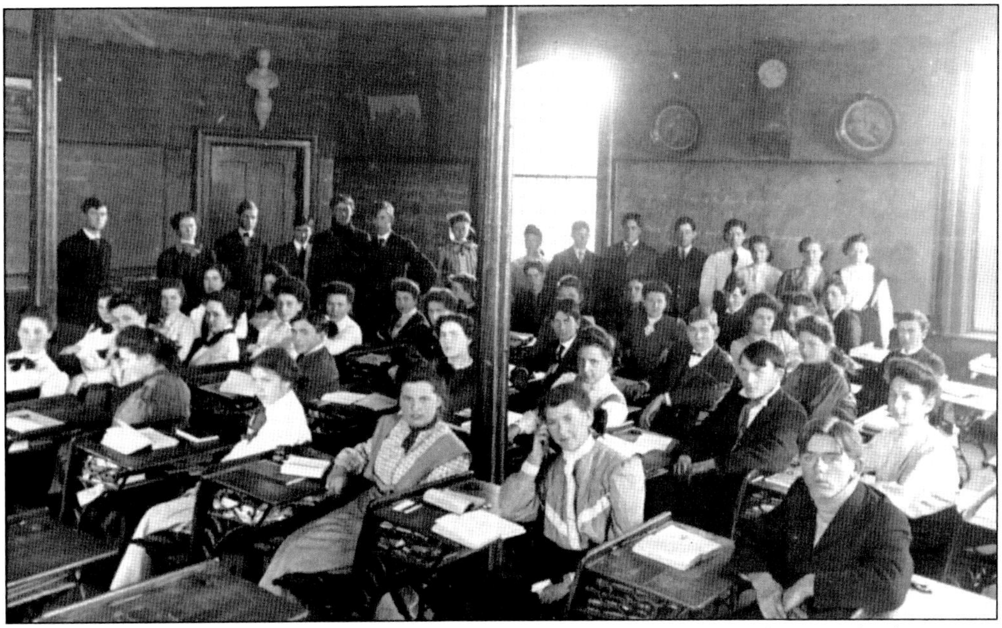

This photograph of an unknown Tecumseh High School class was taken inside the Union School in 1905. As elegant as the building was, it was already too small for the community by the time this picture was taken. It would take 10 years to remedy the overcrowding situation, and many accounts suggest that the Union School building had become structurally unsound some years before its demolition in 1917.

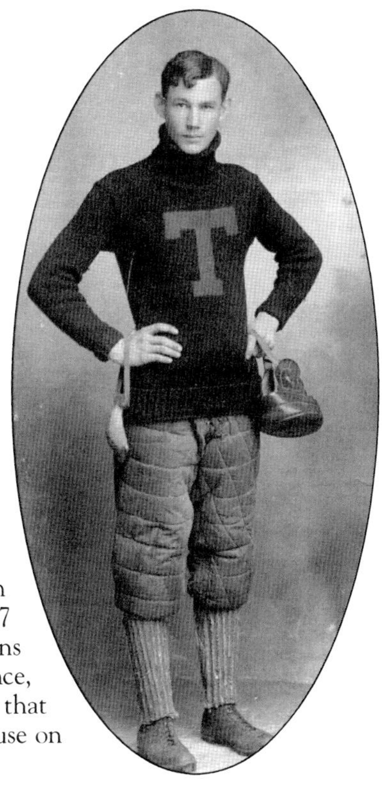

Eugene "Gene" Rosacrans, captain of the Tecumseh High School football team, is pictured during the 1906–1907 school year. Eugene was the son of Fred and Adele Rosacrans and had five brothers and sisters: Leon, Harry, Florence, Marion, and Marjorie. The year 1907 was the same year that Gene's large family moved into their newly purchased house on West Shawnee Street one lot east of Union Street.

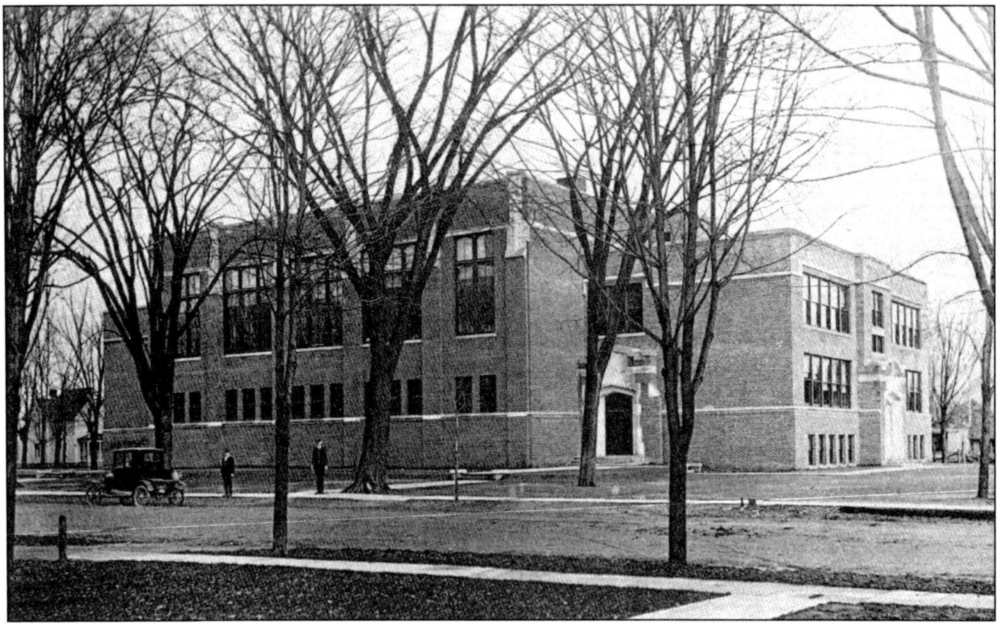

During 1917 and 1918, the Union School was torn down and the "new" high school was built on the same spot. A supervising architect for the project was Roger Waring, who had graduated from Tecumseh High School in 1908. During the 1917–1918 school year, classes were held in a building on South Evans Street that had been the Cummins Carriage Works. Today the "new" high school building houses the Tecumseh School District offices.

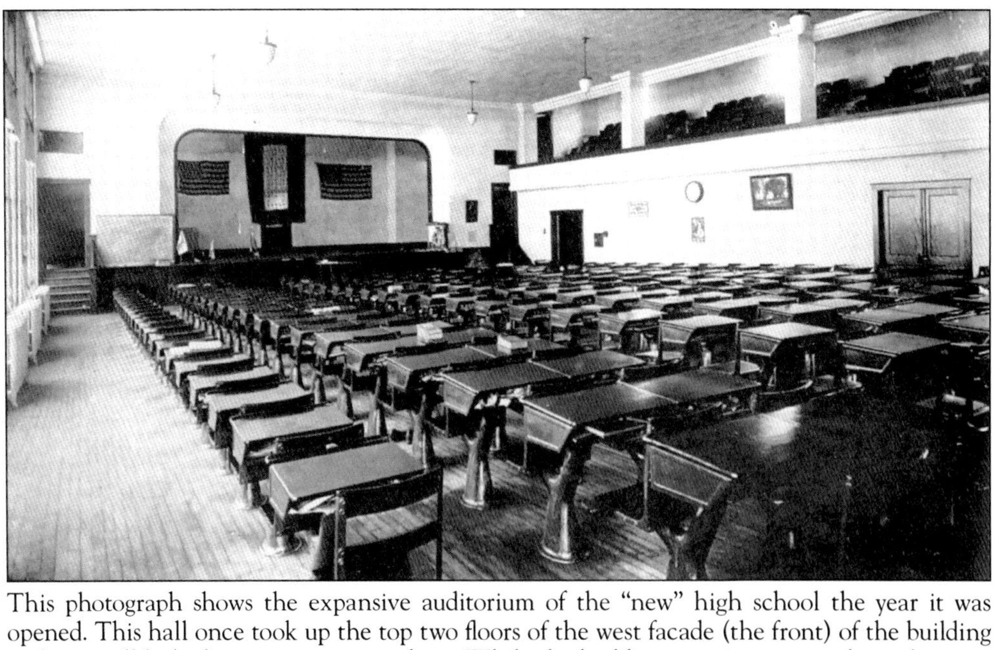

This photograph shows the expansive auditorium of the "new" high school the year it was opened. This hall once took up the top two floors of the west facade (the front) of the building and was well lit by large two-story windows. While the building remains in use, the auditorium was broken up into many individual rooms some time ago.

Three

Residential Tecumseh

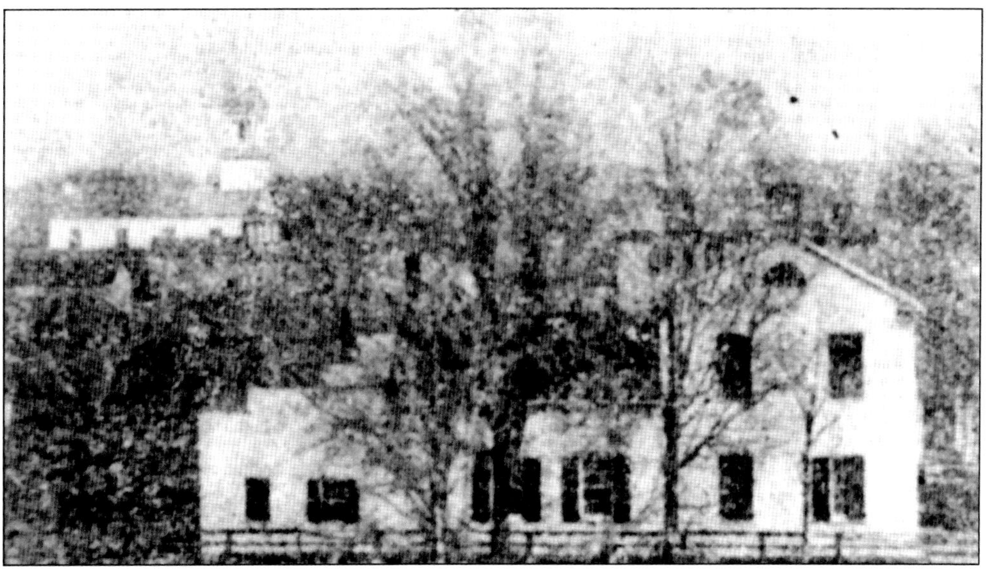

The Musgrove Evans house, built in 1826, is shown in its original location on the northeast corner of Chicago Boulevard and Ottawa Street. Musgrove Evans, one of Tecumseh's original founders, was also a surveyor who set to work laying out the streets of Tecumseh as soon as he arrived. The church in the background is the Presbyterian "White Frame Meeting House," built in 1840 on the site of the original Presbyterian session house, on Maumee Street near Logan Street facing what was then a public square.

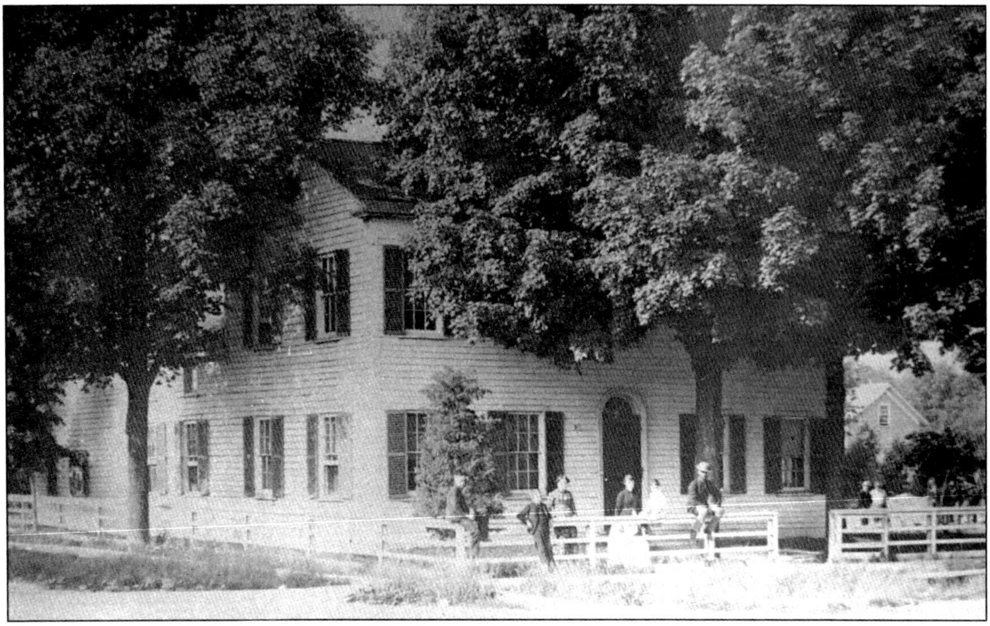

The Musgrove Evans house was still in its original location in 1885 when it was the Shull family residence. Shortly after this picture was taken, the house was moved to its current location on East Logan Street. Pictured from left to right are P. W. A. Fitzsimmons, W. H. A. Fitzsimmons, Mrs. Peter R. Adams, Mary C. Shull, Viola A. Shull, John D. Shull, and on the far right are the workmen who were digging the foundation for the Shull's new house.

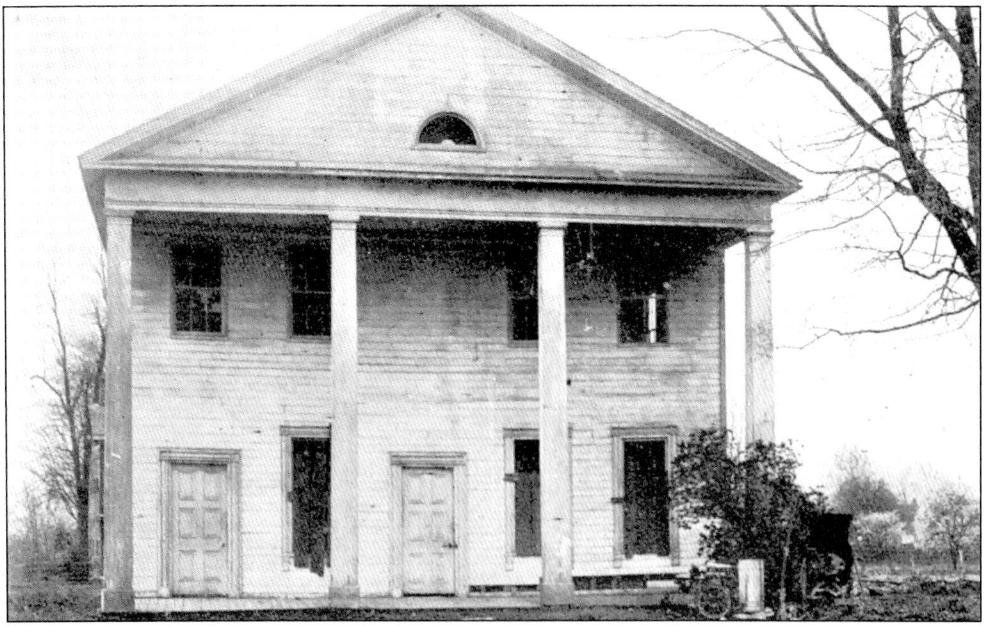

General Brown built the Peninsular House in 1827 as a residence, an inn, and a stagecoach stop for the Western Stage Company, which he also owned. It was located near what is now the intersection of Evans Street and Brown Street, an area that was called Brownville for much of the early history of Tecumseh. The building's grandeur and two of its wings had been lost by the time this picture was taken in 1911, shortly before the Peninsular House was torn down.

Gen. Joseph Brown, along with his brother-in-law Musgrove Evans, recruited a handful of adventurous souls and came west from Jefferson County, New York, to found Tecumseh in 1824. From the very beginning, their goal was not simply to settle in the west, but to establish a thriving community. General Brown died in 1880 "full of years and honors" at his daughter's home in Toledo, Ohio.

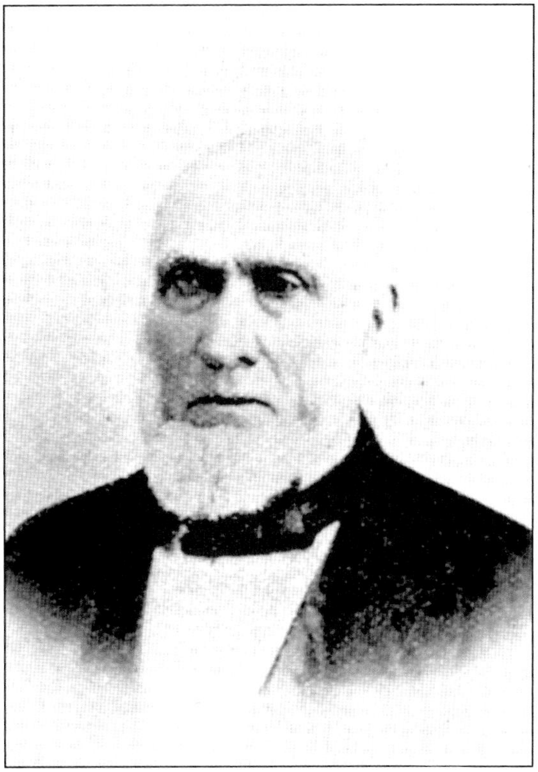

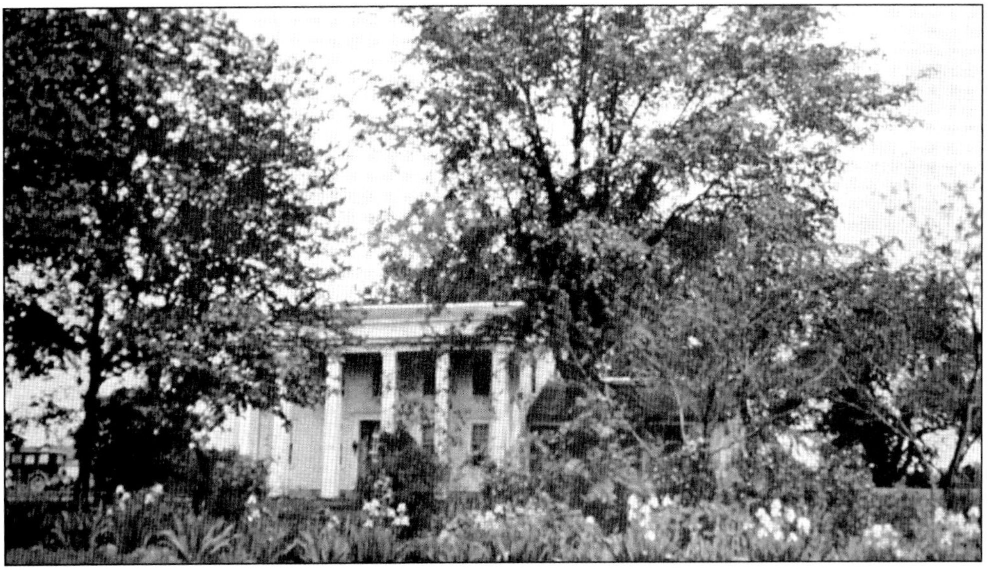

Jacob Ketcham arrived in Tecumseh in 1825, but he and his family spent that winter in Monroe. When they returned in 1826, they built a house on their land along Evans Creek west of town on Chicago Boulevard. It may have been a modest home or it may have been the Ketcham Inn, shown here, making it one of the oldest remaining structures in Tecumseh. This beautiful structure served as an inn under various names and owners, a family home, and an antique shop that was also known for its beautiful gardens. In 1957, the Ketcham Inn was moved to make room for a supermarket, and it now stands on the west side of Occidental Road.

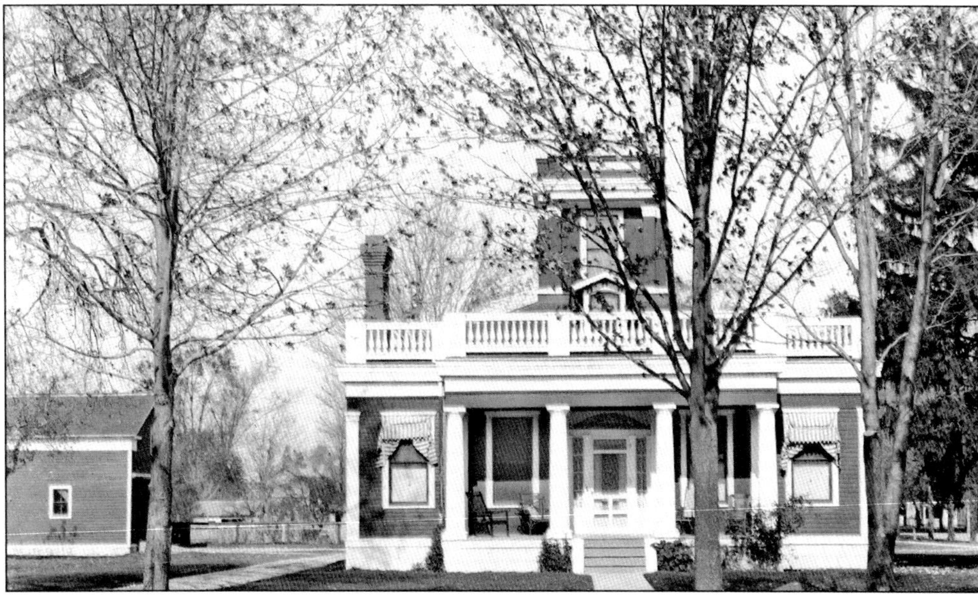

Around 1832, this house at 401 West Chicago Boulevard was built by twin brothers Elijah and Elisha Anderson. It is a popular story in town that there was a tunnel running from this house to the house directly across Chicago Boulevard, also built by the Anderson brothers, and used as part of the Underground Railroad. While there is no hard evidence to prove this story is true, it is known that the Underground Railroad had stops in and around Tecumseh. A newspaper article from 1988 reports the finding of what could have been a tunnel under one of the Anderson built houses, but only four feet of it was excavated at the time.

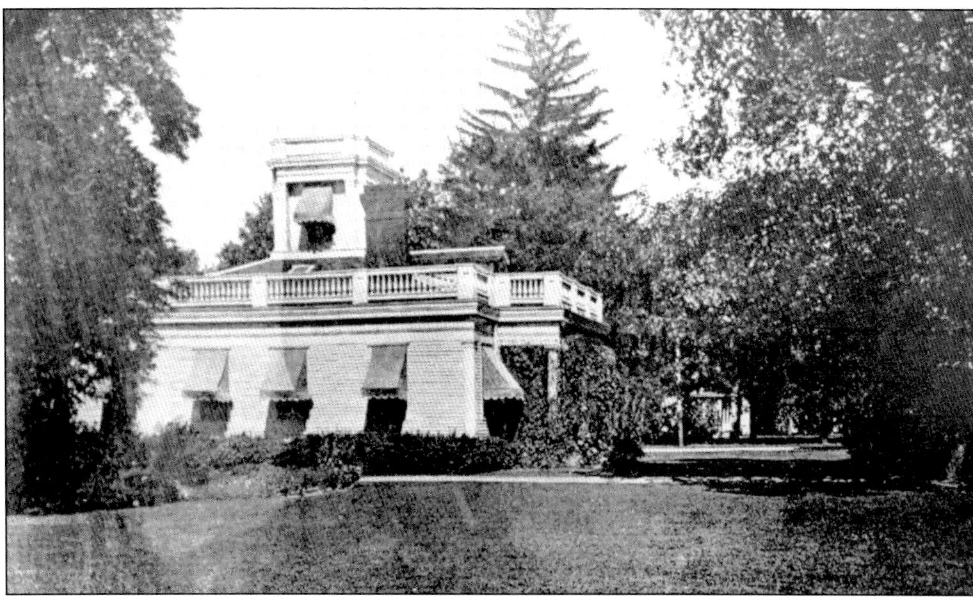

This is a side view of 401 West Chicago Boulevard, also known as the Anderson house, around 1920. This stately home was owned by some notable Tecumseh residents, such as Austin B. Waite and Elijah Anderson's eventual business partner in the Brewer foundry, Horace Brewer. In the 1920s and 1930s, it was a tearoom called the Tecumseh Tavern. It has since returned to being a residence and is still one of the most recognizable Tecumseh landmarks.

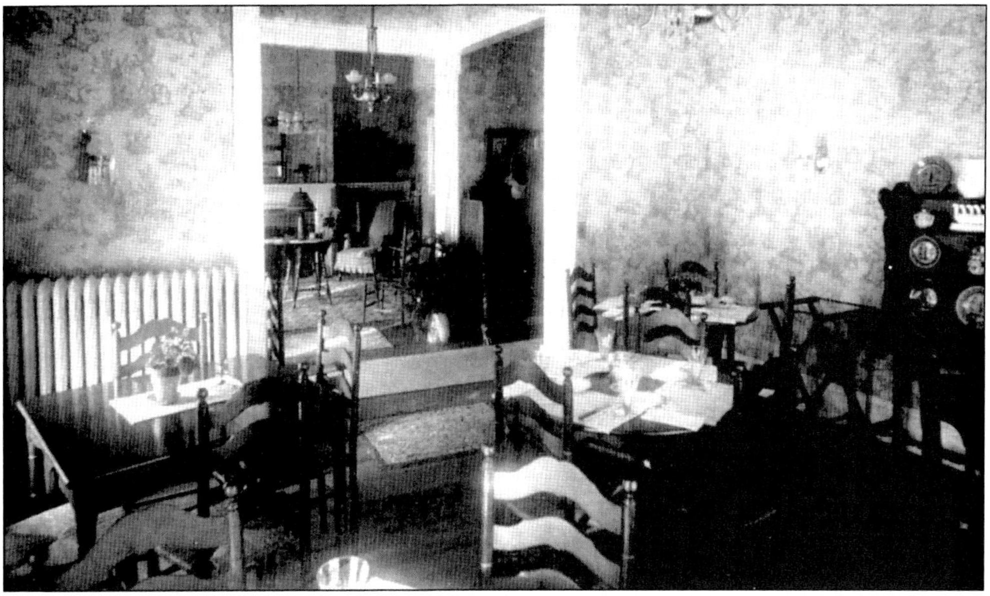

From a postcard advertising the Tecumseh Tavern, which occupied the Anderson house in the 1920s, the caption on back reads in part, "A vista through the dining room and hall into the living room of this quaint colonial tavern discloses its homelike interior . . . [which] after almost a century is now thrown open to the public for the first time."

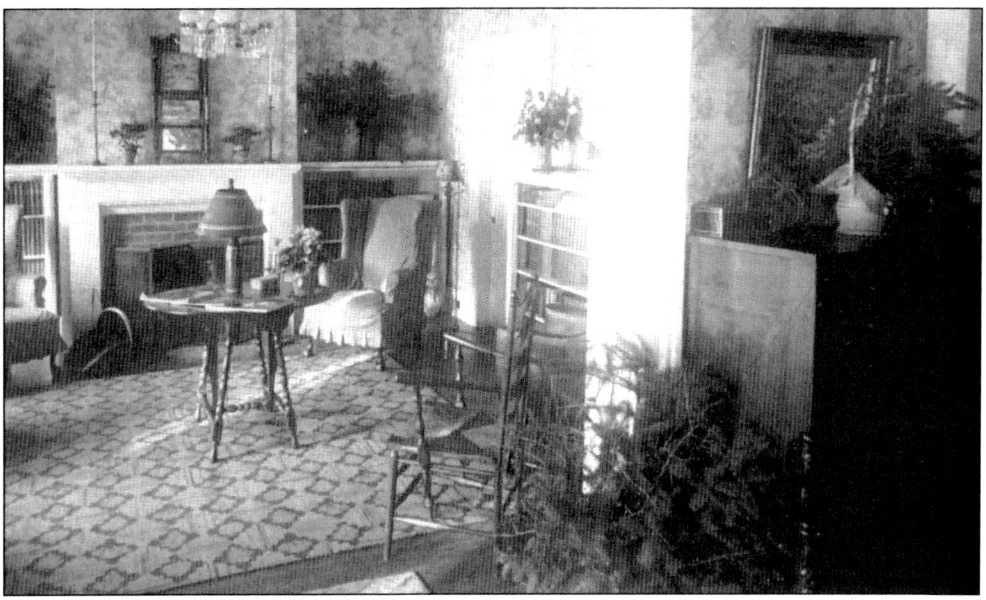

On a different postcard advertising the Tecumseh Tavern, the caption reads in part, "The simple fire place and furnishings . . . old Seth Thomas clock, spiral candle sticks, and sailor andirons, impel one to terry and partake of the good cheer."

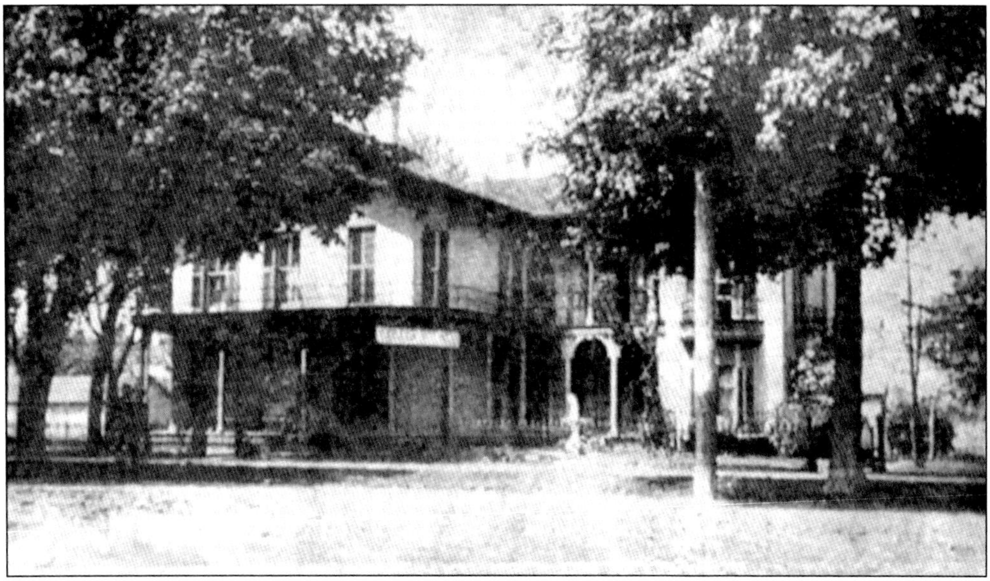

The grand home of extremely successful merchant, farmer, businessman, and real-estate developer B. J. Bidwell once stood on the northeast corner of Chicago Boulevard and Pearl Street. This picture was taken after 1904, when the Bidwell house became the successful Coller House Hotel. The Williamson Brothers Company acquired the house in 1920, and it was torn down to build retail space. (Photograph courtesy of Ashley E. Chase.)

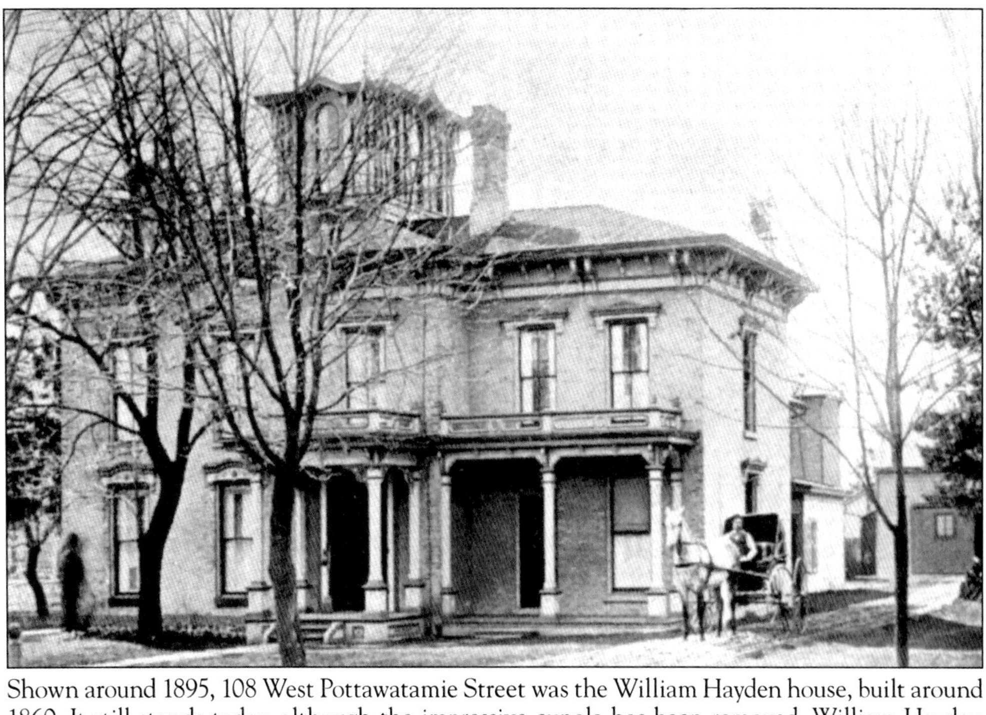

Shown around 1895, 108 West Pottawatamie Street was the William Hayden house, built around 1860. It still stands today, although the impressive cupola has been removed. William Hayden came to Tecumseh in the late 1850s and bought the failed Globe Mill from Stillman Blanchard. Hayden was a successful businessman, and the Hayden family played an important role in Tecumseh history for many generations.

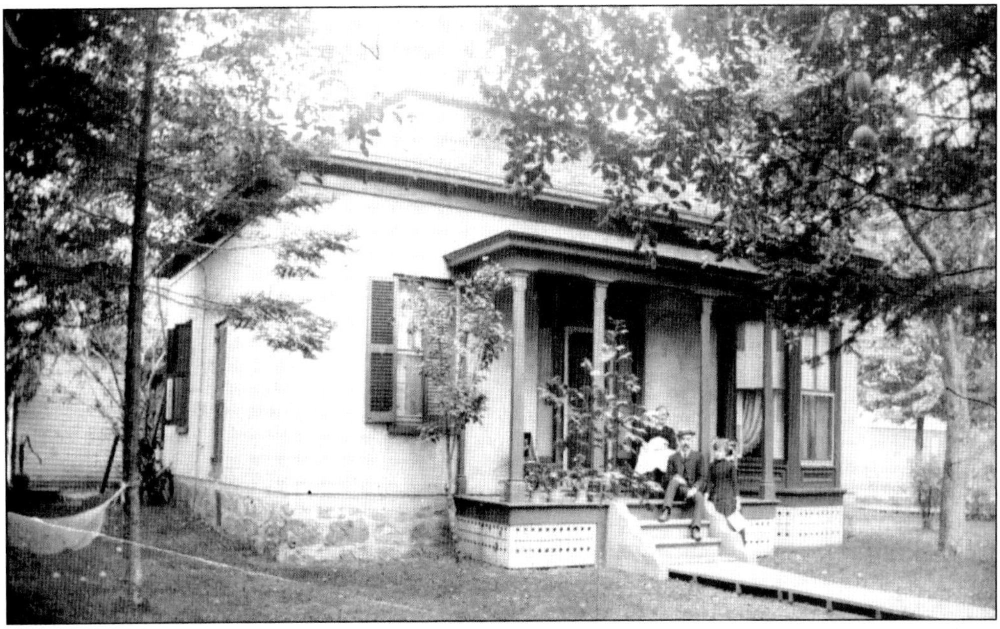

Seen here, around 1910, is the home of Arthur Kennedy and Emma Satterthwaite Kennedy at 123 North Ottawa Street. Of houses in Tecumseh, it was said, " . . . the humbler homes [are] comparatively as attractive as those of greater pretensions." Although the Kennedy Satterthwaite house is gone, dozens of humbler homes from this time still stand as ample evidence of the continuing truth of this statement.

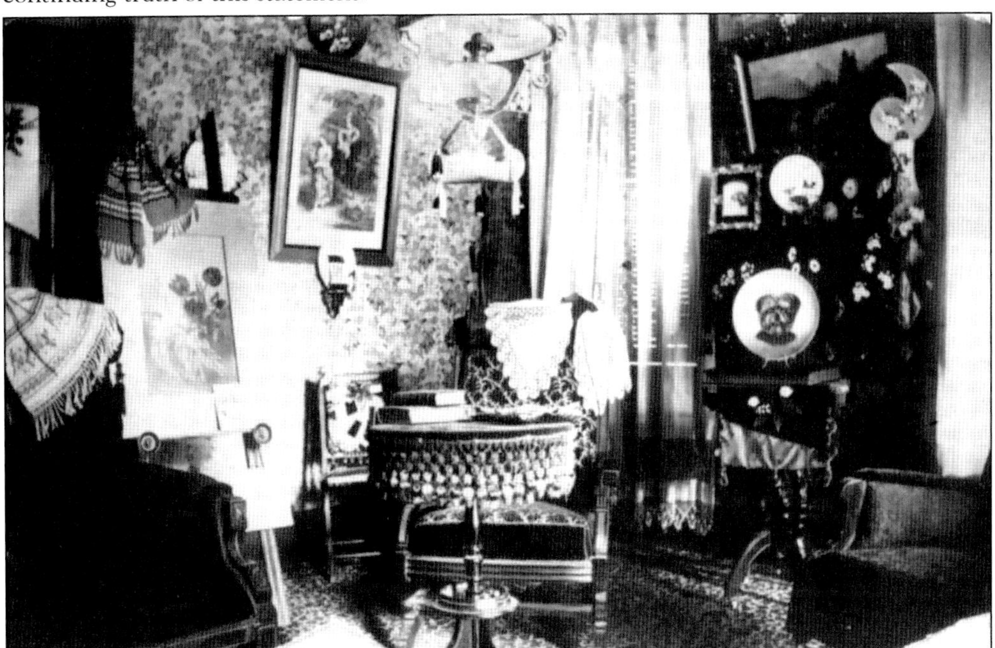

This is a photograph of the interior of 123 North Ottawa Street in the early 1900s, when it was the home of Arthur Kennedy and Emma Satterthwaite Kennedy. Arthur Kennedy was probably from the Kennedy family that owned a grocery, confectionery, and tobacco store downtown in the late 1800s and early 1900s. This house was torn down in 1975.

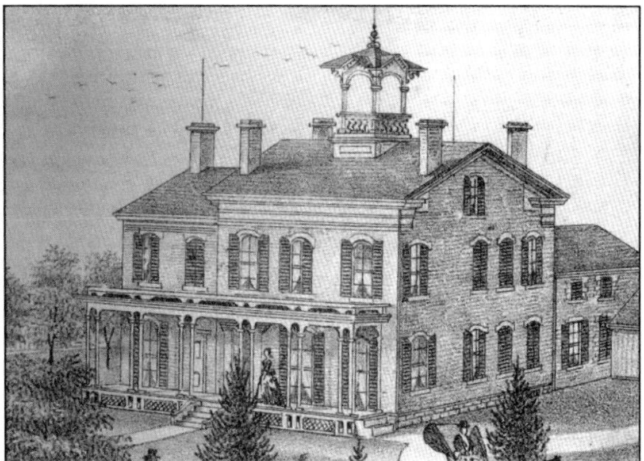

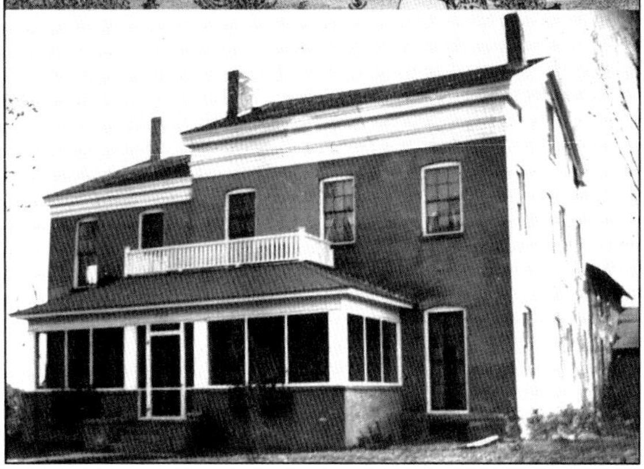

The home of Perley Bills is shown in a lithograph from 1874 and a photograph from the first quarter of the 20th century. Bills arrived in Tecumseh in 1837 and was a school teacher for many years. He eventually served as a member of the state senate, and as a representative at the state constitutional convention. Bills was also a successful developer, a businessman, and a banker, though it took more than one try to find success in banking. The Bills' house once stood on the south side of Killbuck Street at the end of Oneida Street, but stands no longer.

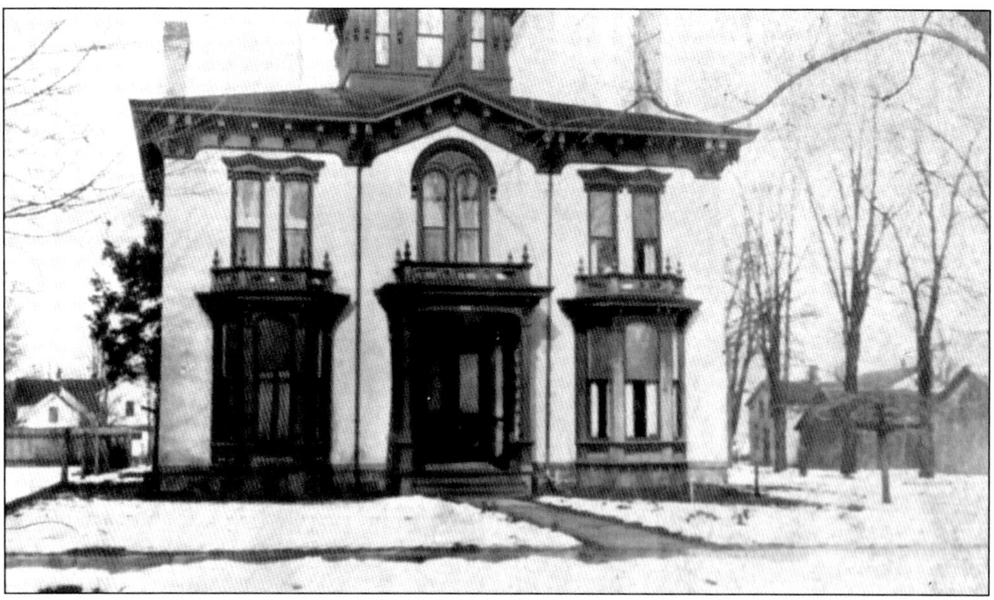

This is 303 West Chicago Boulevard, built in 1850 by Alonzo Murray. Murray was a carpenter who worked with Salmon Crane to construct some of Tecumseh's best buildings, including the Methodist church that was on the northwest corner of Chicago Boulevard and Pearl Street. The daughter of Alonzo and Mary Murray, Abigail, was married in the house on January 1, 1860. (Photograph courtesy of Ashley E. Chase.)

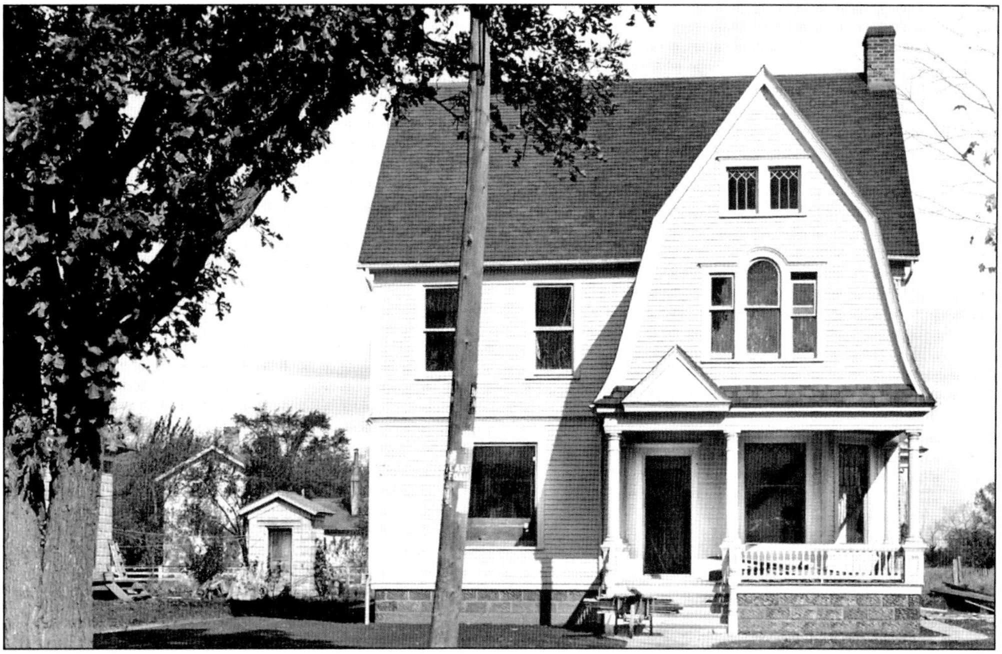

William Sisson, a furniture merchant, built this distinct house in 1901. It stands one lot east of Union Street on Shawnee Street. In 1907, Fred Rosacrans, a successful dry goods merchant, postmaster, and prominent citizen, purchased the house, and the Rosacrans family lived there until 1941.

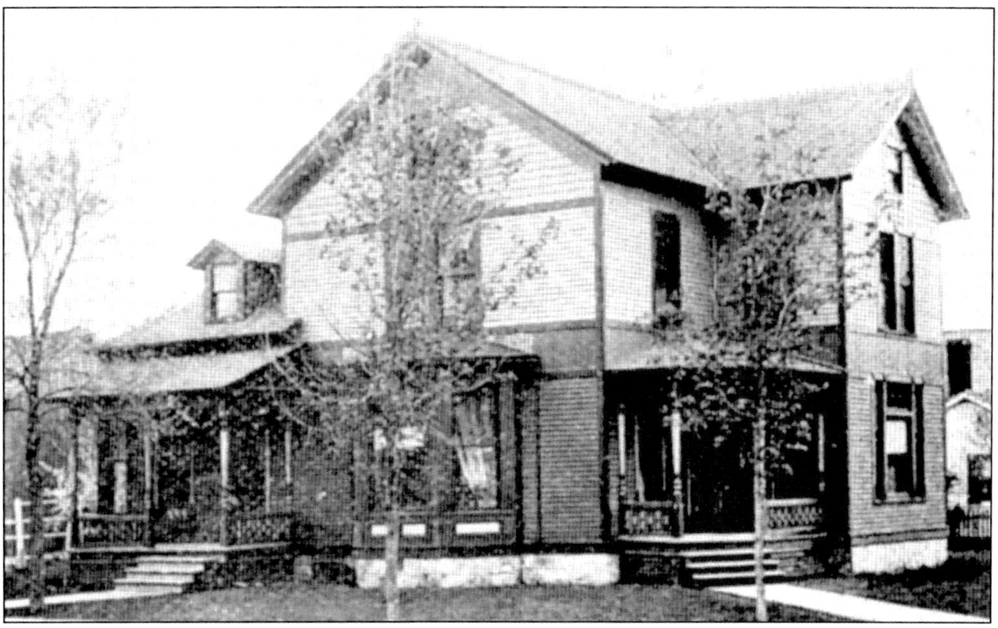

Around 1833, this building 502 West Chicago Boulevard was constructed. William and Lucinda Heck purchased the home in 1883 and extensively remodeled the house in 1889. After Lucinda Heck was widowed in 1893, she sold the house to Carolyn Hyde, widow of Albert Hyde. Albert Hyde Sr., a successful farmer, was the brother of Morris Hyde and had interest in the Hyde Carriage Factory with his nephew Albert Hyde Jr., the son of Morris and Harriet.

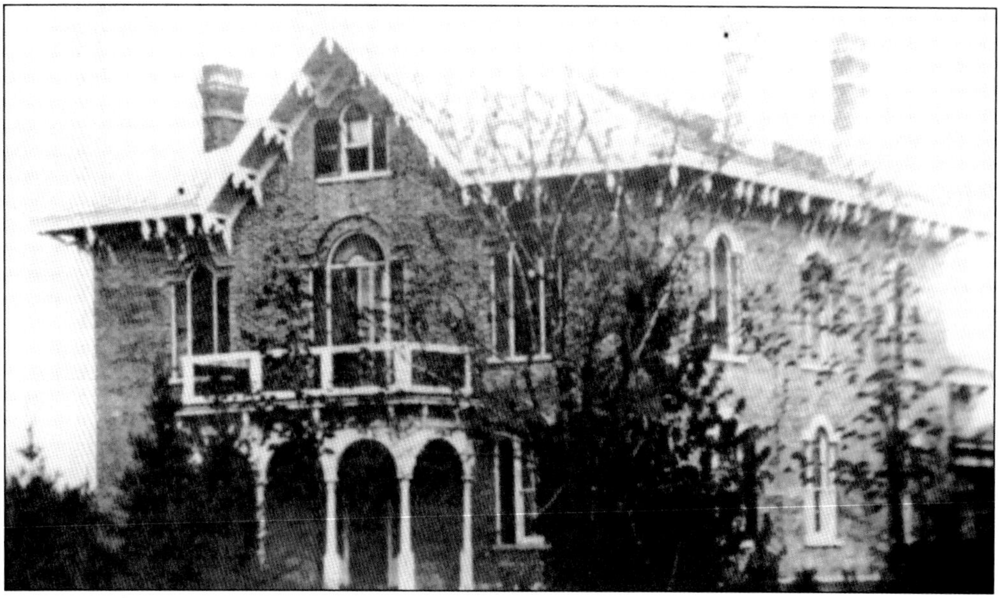

Dr. Michael A. Patterson was one of Tecumseh's earliest settlers, arriving in 1826. Dr. Patterson's first house was on the southeast corner of Chicago Boulevard and Evans Streets, and his second house, shown here, was on the south side of Chicago Boulevard between Ottawa and Oneida Streets. This house reflected the doctor's success not just as a medical practitioner but also as a real estate developer and investor.

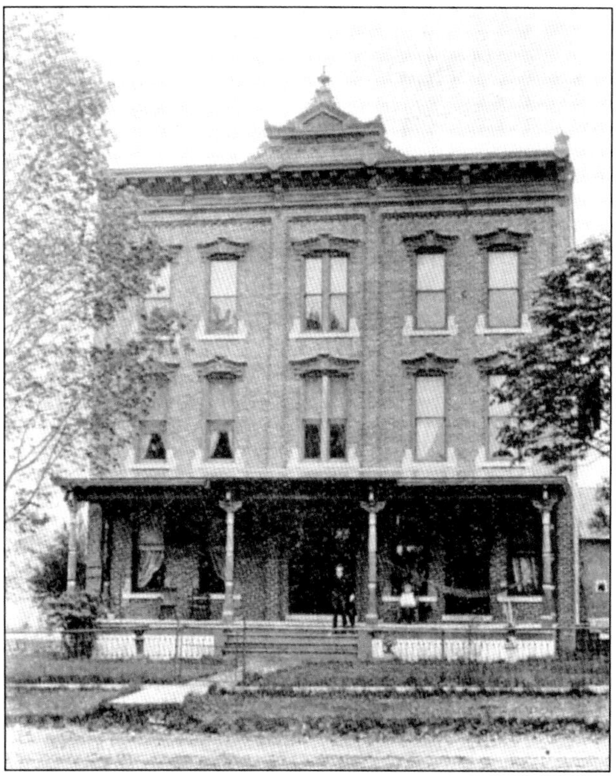

After Dr. Patterson's death, his son-in-law, H. S. Lee, transformed the house into the Patterson House Hotel. While Dr. Patterson had been very successful in business and real estate, his son-in-law was not as fortunate, and the Patterson Hotel was not successful. When this picture was taken in the 1890s, the building had again become a residence of one H. S. Lee. The building was later divided into apartments and then torn down in the 1950s.

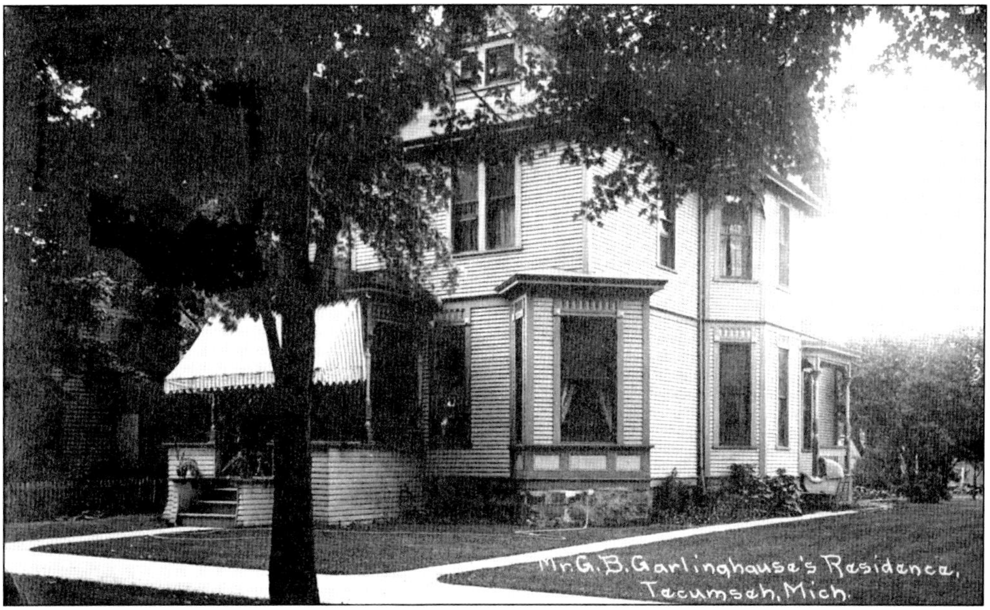

The home at 413 West Chicago Boulevard was built in 1886 for John and Sarah Heck. In 1921, when this picture was taken, it was the home of Gurdon B. Garlinghouse, who purchased the house in 1906. Garlinghouse owned a livery stable that had been established by brothers Ben and Bert Garlinghouse in 1885. In the late 1800s, the Garlinghouse brothers also had interest and management responsibility in the Lilly House Hotel, the Tecumseh Electric Company, and a large farm northeast of town. (Photograph courtesy of Lenawee Historical Museum.)

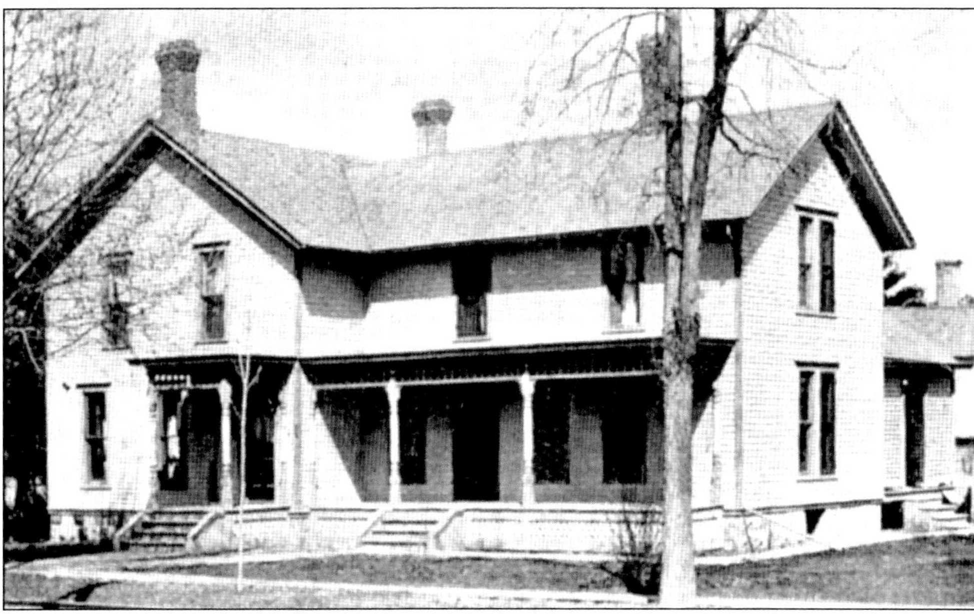

This house was built in the 1870s at 204 South Evans Street. James Elliott, brother of Thomas and Robert, who were all successful blacksmiths in town, purchased it in the early 1880s. He also owned the building directly to the south, which served as his blacksmith shop. A booklet promoting Tecumseh in the 1890s, showing the James Elliott estate, reads in part, "The fine residence and substantial buildings are fair examples of many similar ones in this beautiful village."

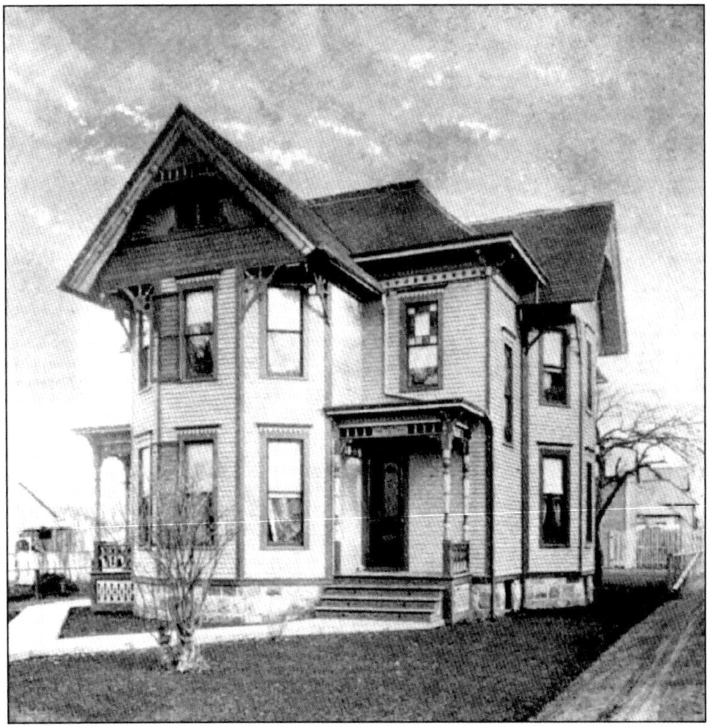

The location of Thomas Elliott's new house was 206 West Chicago Boulevard, photographed not long after its completion in 1892. Thomas, along with his brothers James and Robert, were immigrants from Ireland. They all became prosperous blacksmiths and owned shops in town. In the 1890s, Thomas's business was located on South Pearl Street next to the Hyde Carriage Factory.

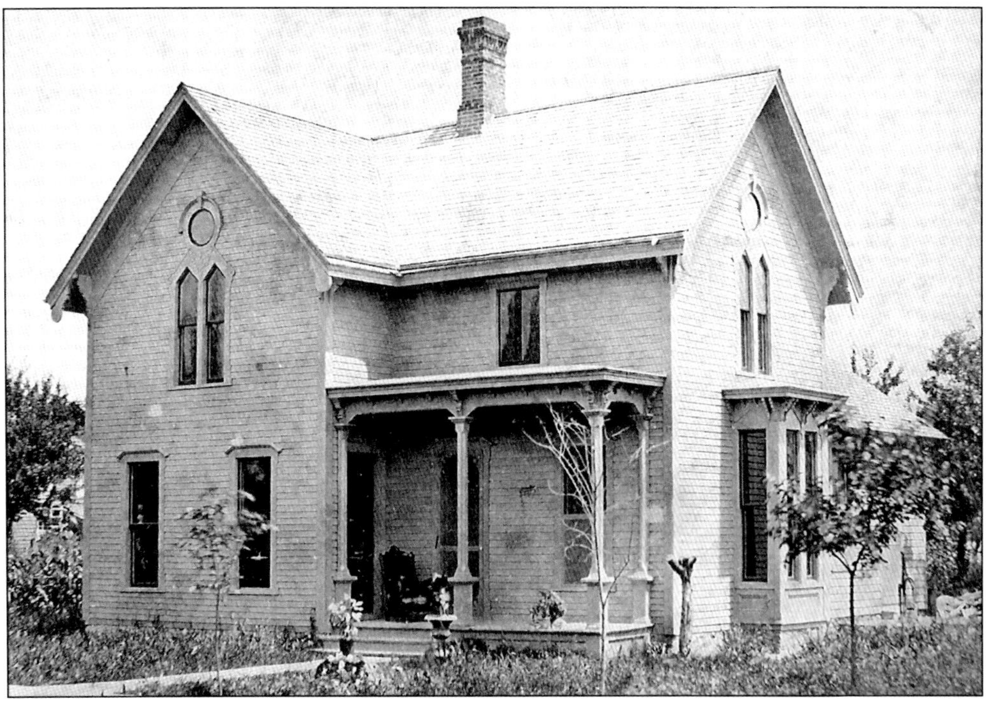

This photograph shows the Tremaine home in 1878, the year it was built and just after the Tremaines moved in. This is quite probably the Mr. Tremaine who was the manager and owner of the creamery on East Pottawatamie Street. The creamery was originally built by Lucius Lilley and a consortium of local businessmen and sold to Mr. Tremaine sometime in the late 1880s or 1890s.

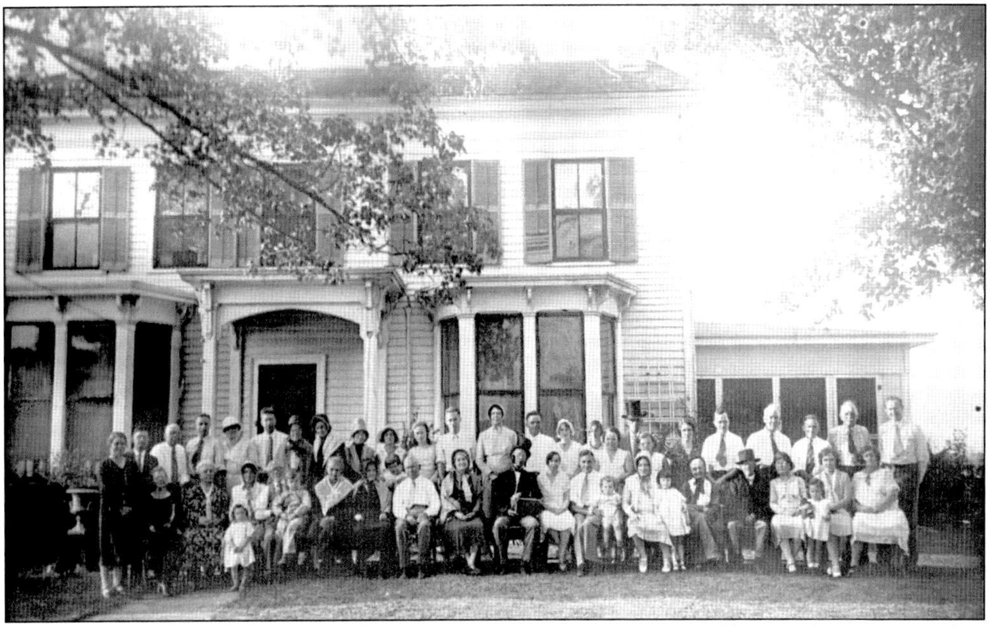

The Satterthwaite house on Shady Lane was built around 1839. Samuel Satterthwaite arrived in Tecumseh in 1831 with his wife, Hanna. During the Satterthwaite's time, the house was said to have been a stop on the Underground Railroad. After the Satterthwaites, the house belonged to the Sutton family. Nehemiah Sutton was a principal in the Sutton Opera House and Sutton and Swan Hardware, which interestingly enough would become Satterthwaite Brothers Hardware.

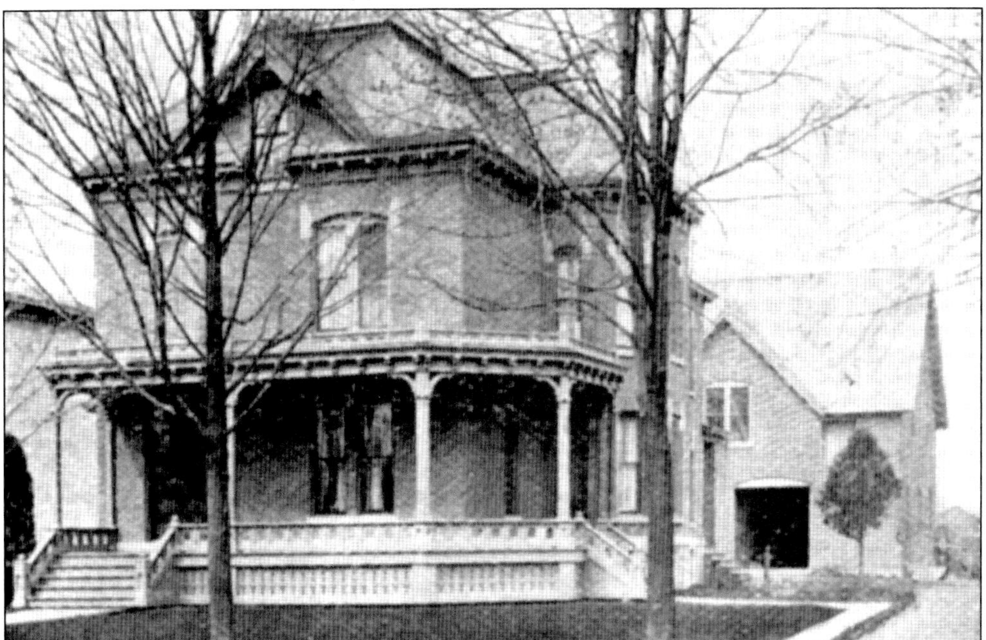

Adelbert W. Mills built the house at 107 South Union in 1884 for his wife Rosa and their six children. Adelbert was a very successful businessman and had interests in publishing, real estate, railroads, framing, hospitality services, and politics. He was also the builder of the impressive Mills Block downtown, built on the corner of Chicago Boulevard and Ottawa Street.

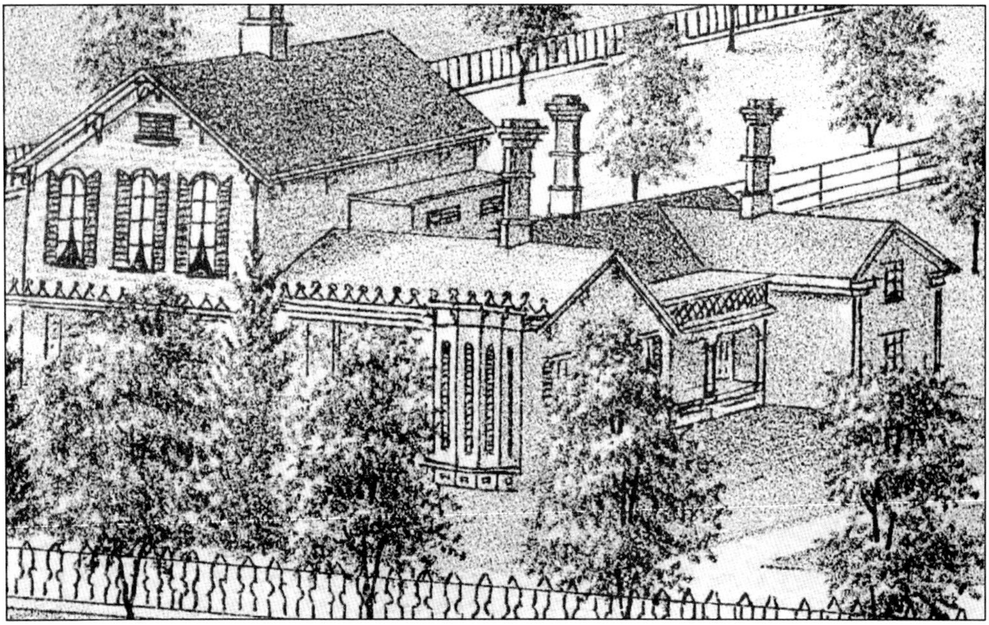

By the 1870s, Samuel W. Temple had dabbled in real estate development and owned a prosperous lumber company, even opening a grocery on Evans Street. His businesses expanded and diversified and appear to have all been successful. His elegant brick house, shown in an artists rendering from 1874, was built in 1866 on the corner of Shawnee and Pearl Streets where it still stands today.

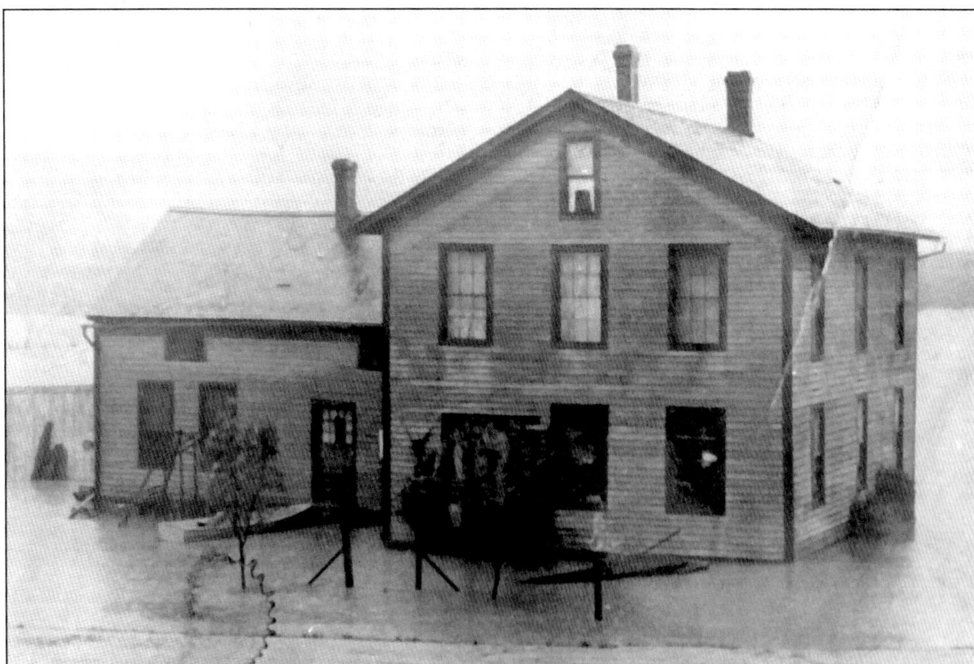

At one time the home of Sheriff John Smith, this house was located on the south side of East Chicago Boulevard, across from the Hayden Mill, close to where the water treatment plant is located today. This picture was taken after a flood in the early 1900s.

This photograph, taken around 1925, shows an unidentified woman standing in front of the large and stately house built by Salmon Crane in 1851. The house still stands on East Shawnee Street at the corner of Ottawa Street. In 1853, Albert and Elona Anderson moved in and would stay for 15 years. Albert Anderson owned a woolen mill and was the founder and owner of Anderson Grocery. (Photograph courtesy of Ashley E. Chase.)

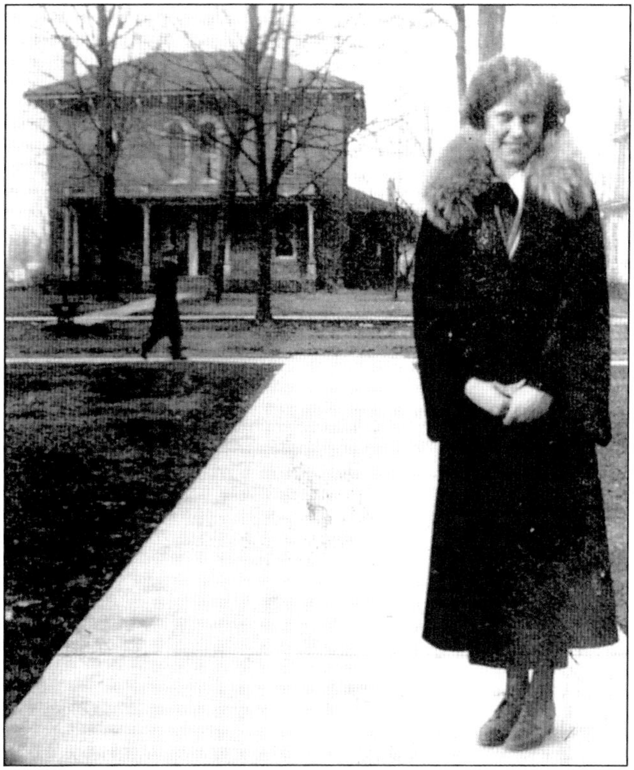

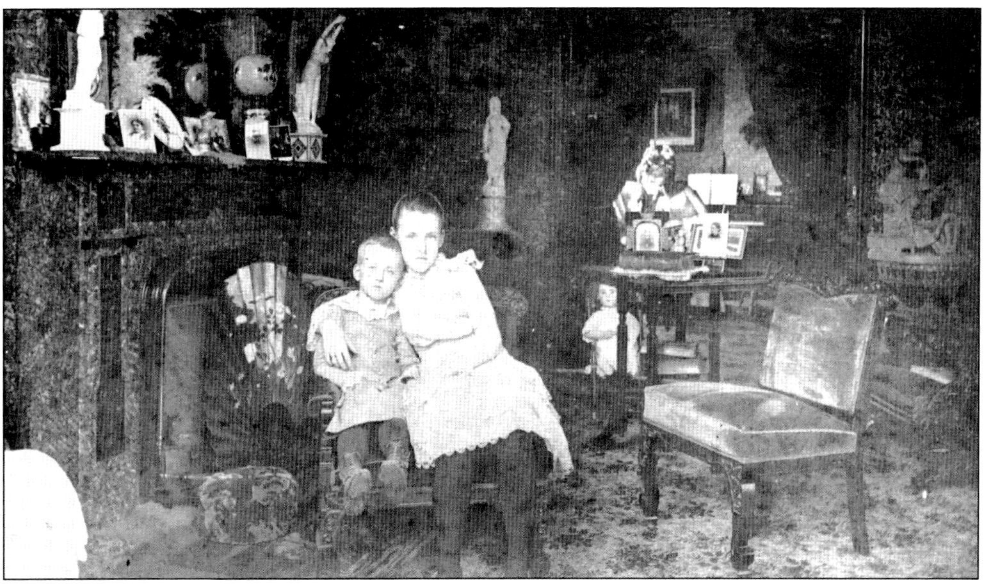

In 1880, Seaton W. Anderson, the son of Albert and Elona Anderson, built a beautiful house at 511 West Chicago Boulevard. Seaton was a principal at the Anderson Dry Goods store and was known for his pleasant manner and excellent salesmanship. This photograph shows Seaton and Ella Anderson's two children, Helen and Faron, sitting in the parlor around 1884.

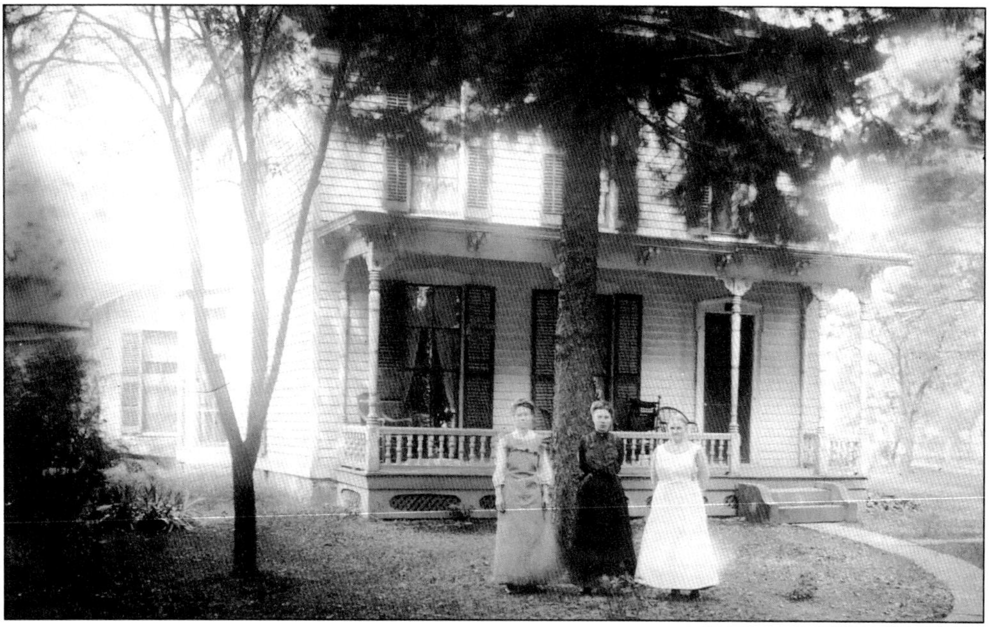

This house at 301 North Union Street was built in 1866 for C. B. Thomas, principal of Union School. William H. Osborn purchased the house in 1881 and sold it to J. Newton Satterthwaite in the spring of 1908. The Satterthwaite family owned it well into the 1970s. Pictured here in 1907 are, from left to right, Carrie Sawyer, Harriet Calkins, and Lucy Lowry. (Photograph courtesy of Lenawee Historical Museum.)

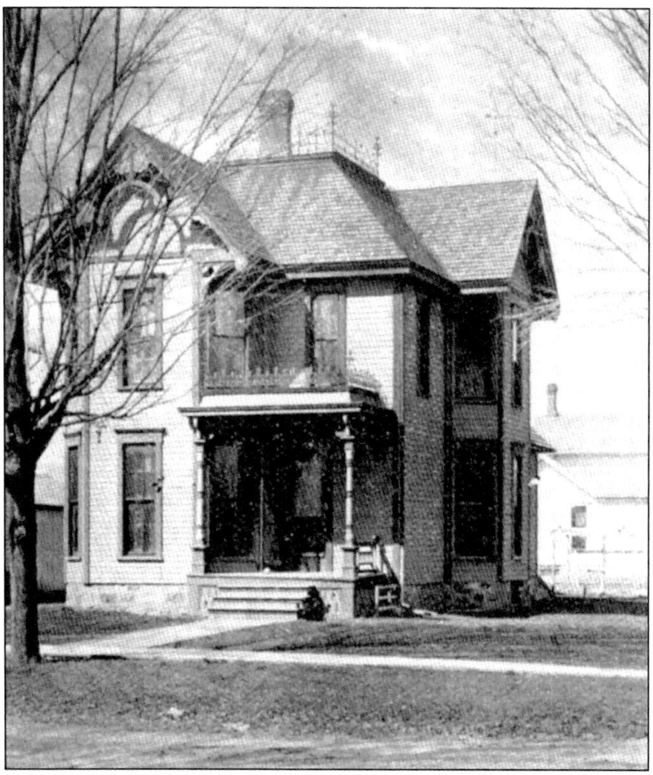

The J. H. Smith House, at 115 North Union Street, shown here around 1890, was built in 1885. Smith held various occupations as a carpenter, a lumberyard manager, a manager at the Tecumseh Table Company, and the cashier at the Lilley State Bank, where in 1913 he became president; in the 1890s, Smith served as the village president. He was also one of the owners of the Tecumseh Indians professional baseball team, in company with other well-known local entrepreneurs such as Brewer, Temple, Faye, Anderson, and Heesen.

Edwin B. Wood, a prominent Tecumseh attorney, built his house in 1867 on the northwest corner of Union and Logan Streets, where it still stands today. Wood arrived in Tecumseh in 1849 with no intention of staying, but instead started practicing law with C. A. Stacy and stayed the rest of his life. He became a respected lawyer and community leader and died in his home in 1885.

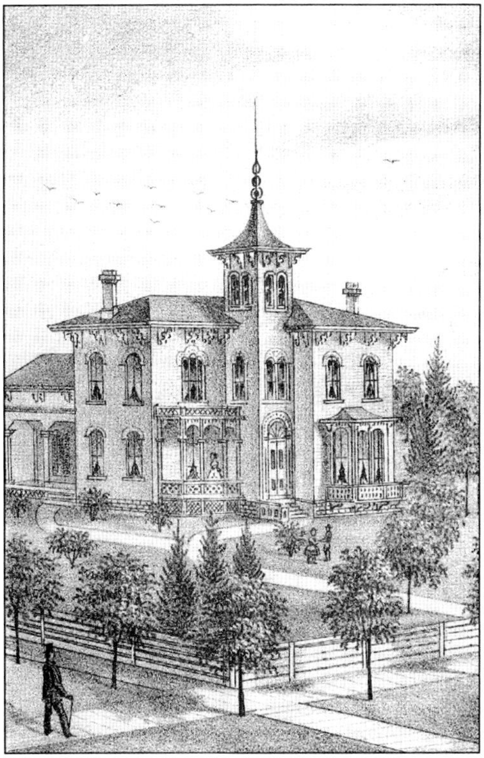

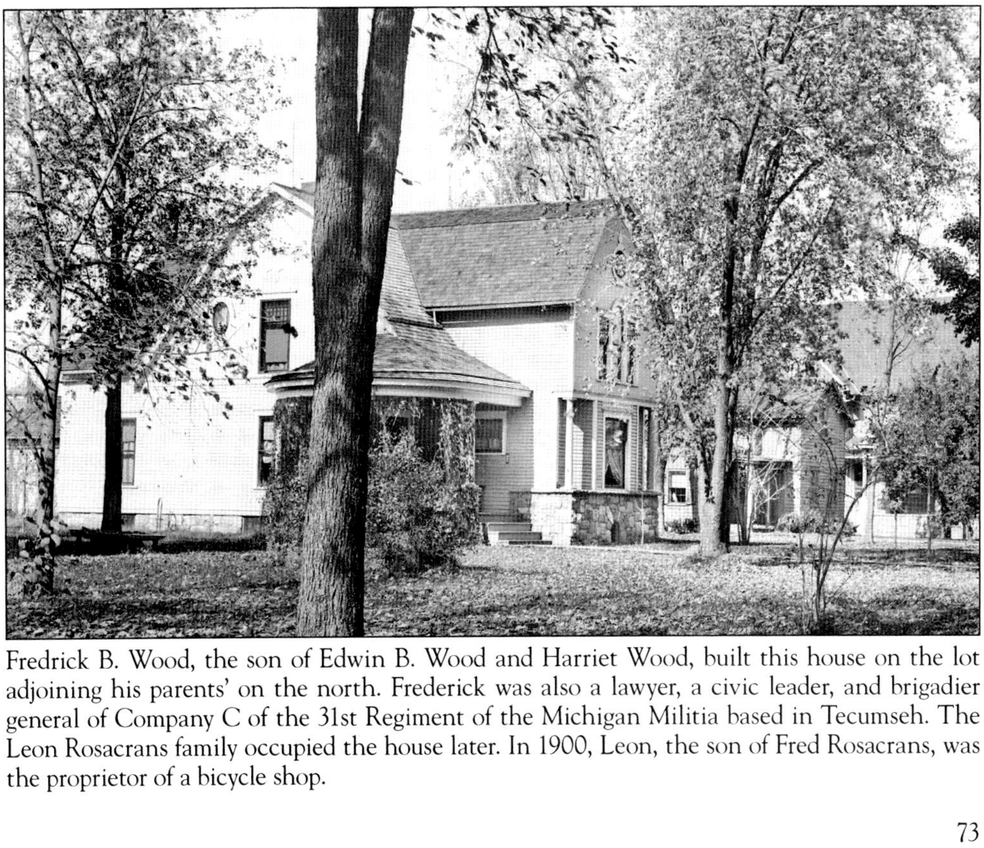

Fredrick B. Wood, the son of Edwin B. Wood and Harriet Wood, built this house on the lot adjoining his parents' on the north. Frederick was also a lawyer, a civic leader, and brigadier general of Company C of the 31st Regiment of the Michigan Militia based in Tecumseh. The Leon Rosacrans family occupied the house later. In 1900, Leon, the son of Fred Rosacrans, was the proprietor of a bicycle shop.

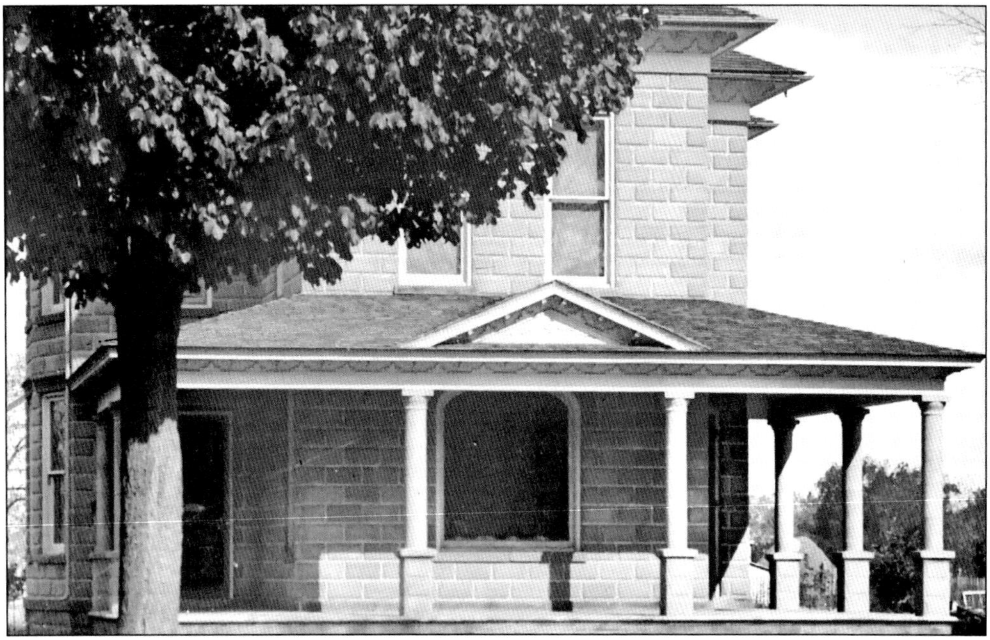

Hendrick and Mary Heesen built this house on the northeast corner of Union and Shawnee Streets in 1899. Although his brother was one of the founders of Heesen foundry, Hendrick worked for the Brewer foundry. Later it was the home of two generations of the Rathbun family. G. Arthur Rathbun was partner in a law practice with F. B. Wood and became a Lenawee County Circuit Court judge.

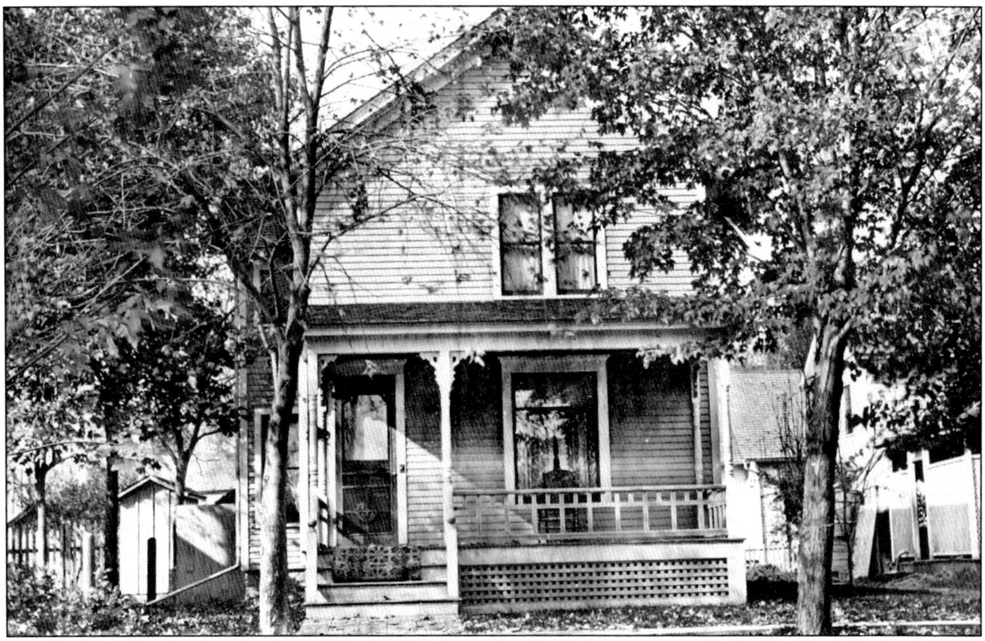

Better know as the Whittier House, 113 North Maiden Lane, shown here around 1900, was built in 1893. It was the home of Harriet Whittier, who was the operator for the first telephone company in Tecumseh. Harriet's pleasant home was a comfortable stroll from Tecumseh Telephone Company, located on the second floor of the Lilley-Wright building.

The J. S. Hendryx house at 307 North Union Street was built over five years from 1860 to 1865, during the Civil War when there was a shortage of wood and skilled labor. In the 1900s, the home was owned by Charles F. Patterson, the grandson of Dr. M. A. Patterson, one of the early settlers and the only doctor in the area for some time. Dr. Patterson was also an entrepreneur and civic leader, attributes that were passed on, as Charles was a successful businessman and farmer.

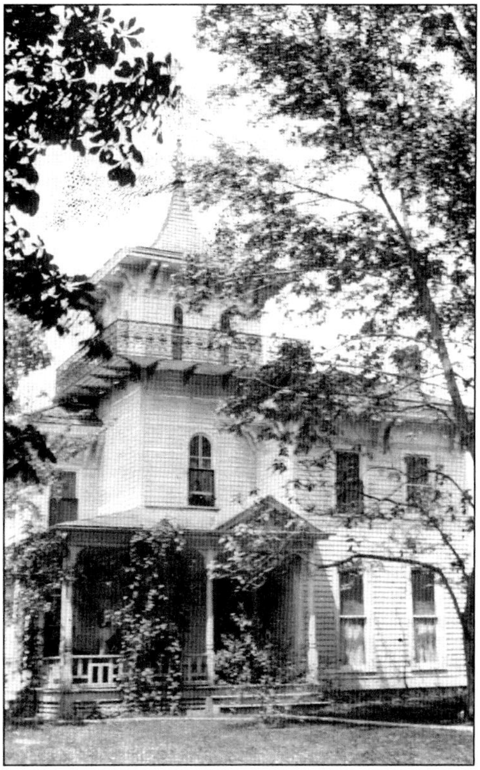

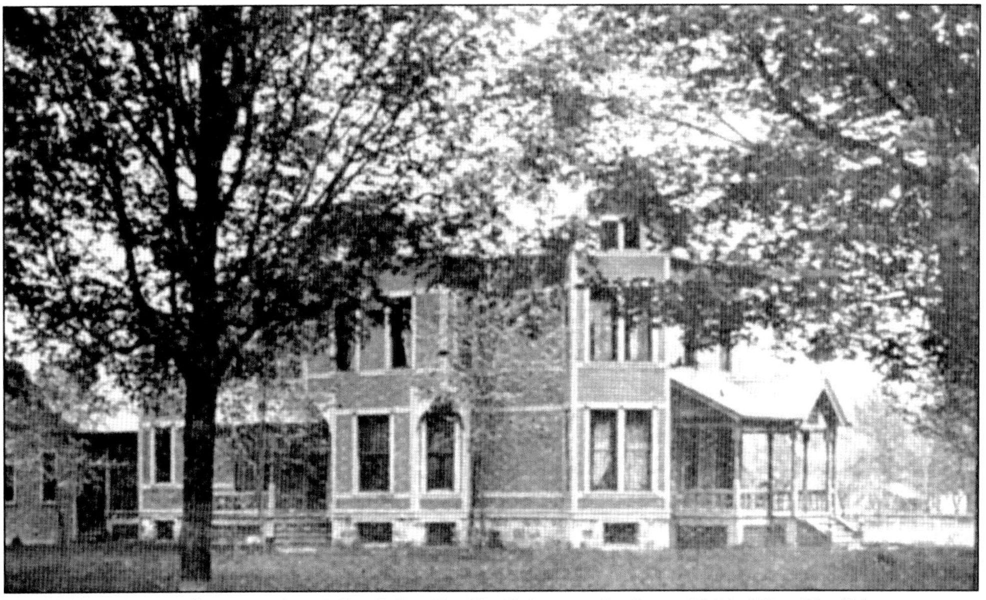

This is an 1890s photograph of the John D. Shull house, built in 1886. The Shull house once stood on the northeast corner of Chicago Boulevard and Ottawa Street, the original location of the Musgrove Evans house. By 1886, the Evans house had changed hands a number of times with Mrs. Shull acquiring it from her father, Peter Adams. Mrs. Shull, however, desired a more modern home and had the Evans house moved to make way for this grand Victorian, which has since been lost to the forces of progress.

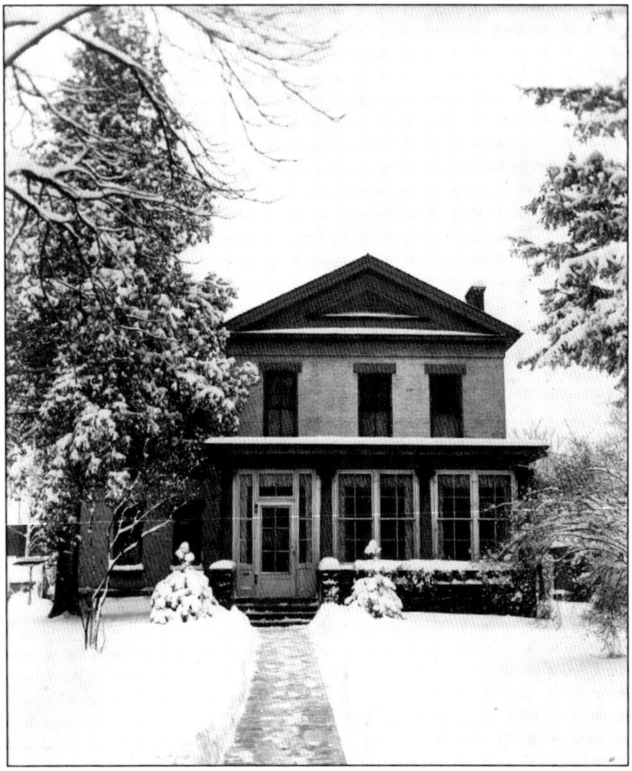

The house at 603 West Chicago Boulevard was built in the 1850s for William Burton, the rector of St. Peter's Church, and his wife, Amelia, although he may have died before it was completed. At one time this was the home of Philo and Mary Mills, the parents of Adelbert Mills who became a successful Tecumseh businessman. When this picture was taken, the DesErmia family, who owned a local furniture store, owned it. (Photograph courtesy of Ashley E. Chase.)

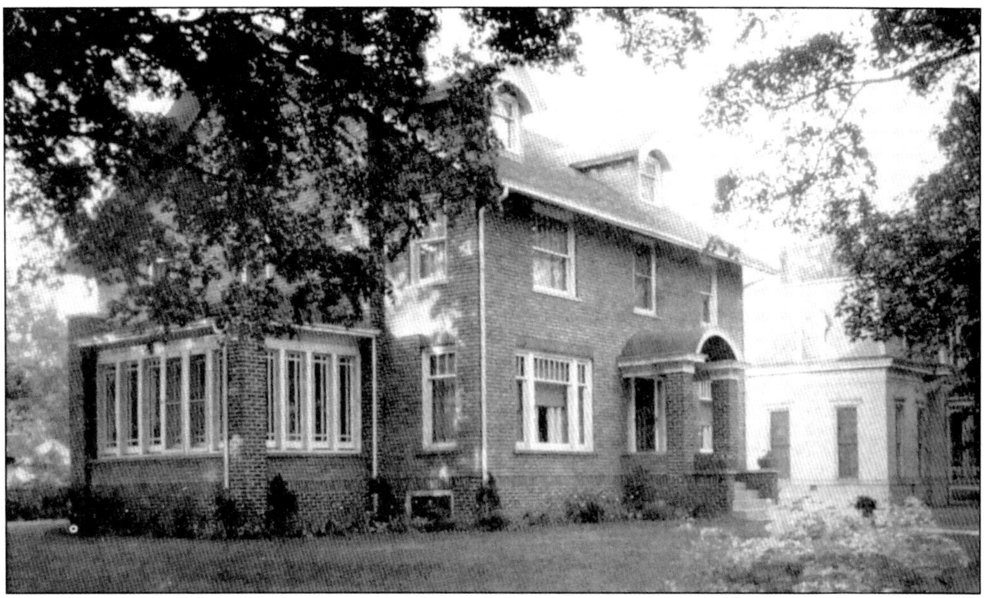

Rudolph A. Heesen, successful merchant, civic leader, mayor, owner of a profitable manufacturing firm, and bank president, built this house in 1922. Heesen had an existing house moved in order to build on this desirable lot at the corner of Chicago and Union Streets, where the Heesen house still stands today. (Photograph courtesy of Ashley E. Chase.)

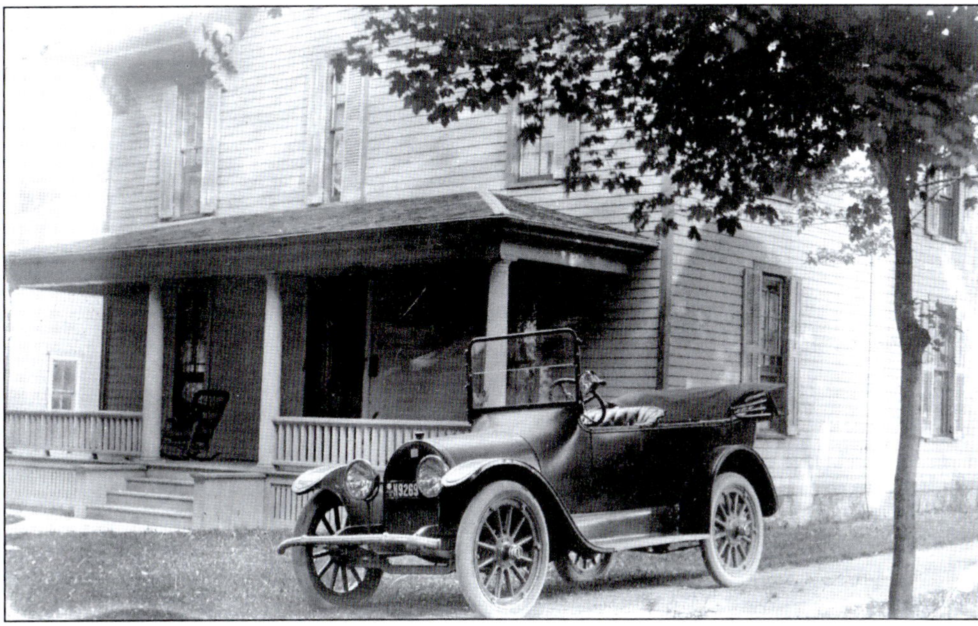

The house at 210 West Pottawatamie Street, seen here in 1919, has been a funeral home for as long as anyone can remember. Around 1900, it was the Guy Belding Funeral Home. Belding also owned a furniture store in the west end of the Merchants Block and started an ambulance service in 1922. After it was Belding's, the house was Green's, then Dunn's, and today it is Purse Funeral Home.

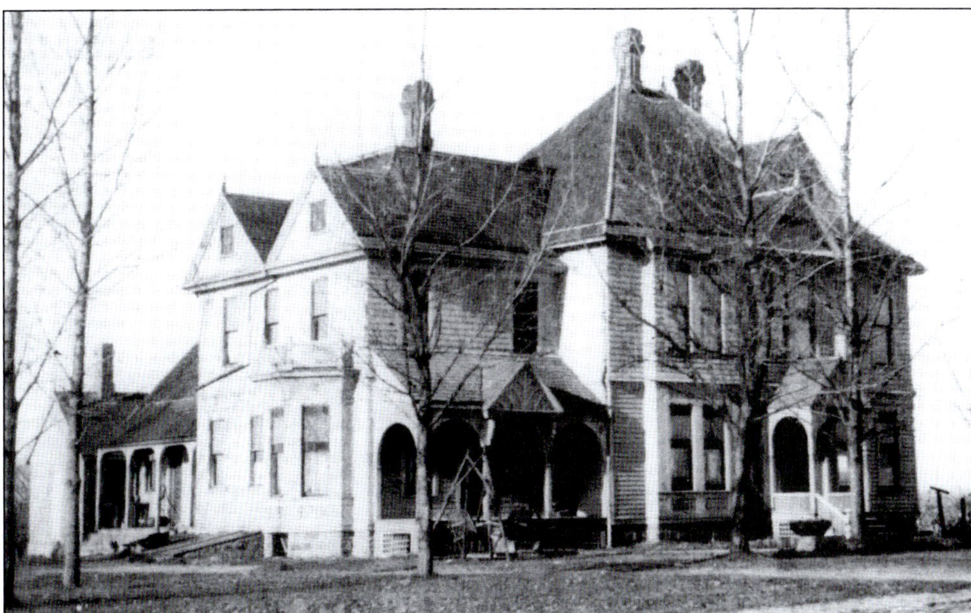

The Edwin R. Smith house, built in 1884 and shown here around 1919, is located three miles north of town. It is an example of the many large farmhouses that can be found just a few miles from Tecumseh and illustrates the success of local farmers. Someone hunting for these castles of cultivation will be well rewarded by a trip up Evans Street, down Rogers Highway, Green Highway, or any number of other rural roads around Tecumseh.

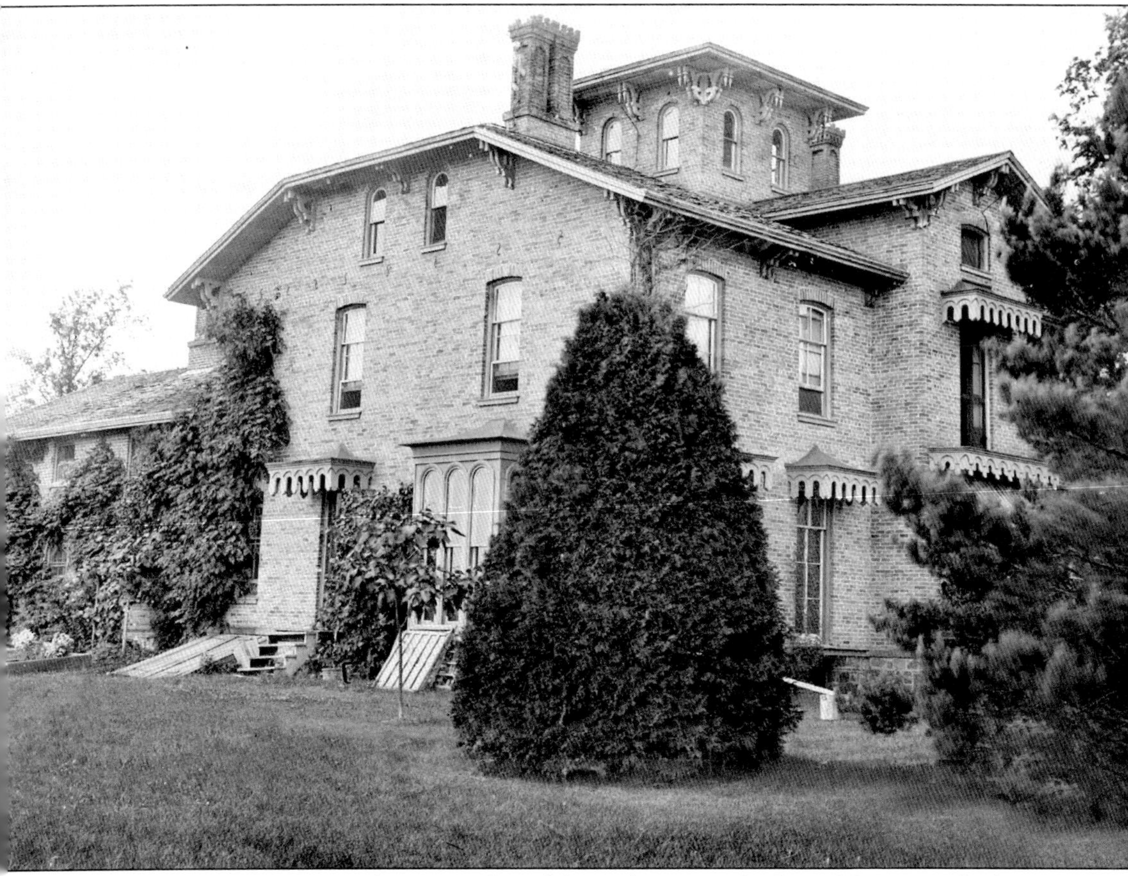

This house at 710 West Chicago Boulevard, better known as the Stacy Manor, was built over an eight-year span (1848–1856) and was constructed of bricks fired on site. Judge Consider Alphonso Stacy was a prominent lawyer, businessman, and judge. This early 1900s photograph, rare for its southeastern vantage point, is from a collection of glass negatives found in the attic of the Stacy Manor that are now at the Tecumseh Historical Society Museum.

Four

TECUMSEH INDUSTRY

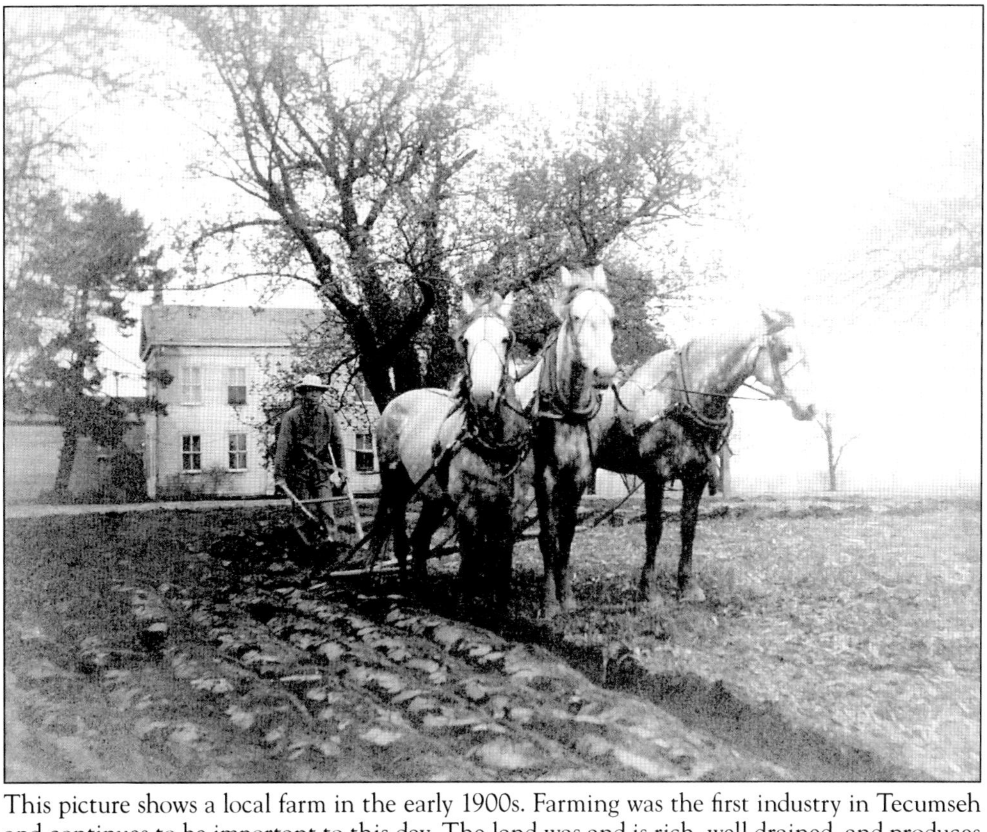

This picture shows a local farm in the early 1900s. Farming was the first industry in Tecumseh and continues to be important to this day. The land was and is rich, well drained, and produces crops in abundance. Successful farmers in Tecumseh's early history would invest their profits in entrepreneurial pursuits, and successful merchants often diversified into farming.

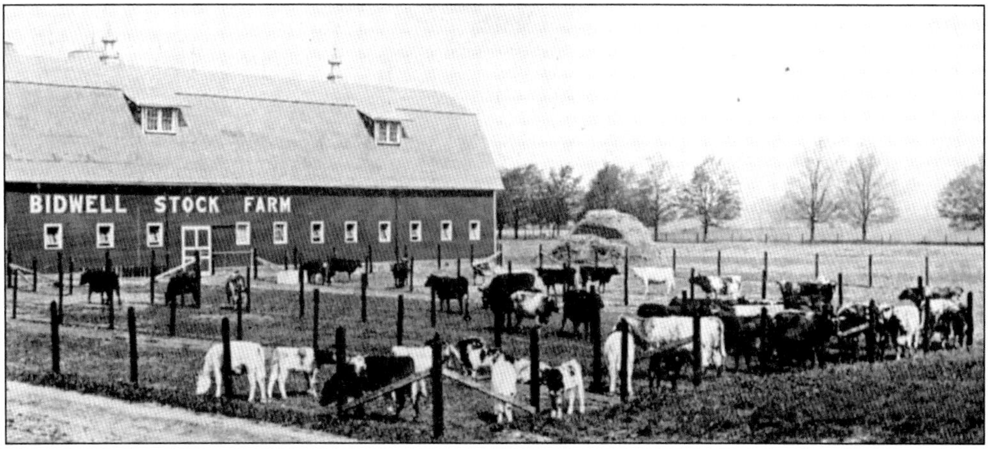

The Bidwell Stock Farm, around 1919, was located at the far west end of Brown Street at what is now known as Ternes Street. Birdsley Bidwell arrived in Tecumseh from New York in 1838 and became a successful merchant. He invested the profits of his success in building ventures, entrepreneurial pursuits, and the Bidwell Stock Farm, which encompassed hundreds of acres. Bidwell retired in the late 1860s to raise cattle, and the farm remained in the family for 75 years.

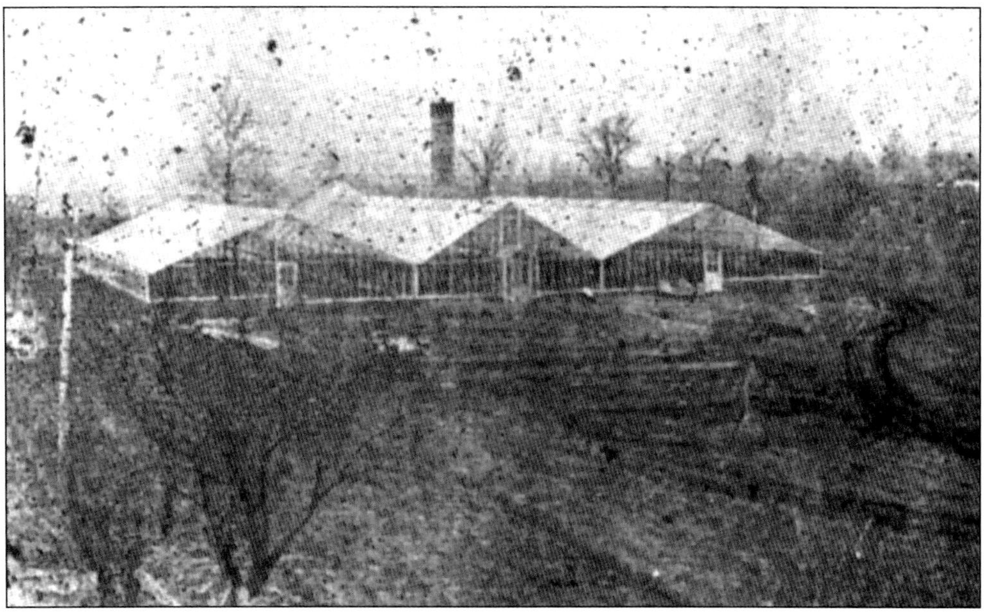

This photograph is of the Prairie Side Celery Company green house in 1911. Celery was big business for a time both in Tecumseh and nearby areas. From the 1880s to the 1920s there were three large celery operations near Tecumseh: Prairie Side Celery Company, Tecumseh Celery Company, and Joseph Russell and Sons. These large farms encompassed hundreds of acres and had their own railroad spurs running to their packing facilities.

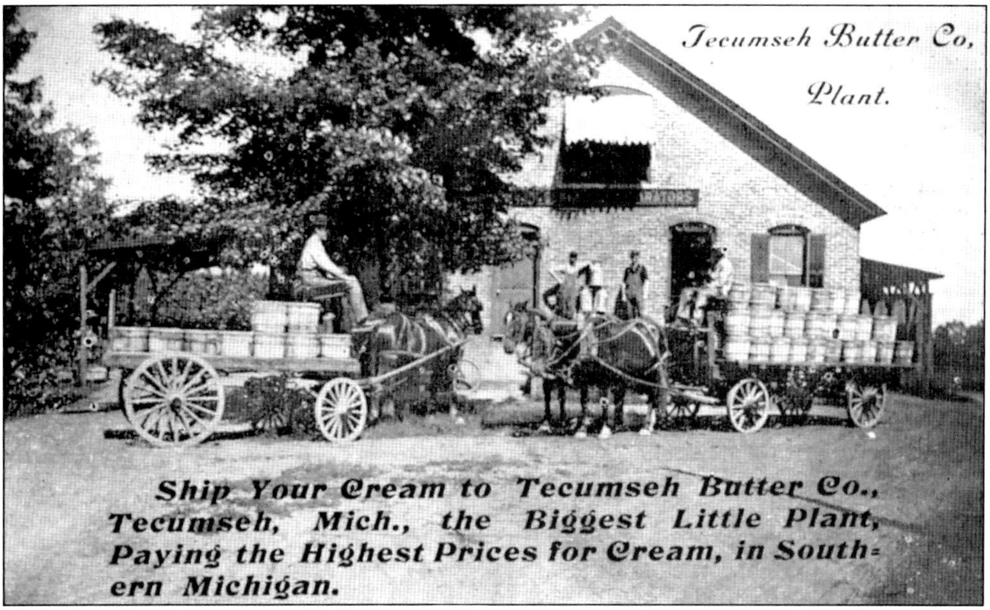

In the 1880s, dairy farming, specifically making butter, became one of the more profitable agricultural pursuits in Tecumseh. The Tecumseh Butter Company Plant was built in 1886 at the end of Pottawatamie Street at Division. Like many of the new businesses in town, it was started by a group of local businessmen that included Lucius Lilley. The business changed hands many times and later burned in 1922. (Photograph courtesy of Ashley E. Chase.)

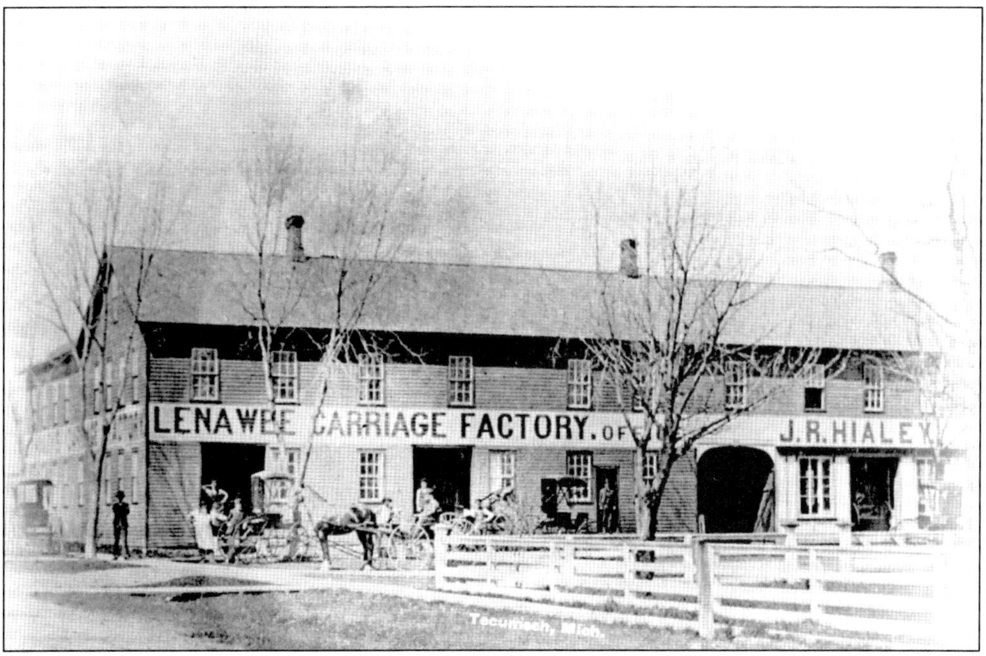

J. R. Hailey owned the Lenawee Carriage Factory, built in 1850. It was located on the corner of South Pearl and Kilbuck Streets. Albert Boyce, Hailey's son-in-law, tore the building down in 1924, and apartments were built on the site.

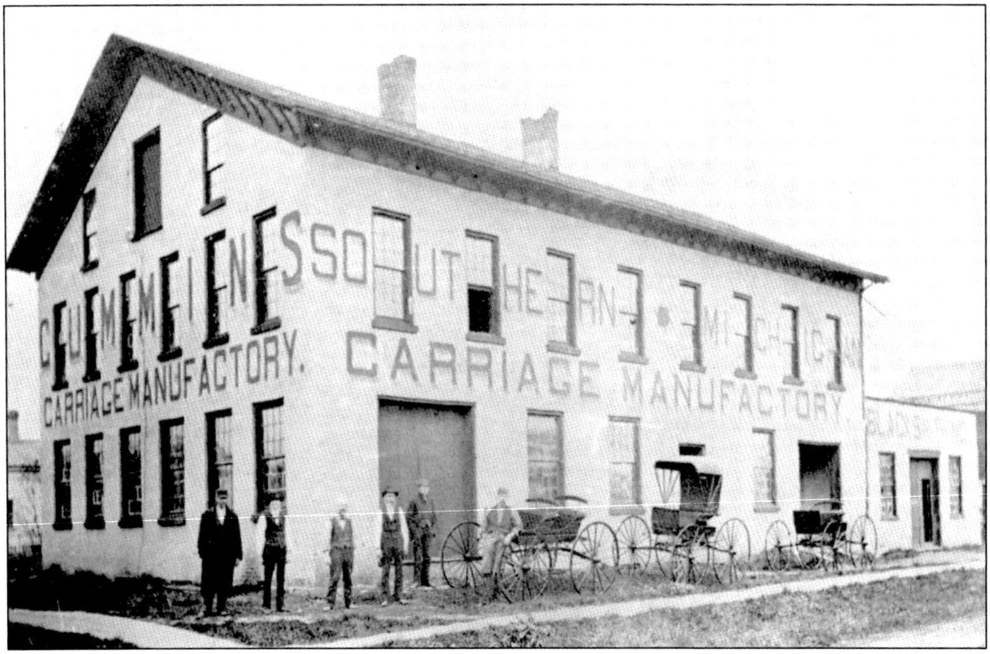

Thomas Cummins moved to Tecumseh in 1840 and built this impressive carriage works on South Evans Street just north of Kilbuck Street. It was one of many carriage manufactories in town and remained in operation until 1880. According to a note on the back of this photograph, the second person from the left is Richard Ford, and the fourth person is Thomas Cummins himself.

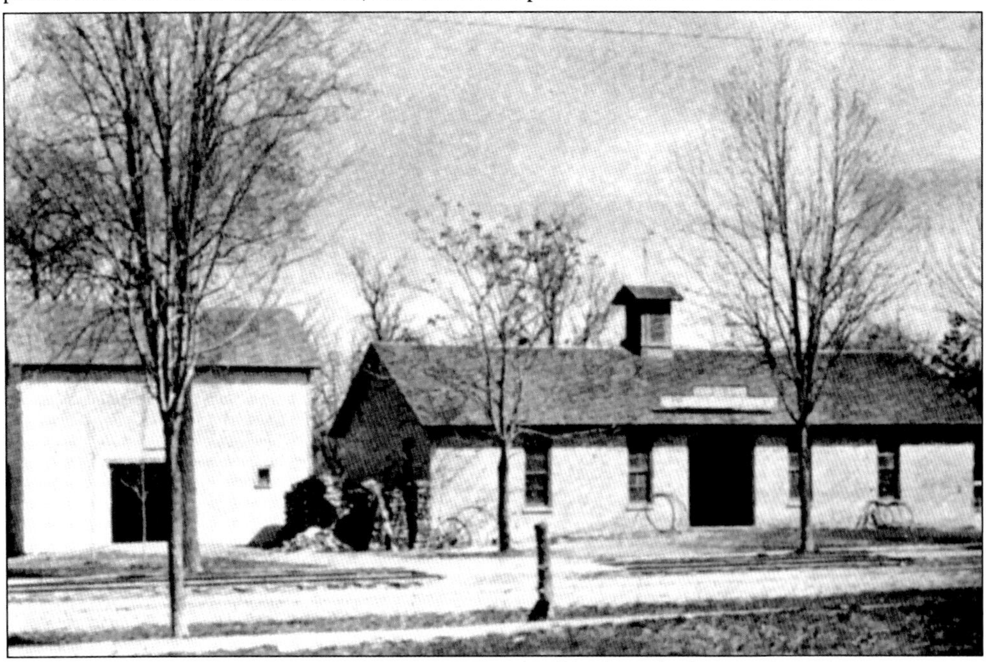

James Pencil constructed this building to use as his blacksmith shop. When this picture was taken, around 1890, it was the blacksmith shop of James Elliott. Elliott lived in the house directly north of the shop and was a prosperous businessman who also served as village president. His son Floyd carried on the family business until the 1960s.

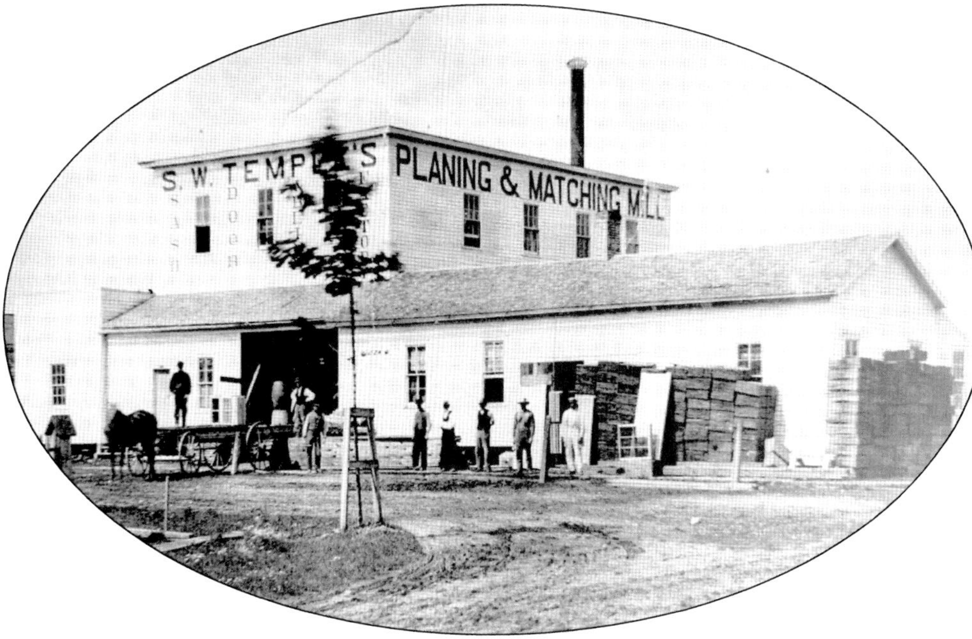

Samuel W. Temple arrived in Tecumseh on June 15, 1859. He built a small workshop on Shawnee Street and began making gates, sashes, and doors by hand. His business grew, and by 1874, it included a lumberyard and took up the entire south end of the block from Evans Street to Pearl Street. This photograph shows Temple's mill in the late 1800s, a far cry from the workshop he started with.

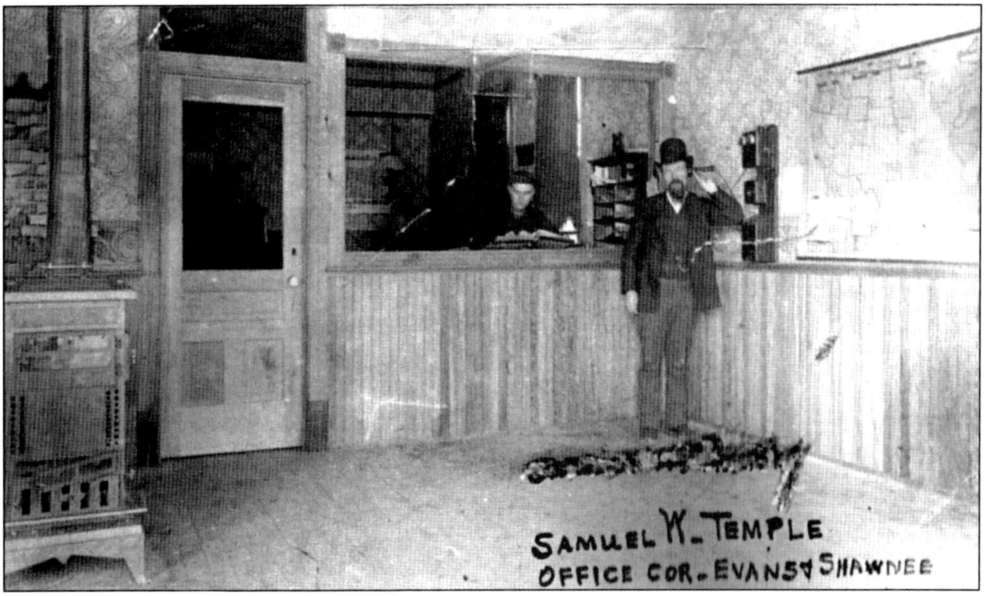

Samuel W. Temple, shown here on the phone in his lumber company office around 1900, had found success in many other business ventures as well. Temple acquired his office building by purchasing the first church building of the Methodists in the late 1800s and moving it from the southeast corner of Pearl and Shawnee Streets to the corner of Evans and Shawnee Streets.

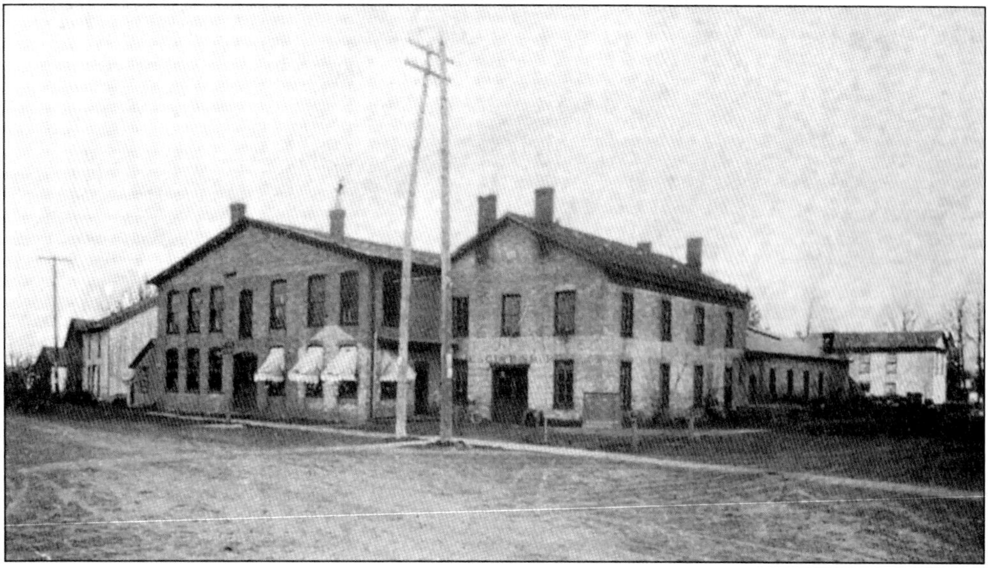

H. Brewer and Company, pictured around 1893, was located south of Evans Creek between Evans Street and Ottawa Street. Originally a foundry established by Stoughton Strong and Elijah Anderson in 1848 to build steam engines, the foundry changed ownership numerous times before Horace Brewer bought out his partners and brought in his son Albert. Horace Brewer died in 1880, and in the 1890s, the firm was jointly owned by A. Brewer, H. Heesen, P. S. McKinnon, and H. E. Stout. It supplied all manner of goods from the original product, steam engines, to specialized masonry and clay working machinery.

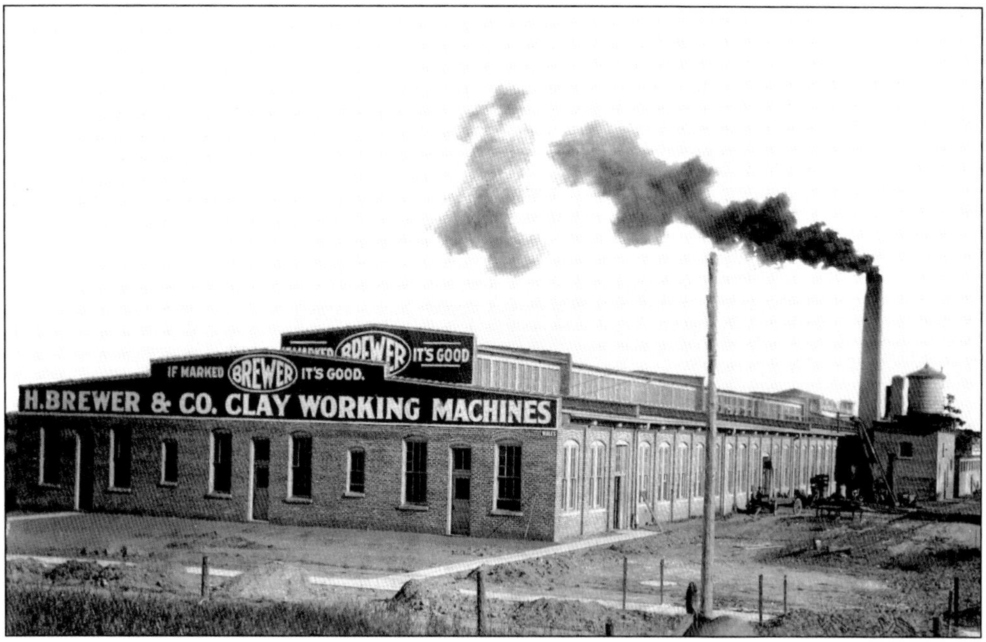

The Brewer Foundry, originally the Tecumseh Foundry, was incorporated as a stock company in 1900. In 1909, H. Brewer and Company built a new facility, pictured here, east of the Anthony Fence Company Factory and west of Ottawa Street. In 1935, this building became part of the Tecumseh Products plant.

Harold M. Kolkloesch, son of Fred and Sarah Kolkloesch, is shown at the Brewer Machine Shop around 1912, when he was about 18 years old. This was in Brewer's new buildings, not more than three years after their construction. Kolkloesch's father owned a saloon downtown, but it appears that Harold found gainful employ at Brewer Foundry.

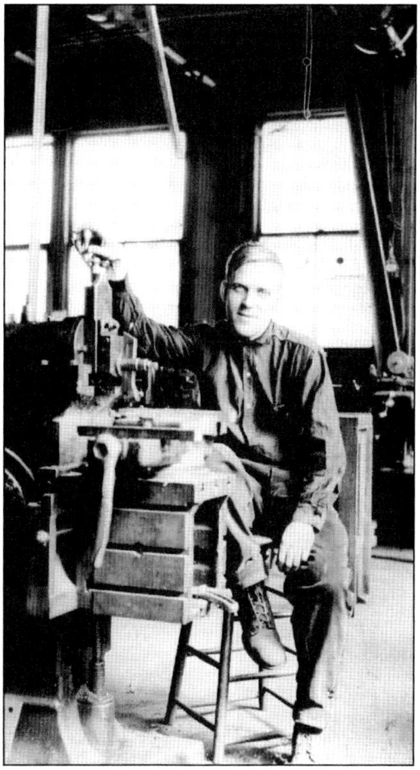

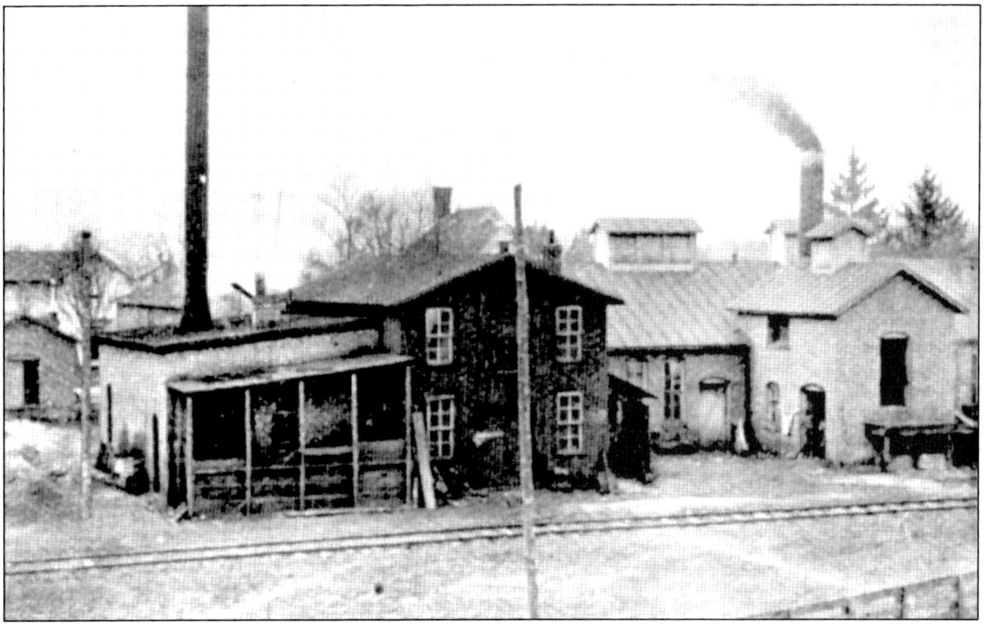

Heesen Brothers and Company is shown around 1895. The Heesen brothers, George and John, emigrated from Holland in 1852 and owned a clothing store downtown. The brothers then started manufacturing hog rings and the "Hog Ringer," a pair of patented hog ring pliers, in a shed behind their store. The brothers met with success and moved manufacturing from the shed first to South Pearl Street and then to these buildings located on North Pearl Street by the railroad tracks.

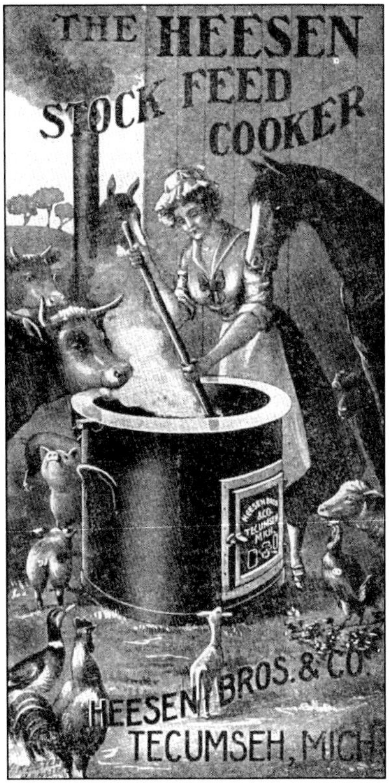

In 1895, Henry Nyland joined the Heesen brothers in their manufacturing business, but the company retained the Heesen Brothers and Company name. By this time, the company was manufacturing more than hog rings and hog ringers, they were also making hollowware and light grey castings, as well as the Heesen Stock Feed Cooker shown here in an 1890s advertisement.

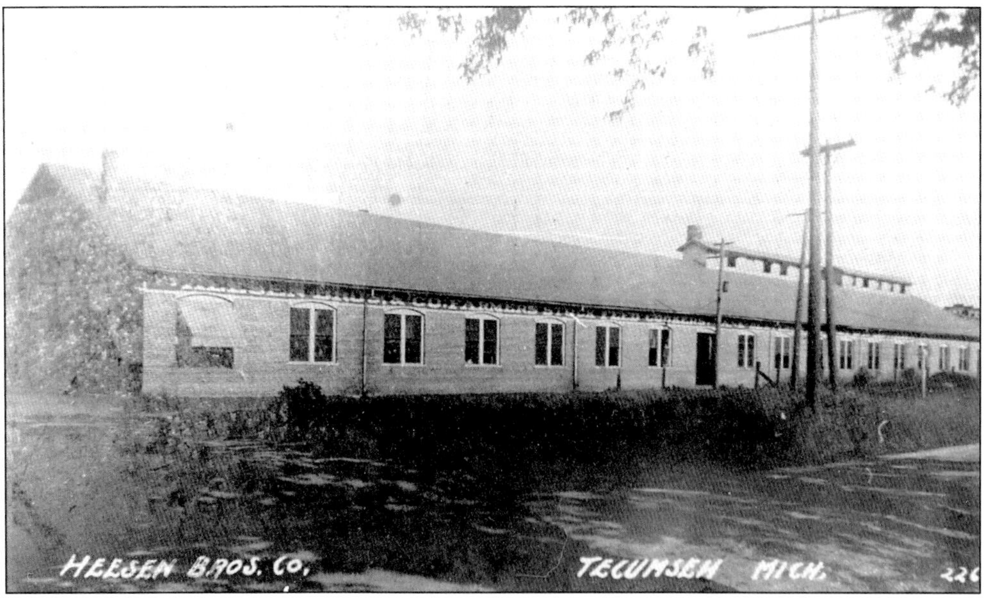

In 1890, Charles Tiffany established the Tiffany Foundry on Cummins and South Evans Streets. The Tiffany Foundry manufactured brick and clay working machinery, competing directly with Brewer Foundry. Tiffany was not successful and went out of business in 1899. Not long after Tiffany dissolved, the Heesen brothers purchased the building and moved in. It remained a foundry for some time, becoming the Carson and then the Bruce Foundry. The building shown here was torn down, but the foundry office remains.

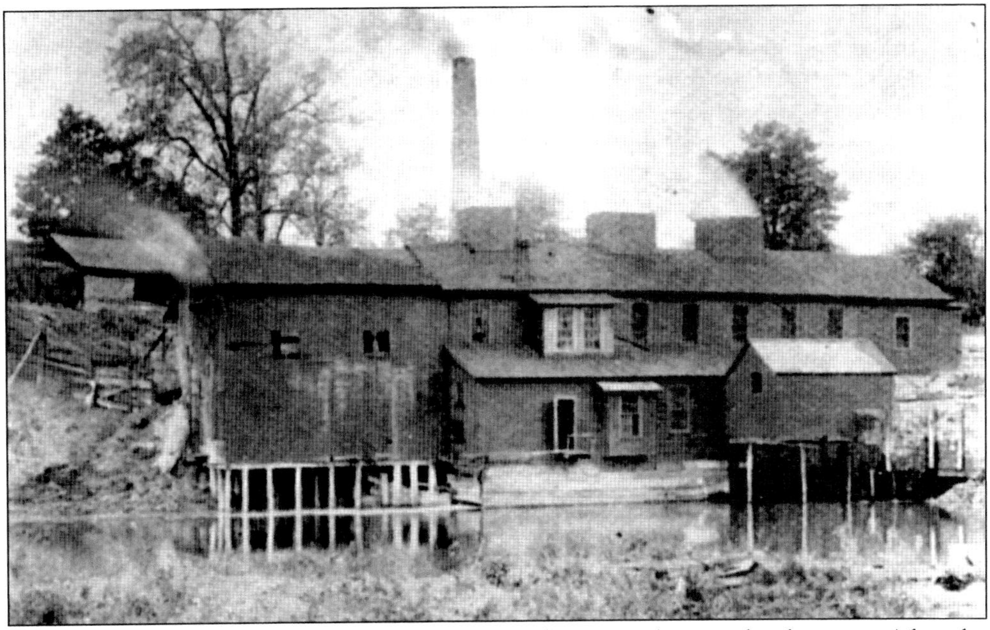

In the 1860s, Henry Smith bought the VanTyne furniture plant at this location. After the furniture plant burned in 1869, Smith built the Tecumseh Paper Mill and began using straw to make brown paper. This photograph, around 1895, shows the paper mill on the south bank of the River Raisin, just under the Red Mill Dam. The paper mill was damaged beyond repair in a flood in the early 1900s.

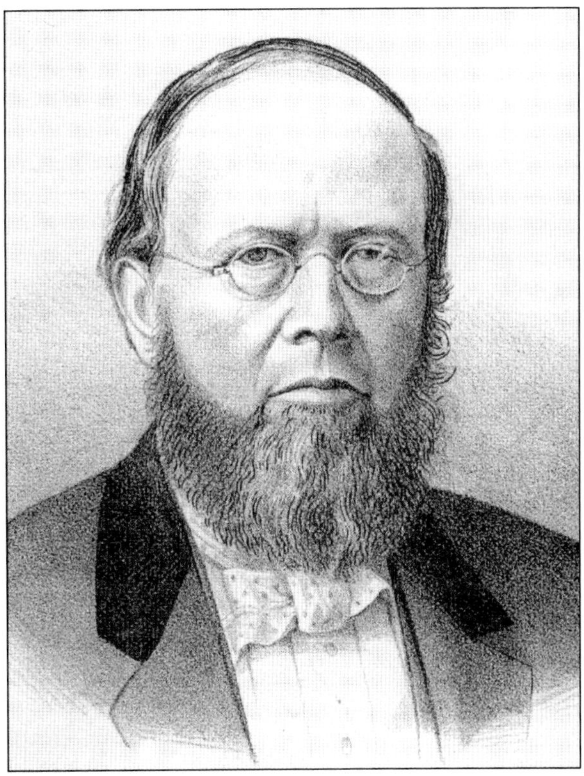

This is an artist's rendition of Judge Consider Alphonso "C. A." Stacy as he appeared in the 1870s. C. A. Stacy arrived in Tecumseh in August of 1836 at the age of 19 filled with determination, drive and, if reports are to be credited, an abundance of charisma. Judge Stacy played a prominent role in Tecumseh's history. Stacy was among other things a lawyer (he passed the bar in 1837 at 20 years of age), a judge, a banker, a developer, a civic leader, a gentleman farmer, one of the founders of Eastern Michigan University, and father of seven with his wife Mary Walker Stacy. He is even reputed to have aided many escaping slaves on the Underground Railroad through Tecumseh.

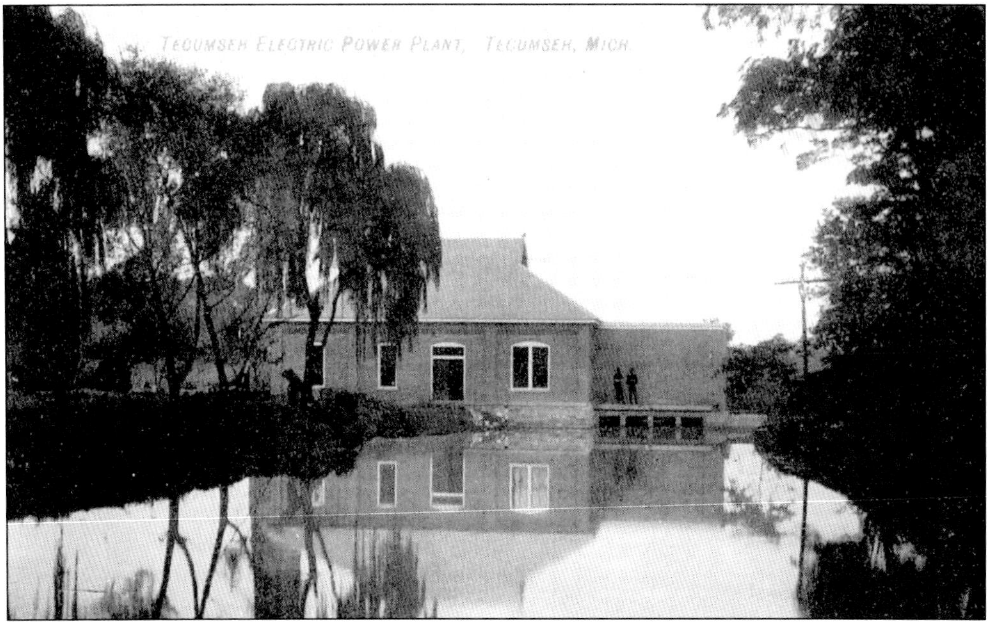

The Tecumseh Electric Power Plant was built in 1901 by George U. Smith, son of Henry Smith, and Louis Schneider. The plant generated power using water from the Red Mill Pond to drive a turbine but could also generate electricity with a supplementary steam boiler. Prior to the construction of this plant, electricity was supplied to Tecumseh by a steam generator at Evans Street and Evans Creek.

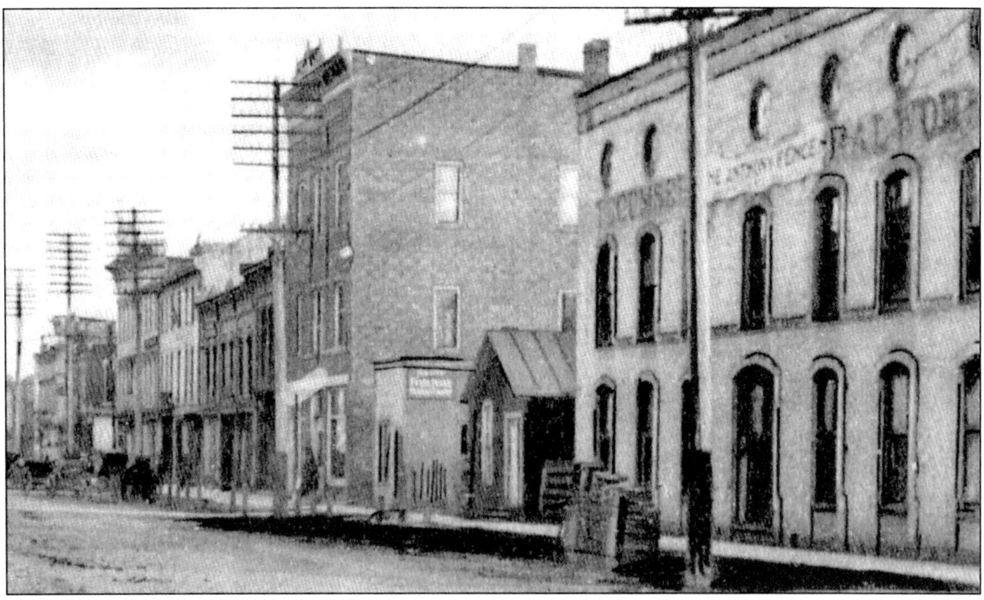

Anthony Fence Company (far right foreground), seen here around 1905, was located on the southeast corner of Chicago Boulevard and Pearl Street, originally the location of Beers blacksmith shop. In 1836, the Tecumseh Furnace Foundry was built here but burned down in 1856. Thirty days later, the brick building shown here replaced the burned foundry. This building housed the Tecumseh Table Factory from 1890 until 1897, and then the Tecumseh Agricultural Works. It was raised in 1924 to make way for a gas station. (Photograph courtesy of Lenawee Historical Museum.)

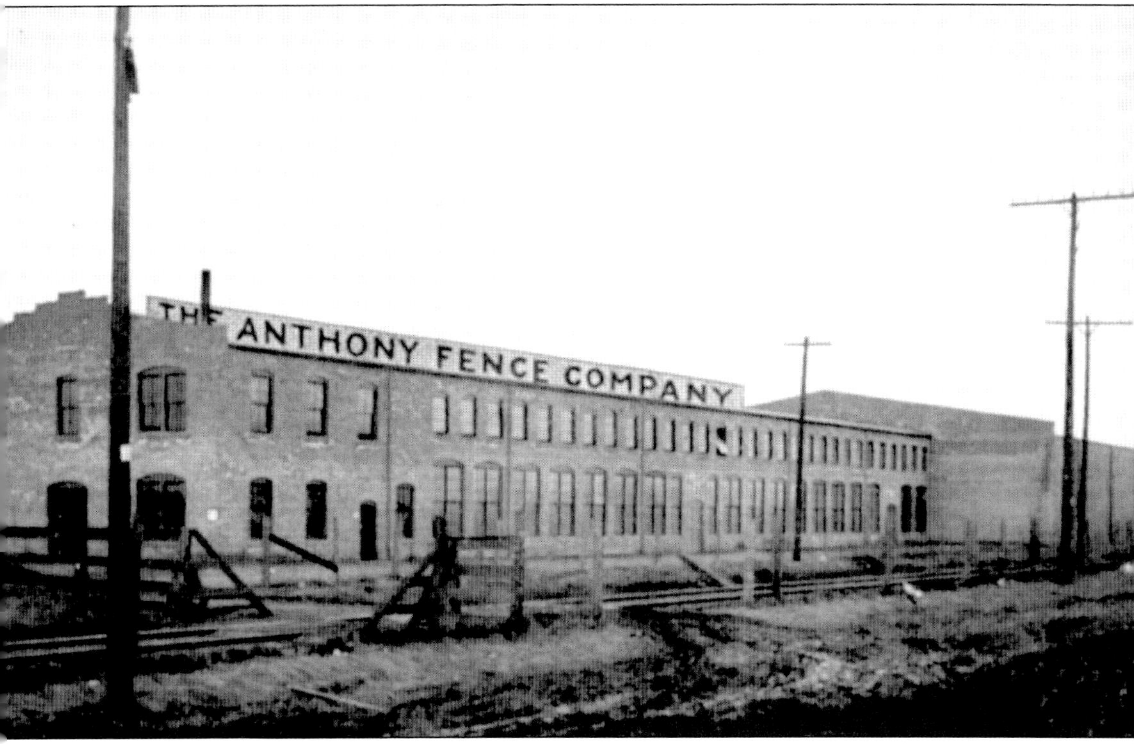

In 1906, Alley S. VanWinkle built the Anthony Fence Company factory for $25,000 on a four-month schedule. VanWinkle had just completed an addition to the Clinton Woolen Mill. The new factory was located on South Evans Street just south of Patterson Street. The Anthony Fence Company had been founded earlier by P. D. Anthony and had occupied the old Tecumseh Table Company building. By 1907, this factory had five looms weaving wire fence 24 hours a day. The company was sold to American Wire Fence in 1910 and continued to make wire fence until 1925. The building eventually became part of the Tecumseh Products plant.

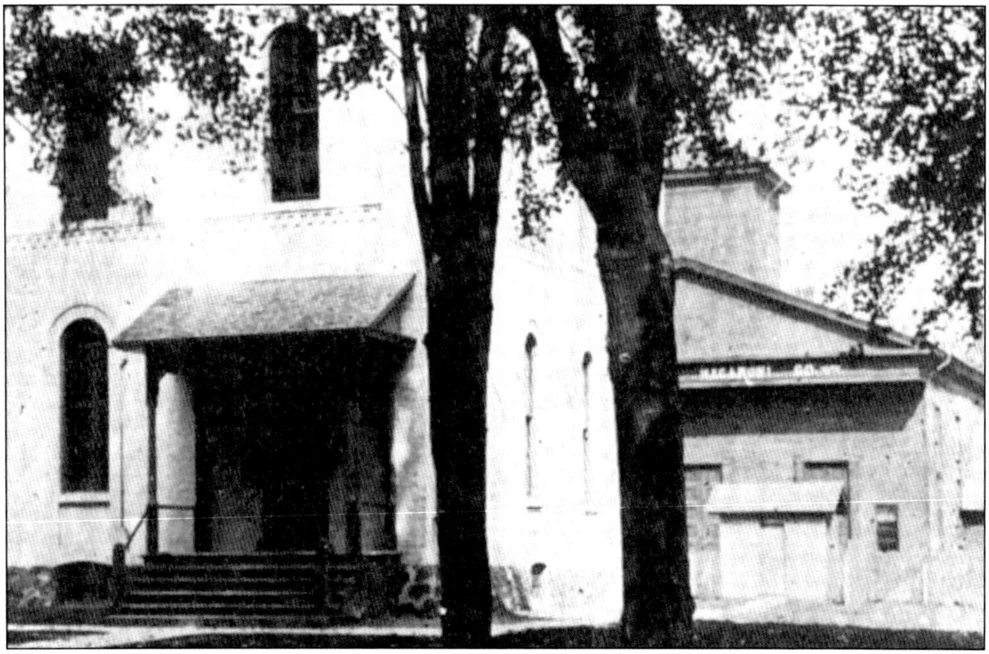

On the right, behind the East Branch School, is the Presbyterian White Frame Meeting House. This photograph was taken prior to 1911 and shows the old church had become the home of either the Michigan Macaroni Company (1904–1908) or its successor, Uncle Sam's Macaroni Company (1908–1911), before it moved into its new factory on South Evans Street.

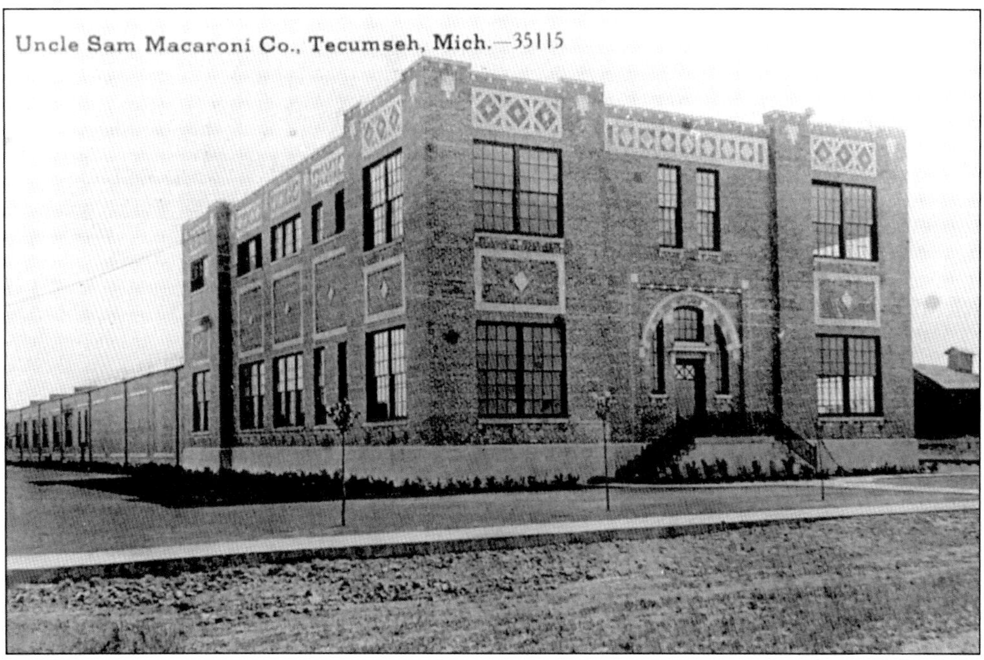

Uncle Sam's Macaroni Company met with great success, so it reorganized and raised funds to build this new factory on the east side of South Evans Street in 1911. The expenditures for the new factory proved to be too much to overcome, and Uncle Sam's went under. The plant was sold to Quaker Oats, and today it is the core of the Tecumseh Corrugated Box plant.

Stillman Blanchard purchased over 600 acres of land north and east of town and started his Globe Mill project in 1832. The mill's location was to be where Evans Creek met the River Raisin. This was close to the very spot where Tecumseh's original settlers spent their first night in seasonal shelters left behind by the Pottawatomie, who traveled through the area on the Saulk and LaPlaisance Bay Trails.

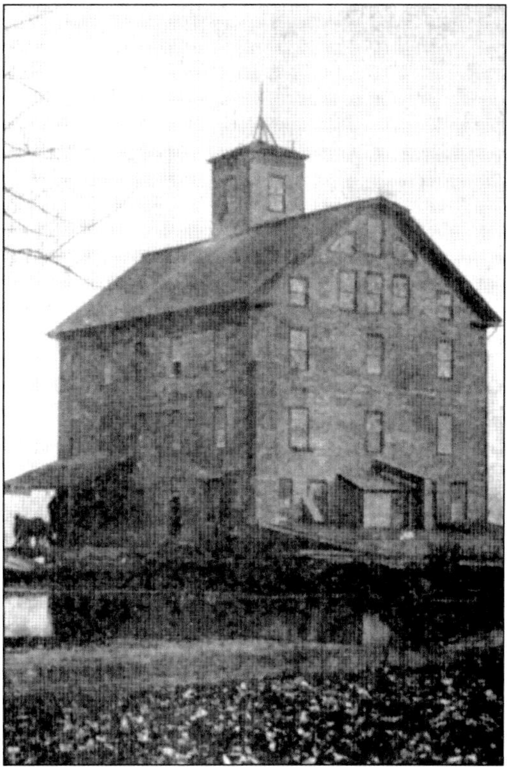

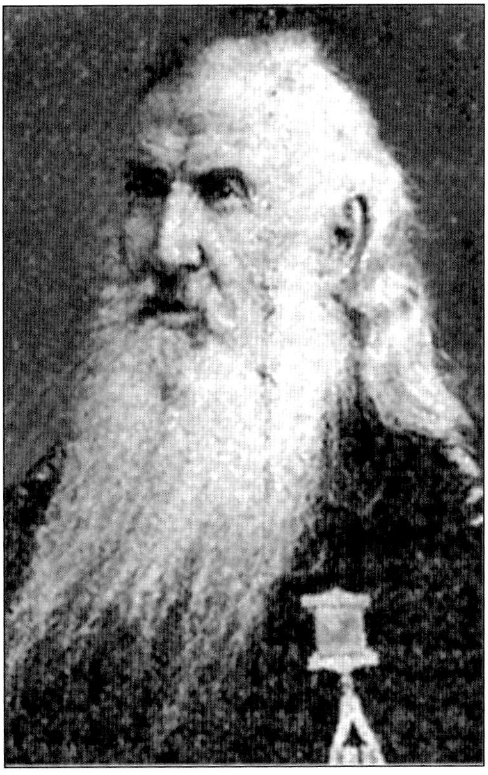

The Honorable Judge Stillman Blanchard arrived in Tecumseh in 1826 at the age of 30. He was one of the first merchants to have a store on Chicago Boulevard and eventually had his hands in almost every civic and business venture in town. Many of those ventures were profitable, but eventually Blanchard found himself in possession of some of the most dramatic business failures in Tecumseh's history. (Photograph courtesy of Ashley E Chase.)

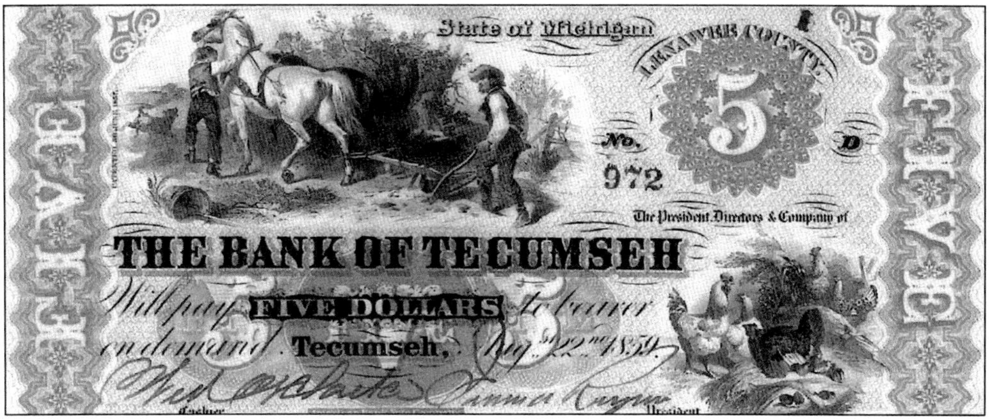

An 1859 $5 bank note from the Bank of Tecumseh is pictured. The bank was founded on July 25, 1836, as part of the charter for the River Raisin-Grand River Railroad. Stillman Blanchard was a driving force behind both projects and the first president of the bank. The railroad project never got off the ground, and the bank was closed in 1839. It was reopened in 1855 and permanently closed in 1861. (Photograph courtesy of Ashley E Chase.)

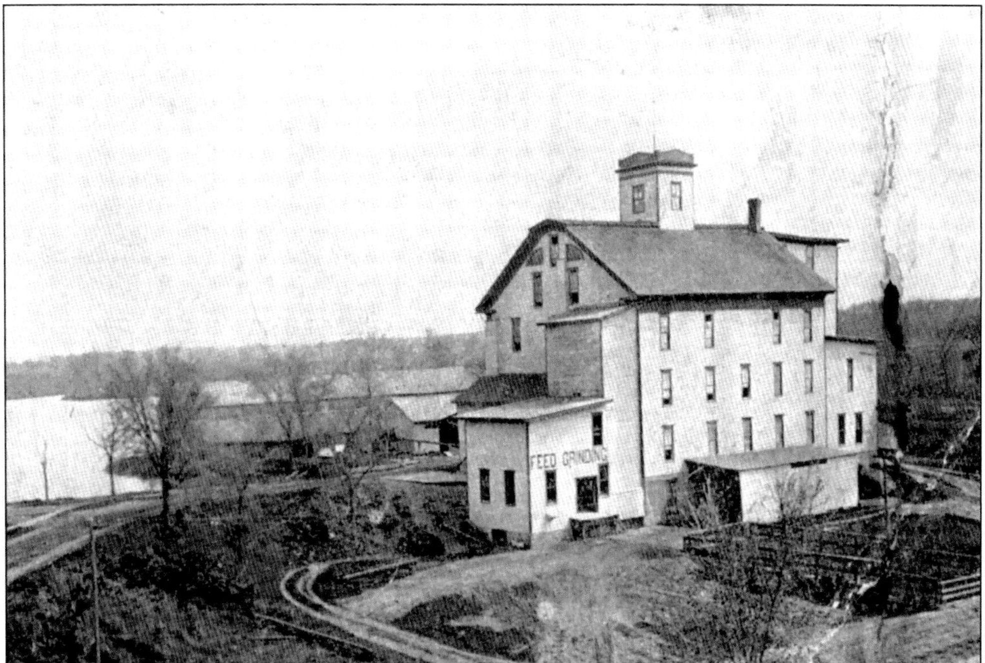

Stillman Blanchard's Globe Mill required a colossal effort to complete. Construction took seven years, two dams to raise the river level, an earthwork to keep it at that level, and about $32,000, an enormous amount of money in the 1830s. The Globe Mill started its life massively in debt, and Blanchard was hopelessly attracted to risky business ventures. In 1858, Blanchard's many speculative enterprises fell apart and he went bankrupt. The mill was sold to William Hayden and became quite successful under Hayden's management. This picture was taken in 1896, during the mills glory days. Less than two years later, this mill would burn to the ground.

William Hayden came to Tecumseh, purchased Blanchard's Globe Mill, and founded a dynasty. Hayden's early life was something for the storybooks. He was born in New York as one of 12 children and orphaned at the age of four. He and went to California in the gold rush of 1849, and on his way to California, he was one of the first in his group to be struck with cholera, and his companions left him behind with little food and water. Eventually a more compassionate member of the group came back to help him. His luck appeared to have changed when he found a modest fortune of $3,000 in gold, but he lost it all when the ship he was returning east on sank. Eventually Hayden made his way to Jackson, Michigan, where he married, and came to Tecumseh in 1858. He and his wife, Sarah Hayden, had eight children. Their son Levi would take over the Hayden Milling Company and bring it into the new century.

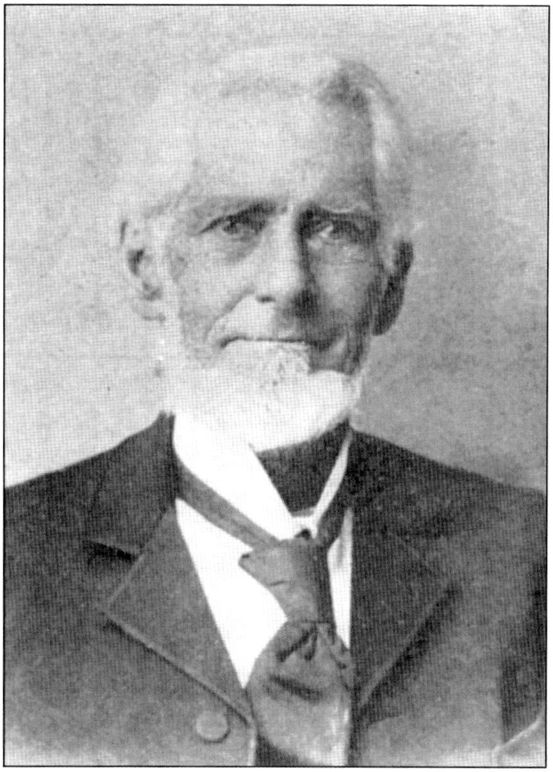

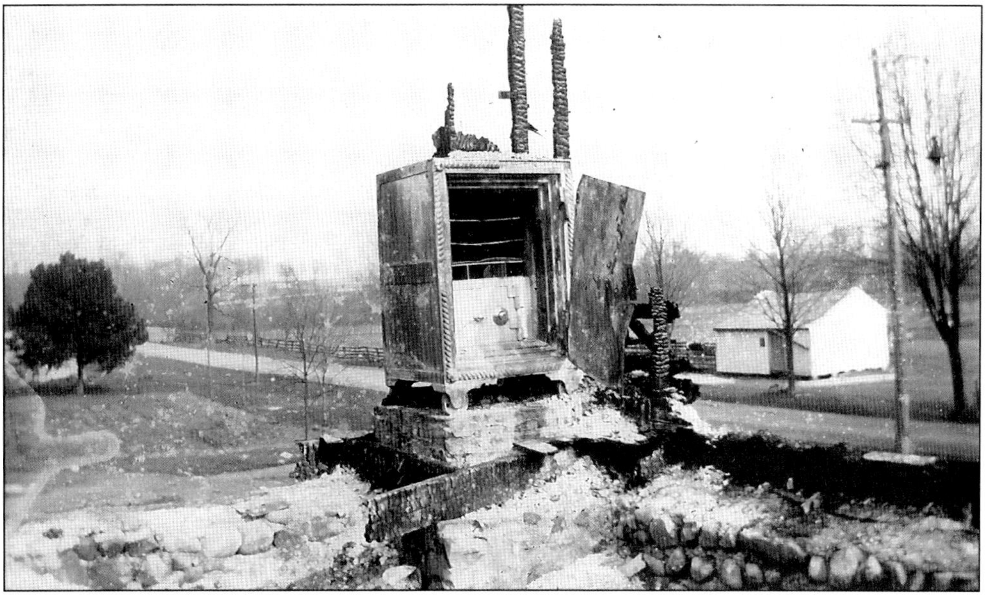

On March 25, 1898, the original Globe Mill burned, the unfortunate result of an employee "who tried to mix liquor with milling." The mill had lasted almost 60 years and had been capable of producing as much as 250 barrels of flour a day. After the fire, nothing was left, even the safe shown here had taken a beating, and to make matters worse, the mill had not been insured. Much of the money needed to rebuild was raised by selling shares to the citizens of Tecumseh, who knew the mill's importance to the community.

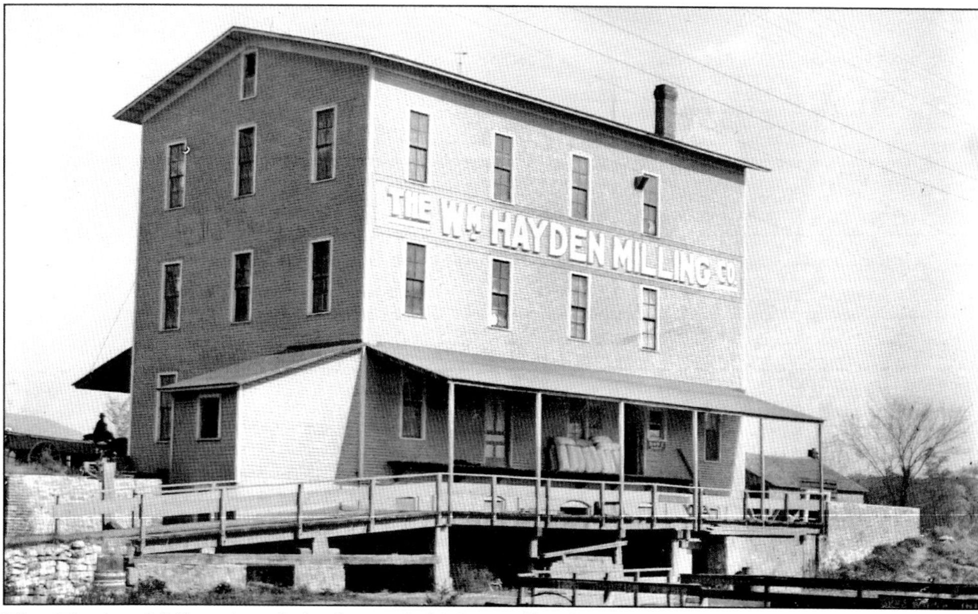

The Hayden Mill replaced the burned Globe Mill. This new mill was to have all the latest technology in milling, a roller grinding system, a "cockle machine," a Wolf Level Sifter, and a Carter Disc Separator. The new mill was prosperous and profitable, and both the Haydens and Tecumseh benefited by it. Eventually Perry Hayden sold the mill to Henry Ford for $1. Ford razed the mill and built a new one, which stands today.

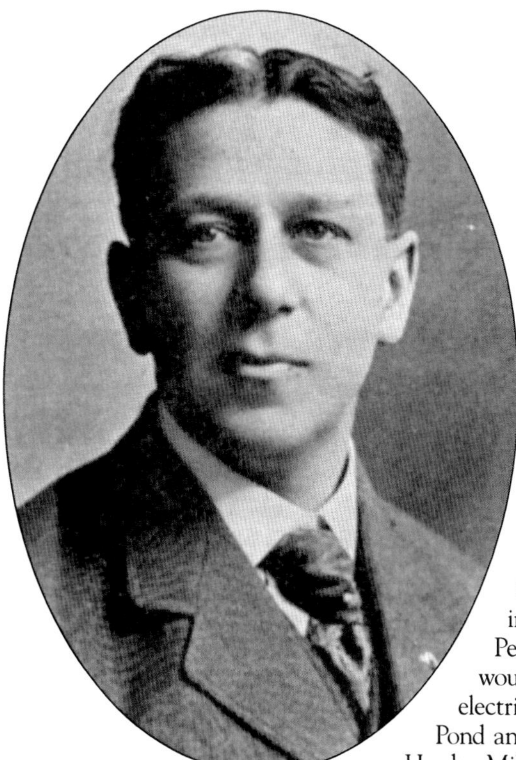

Levi Hayden expanded his father's business concerns, the Hayden Milling Company, and diversified them as well. Perhaps out of his love for the automobile, he also played an active role in management of the Hayden Garage. His son Perry Hayden and son-in-law Perry Satterthwaite would continue the Hayden dynasty, adding an electric power plant by the Hayden Mill at Globe Mill Pond and managing Hayden Fuel and Supply and the Hayden Milling Company.

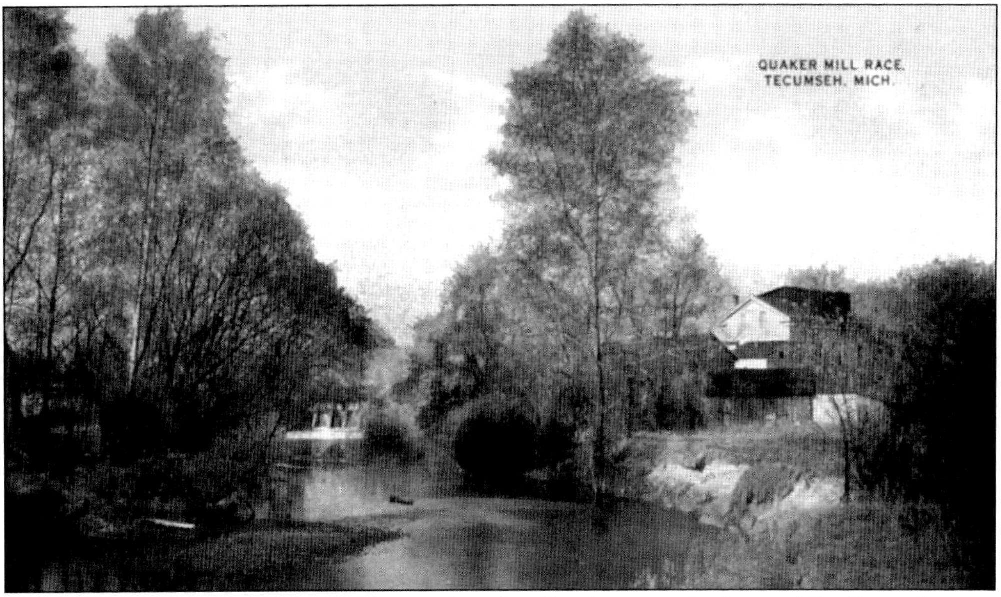

This view shows the Quaker Mill Race on Comfort Road just south of town. The Satterthwaites constructed Quaker Mill in 1847 next to their existing sawmill. The enterprise was originally known as Raisin Mills and was a cooperative effort with the Comforts. This collaboration between the Comforts and the Satterthwaites was successful in business and at home, as three of the Satterthwaite children were married to three of the Comfort children. (Photograph courtesy of Lenawee Historical Museum.)

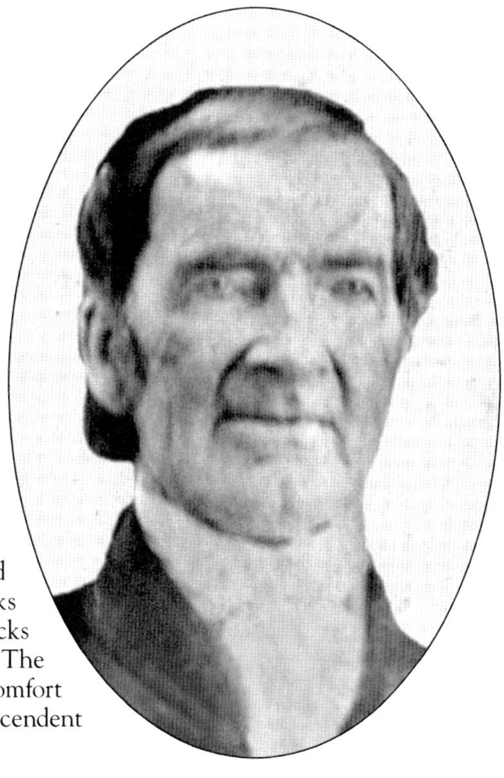

Aaron Comfort settled southeast of town in the 1840s and was part owner of the Quaker Mill. The Comfort house on Green Road is said to have been one local stop on the Underground Railroad. Aaron's son Elwood Comfort founded a very successful brick works in the late 1850s, which made many of the bricks that were used to build Tecumseh buildings. The brick works existed into the 1970s, and Comfort Enterprises on Rogers Highway is a direct descendent of that business.

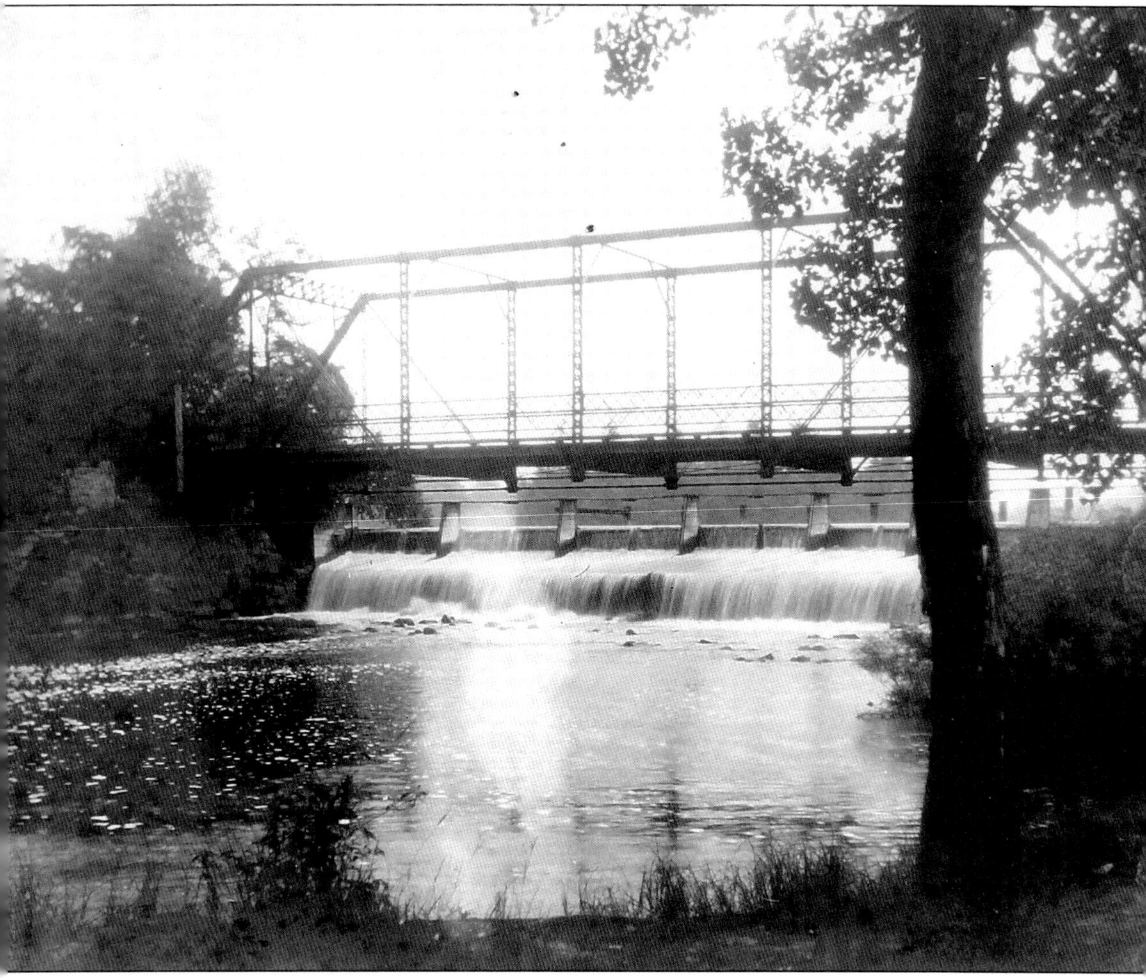

The Quaker Mill Dam and bridge on Comfort Road are pictured here around 1906. The location for Tecumseh was determined in part by the availability of water, the course of the River Raisin, and where it could be dammed, allowing various ponds to be formed and mills to be built. Nearby mills were located at Newberg, about three miles north of town; Red Mill pond; the Globe Mill pond; on Ezra Blood's land just south of town; and on Aaron Comfort's land where Quaker Mill Dam and pond provided power for various manufacturing enterprises.

Five

TECUMSEH TRANSPORTATION

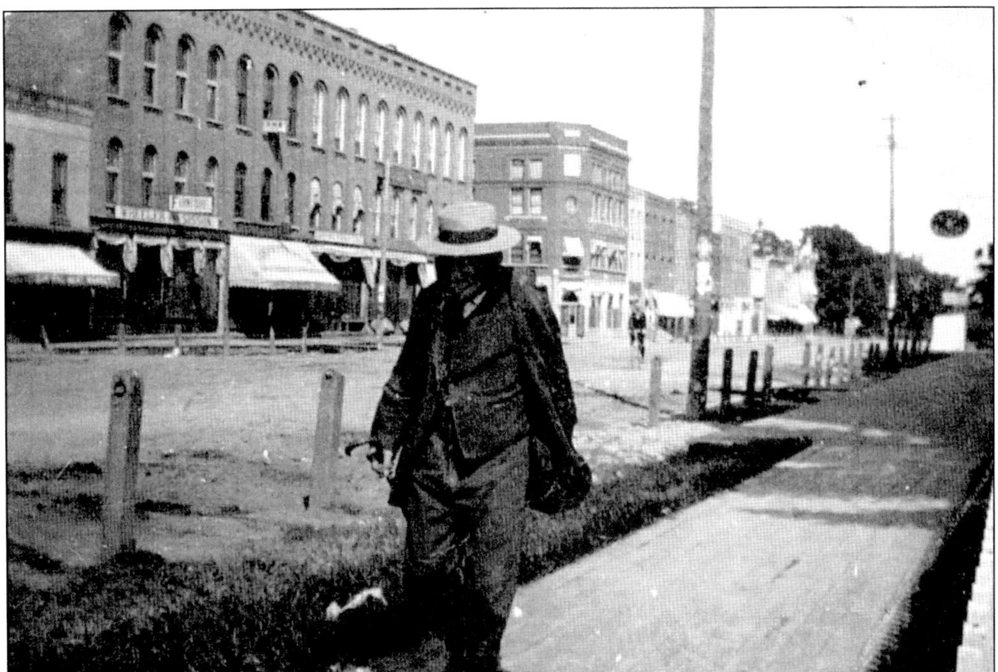

Walking was a common means of transportation in the town's first century. Today it is still a pleasant way of getting around this lovely city. This picture is of one of the Satterthwaite family members, most likely Joseph C., walking along the wooden sidewalks of downtown in the mid-1890s. The wooden walks were big news, and many articles in the *Tecumseh Herald* were devoted to where the new wooden sidewalks were being constructed or where the old walks needed repair. In 1895, the city began to replace all wooden walks with cement.

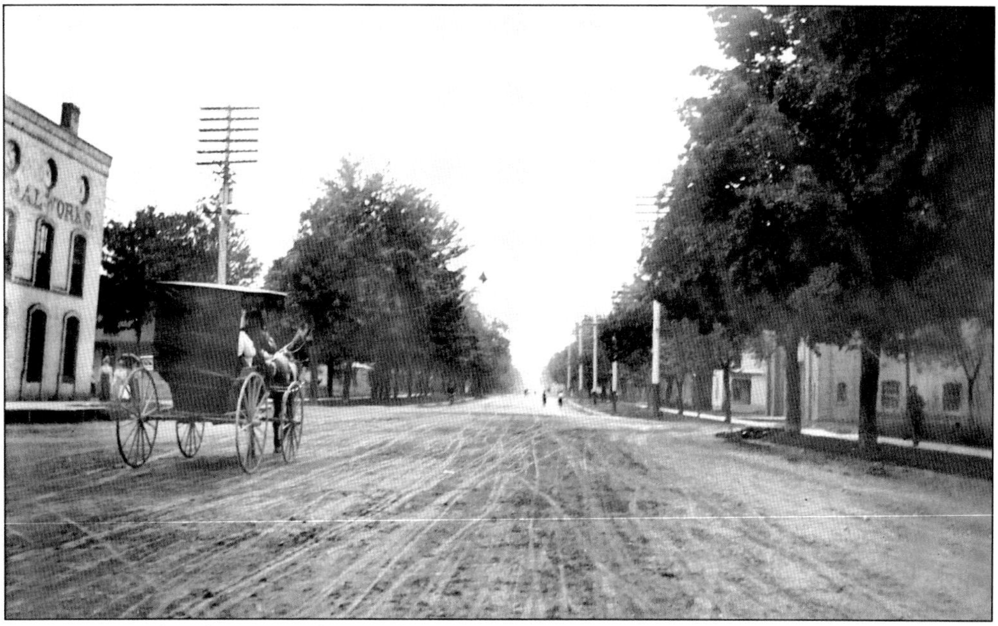

This photograph taken around 1906 shows a horse and carriage traveling west down Chicago Boulevard. This was the primary means of rapid transportation around town for quite some time. The horse and carriage were also important to Tecumseh commerce, as there were several successful blacksmiths and carriage manufactures located around town in the 1800s and early 1900s.

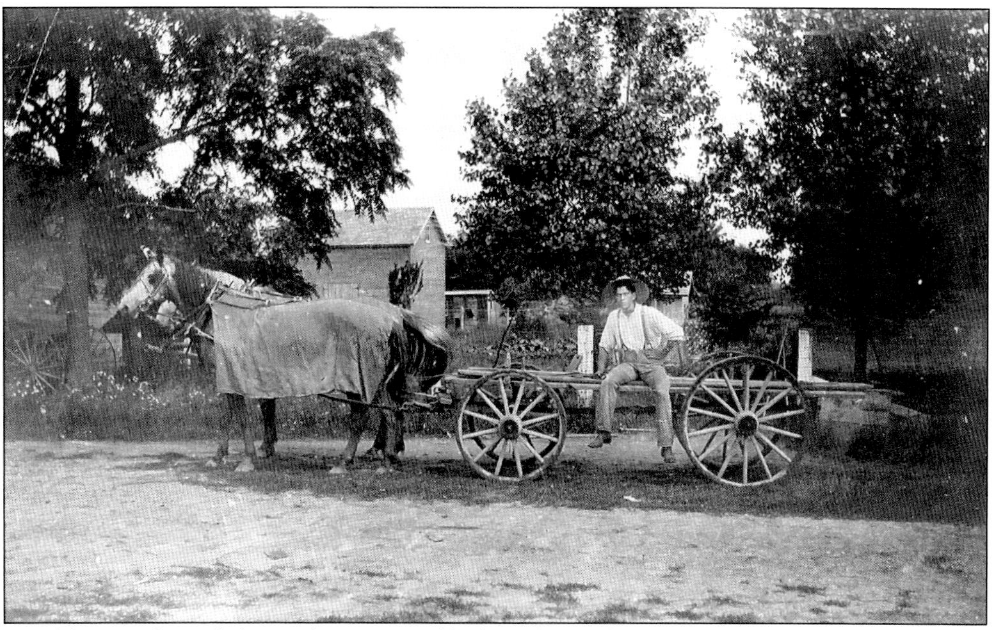

Local farmers depended upon horsepower, blacksmiths, and wagon works to help run their farms and bring their crops to market. Here J. G. Waldron rests on a horse-drawn farm wagon in a photograph taken in the early 1900s. The Waldron family arrived in Tecumseh in 1825, amongst the first settlers. Several family members became important farmers and civic leaders in the village, including veterinarian C. A. Waldron and the historian Clara Waldron.

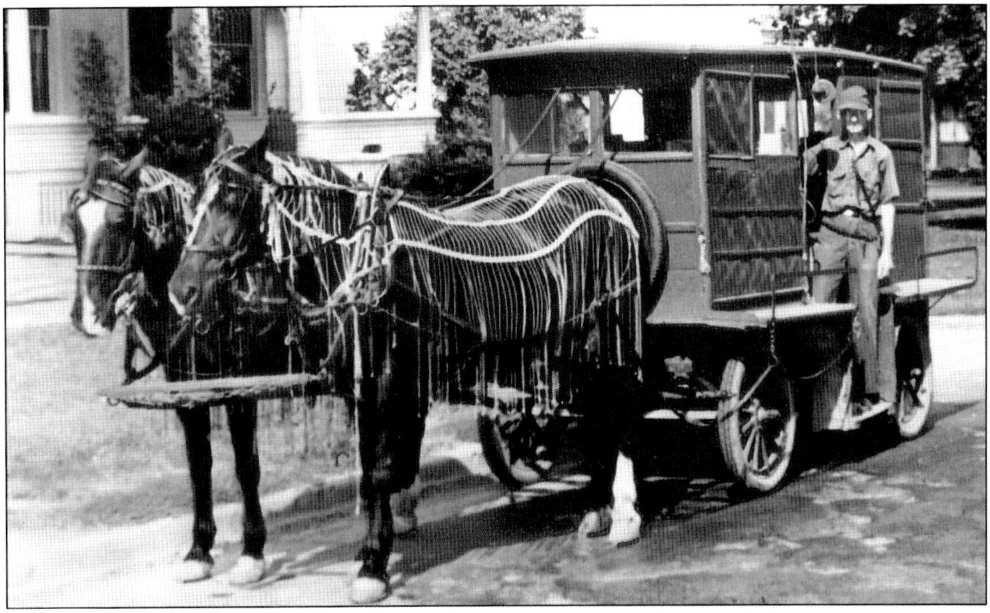

Ernie VanVleet came to Tecumseh in 1906 and purchased a horse-and-carriage grocery delivery service from Charles Shaw. Taken several years later, this photograph is of Ernie in his delivery wagon. In his 50 years of business, this was the only means of delivery he used. George Elliott, grandson of local blacksmith James Elliott, remembers that Ernie had a heavy weight tied to the reins. At each stop Ernie would toss the weight on the road behind the carriage to keep the horses from wondering off. When Ernie retired in 1956, the last horse-drawn vehicle disappeared from the streets of Tecumseh.

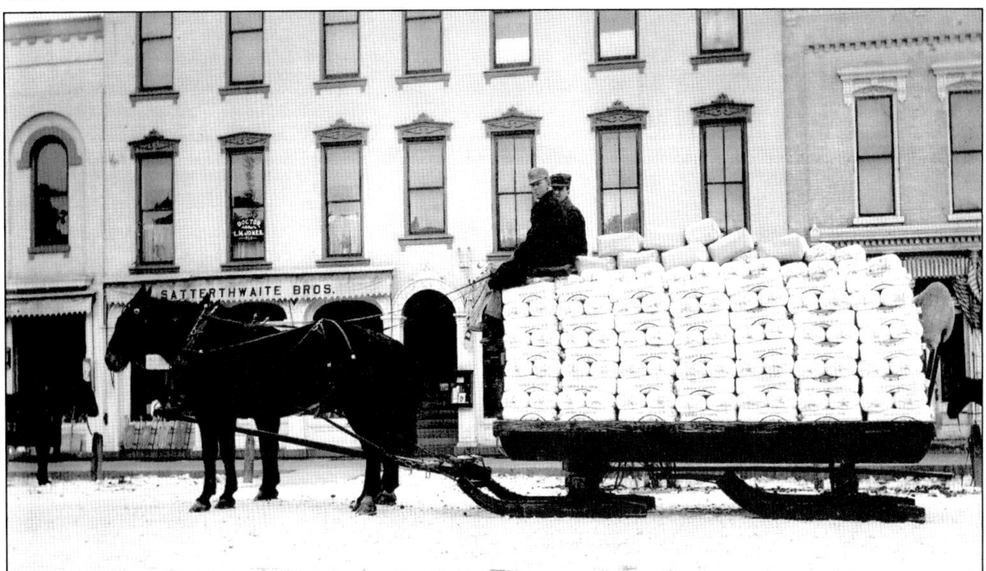

A horse-drawn sleigh loaded with bags of Hayden's "1900" brand flour is coming from the Hayden Mill in 1919, most likely on its way to the warehouse to be loaded onto a freight train. The sleigh is parked in front of the Anderson block, built by Albert Anderson or perhaps Anderson and Perley Bills in 1859. The building succumbed to fire in 1954. (Photo courtesy of Lenawee Historical Museum.)

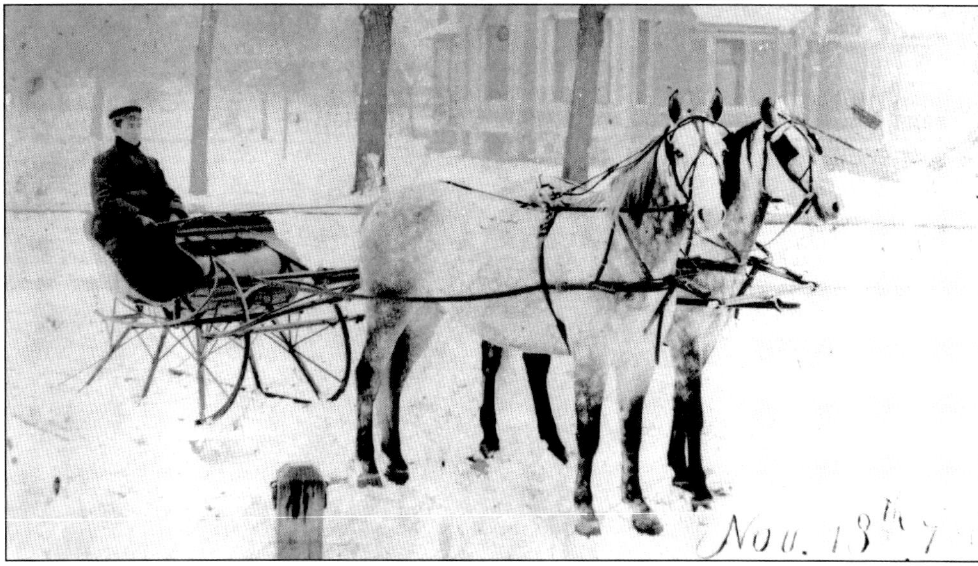

This appealing winter scene is of William Hayden, son of William and Sarah Hayden, in an elegant sleigh on November 13, 1894. He is photographed on the corner of Chicago Boulevard and Ottawa Street. The house in the background is the Shull House that once stood on the northeast corner. (Photograph courtesy of Ashley E. Chase.)

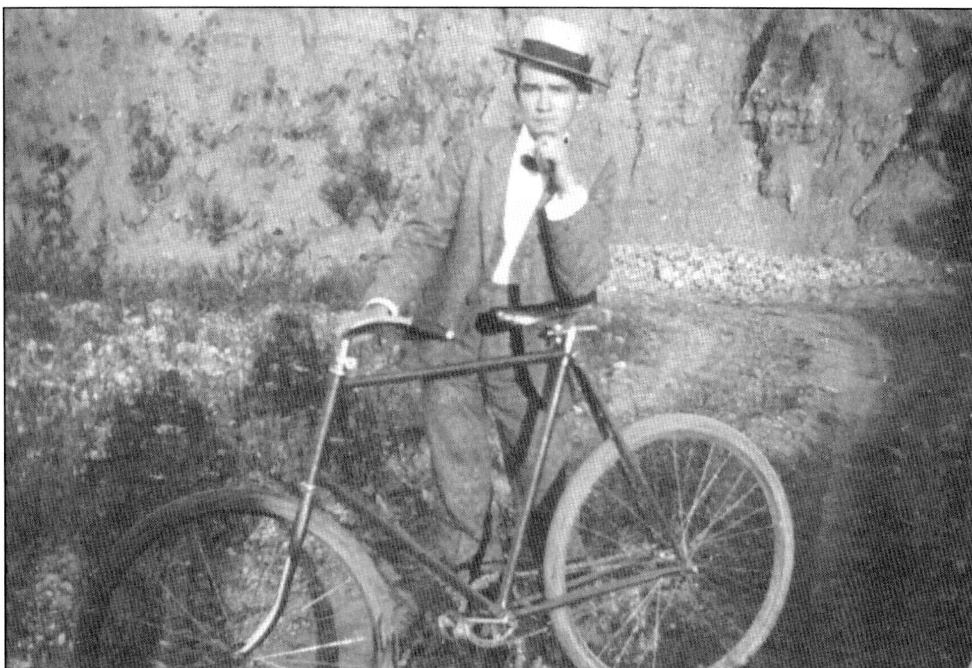

An unidentified cyclist is posing with his transportation on an excursion around Tecumseh. Bicycling, including bicycle racing, was very popular in Tecumseh in the late 1800s and early 1900s. The Tecumseh Bicycle Association was formed to promote races, and in 1896, an officially sanctioned race was held at Bill's Racing Park with over $1,000 in prizes offered. Professional riders came from far and wide, including Bernea Oldfield who later took up automobile racing, where he was known as "Barney" Oldfield.

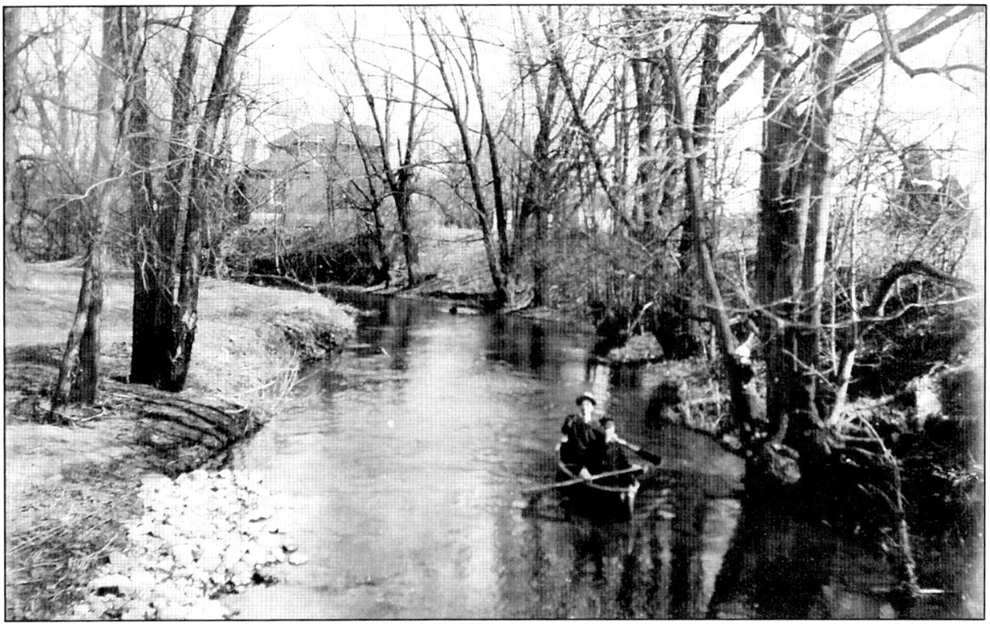

Canoeing along the River Raisin was an agreeable diversion around 1910. The River Raisin, named by French explores for the many grape vines found along its banks, and the many millponds that surround Tecumseh are still used today for recreational entertainment. The numerous dams and bends along the River Raisin as it works its way to Lake Erie make it impractical for any type of serious transportation.

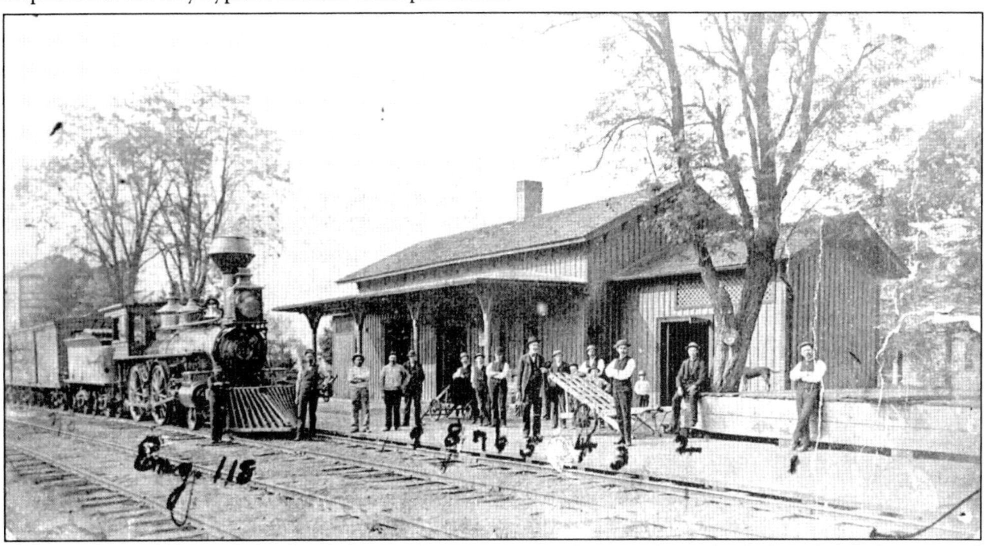

The first railroad to arrive in Tecumseh was a spur from Adrian built by the Palmyra and Jacksonburg (Dr. M. Patterson, president) in 1838. It ran on wooden rails and stopped just north of downtown behind St. Peters Church. Falling on hard times, the railroad was taken over by the state in 1844. In 1846, it was purchased by the Michigan Southern and Indiana Northern Railroad, which covered the old wooden rails with strap iron and put the spur back in service. This 1880 photograph shows the Michigan Southern Depot, which was built in 1854 along the tracks behind St. Peters and burned in 1893. Number eight in the photograph is Newberry S. Satterthwaite, who retired in 1903 after holding the position of station agent for 33 years.

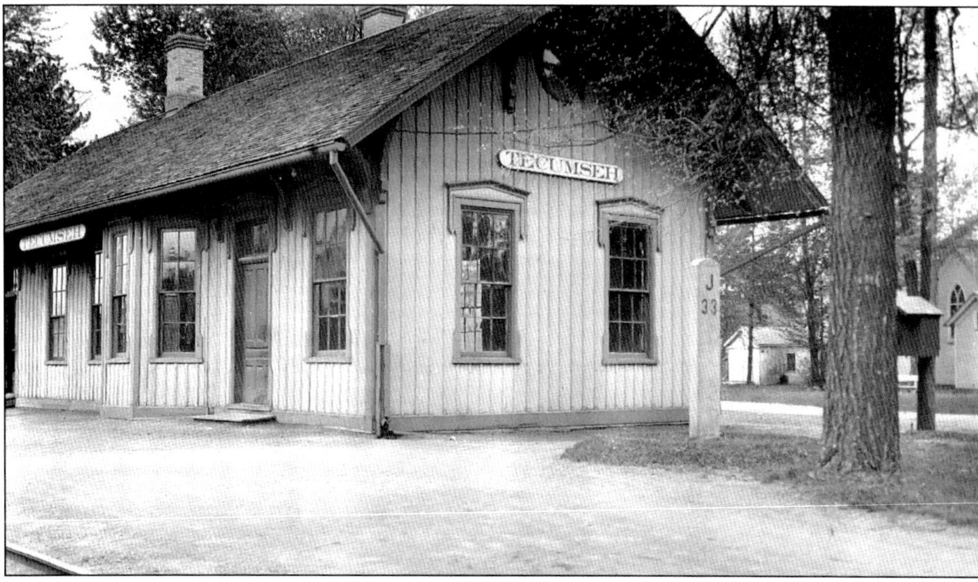

This depot was completed in November 1895 to replace the original Michigan Southern and Indiana Northern depot that burned in 1893. The strap iron rails put down in 1846 over the wooden rails of the Palmyra and Jacksonburg were replaced by iron T-rails in 1856, and the line was completed to Jackson. The distance marker by the depot "J 33" reports the number of miles from this point to Jackson. The back of the original St. Peters Church can be seen on the far right.

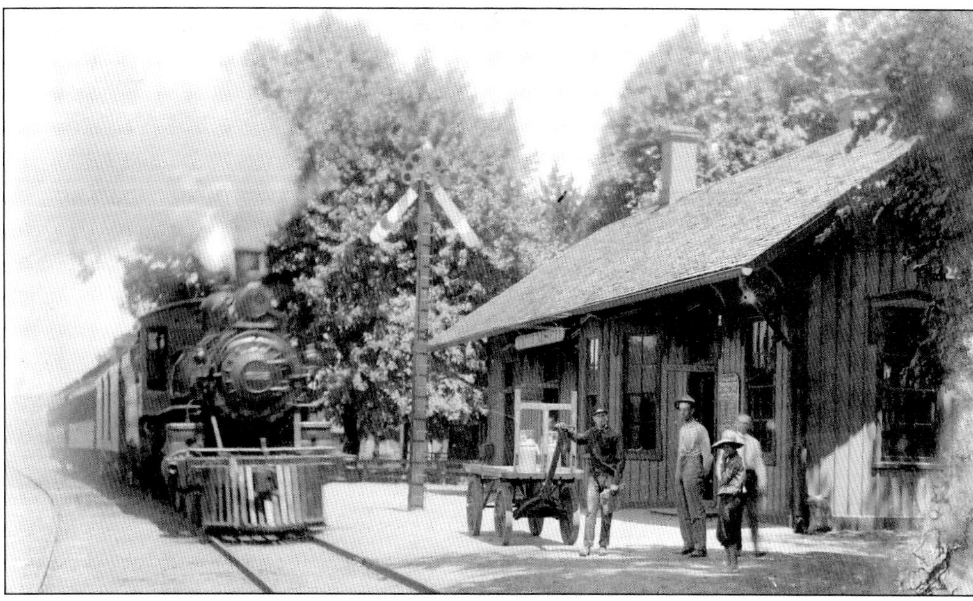

Much of the money needed to start and maintain the original railroads was raised by selling stock to Tecumseh residents and businesspersons who understood the importance of having a rail line in town. Over the years, the railroad changed owners and names many times. When this picture was taken, sometime between 1905 and 1914, it was the Lakeshore and Michigan Southern Rail Road. The 1895 depot, shown here, was torn down in the 1950s. (Photograph courtesy of Lenawee Historical Museum.)

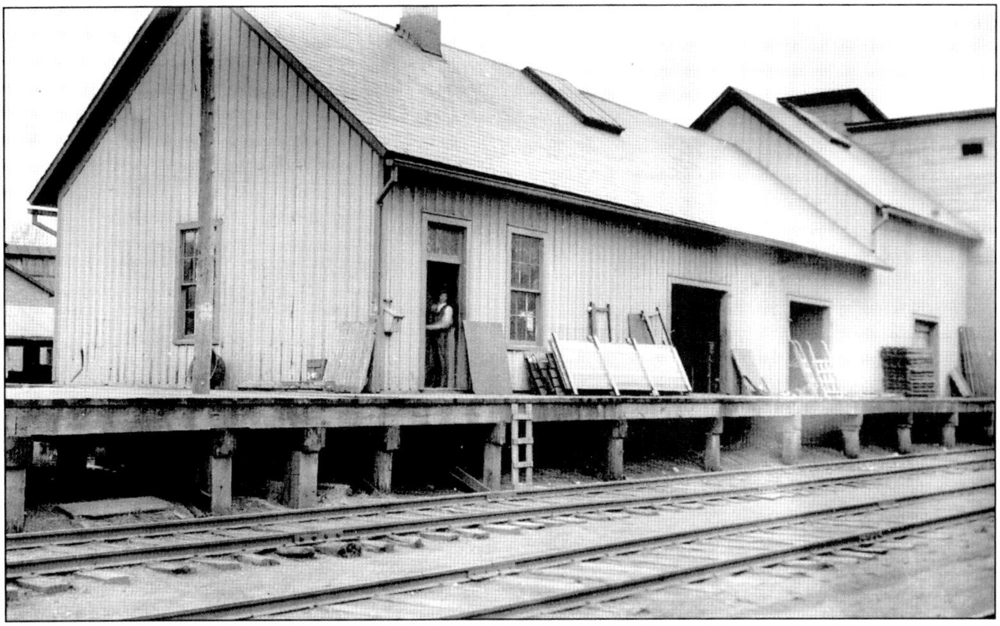

This railroad freight house, shown here around 1919, was built in 1891 north of downtown and directly across the tracks from the depot. It is the second freight house to have been built on this spot, the first being lost to fire in 1891. The building shown connected to the freight house on the north was C. A. Slayton's grain elevator and grain dryer, built in 1898. In the 1960s, this freight house was torn down.

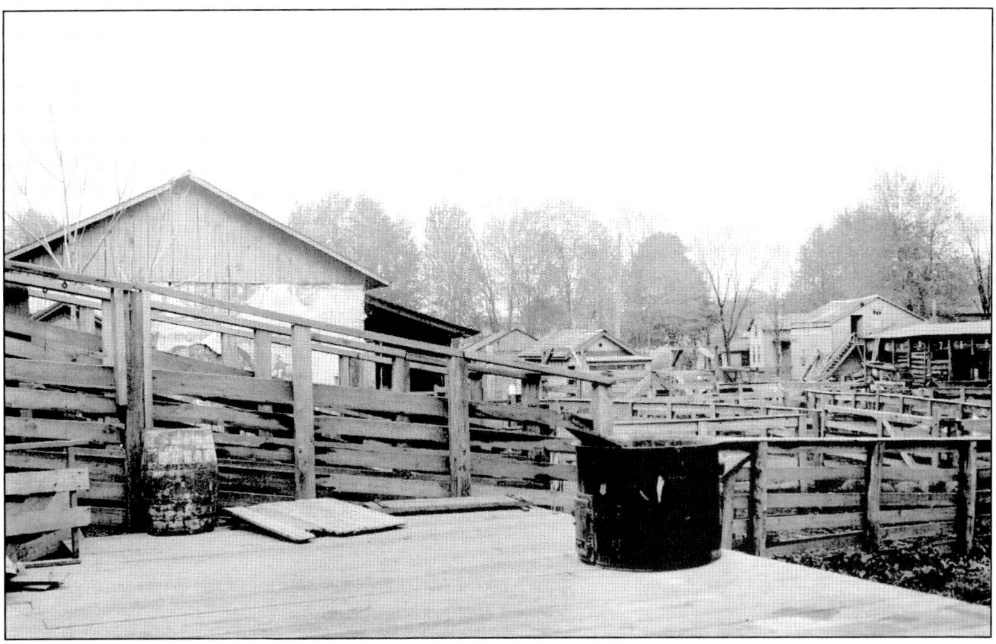

Looking south from the freight house was the Tecumseh stockyard, shown here around 1919. The local farmers exported both grain and livestock as a source of income. Here the livestock was loaded on trains for shipment to markets across the country. In the late 1800s, S. W. Temple's lumberyard was just southwest of the stockyard.

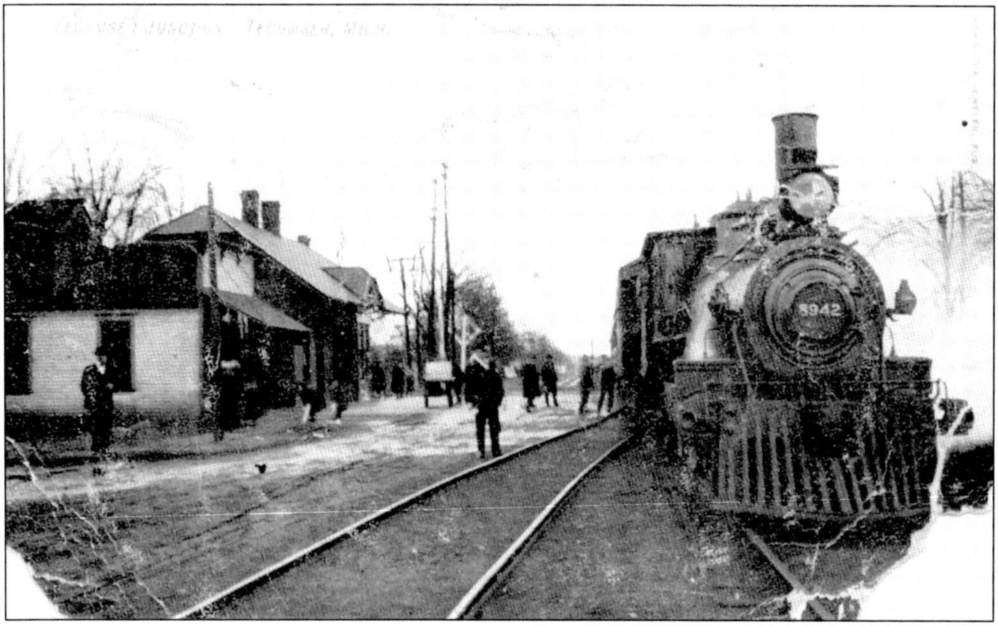

Eventually a second depot was built in Tecumseh, and multiple railroad companies came through town. The various roads went south to Adrian and on to Lima, Ohio, or south to Lenawee Junction and on to Toledo, Ohio; north to Jackson, east to Dundee, and west to Marshall. Tecumseh Junction, shown here facing east, was where all these roads met and crossed each other.

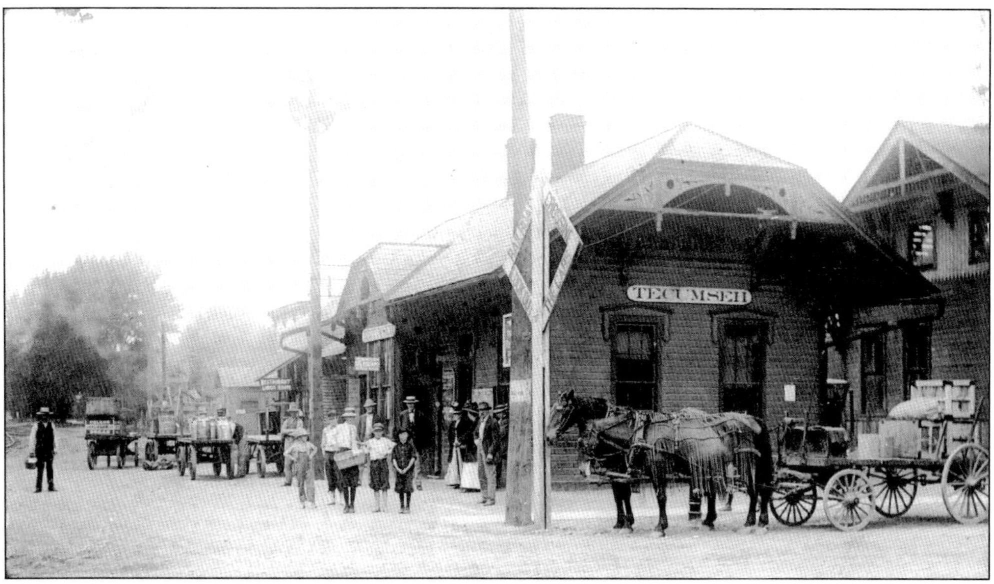

Tecumseh Junction Depot is pictured around 1905 from across Evans Street looking west. The boy with the basket is Perry Satterthwaite, who earned about $1 a week selling newspapers and popcorn (most of which he said he ate himself) to the passengers. Perry would also run to the store and buy cigars for the engineer and fireman, who could not leave the train.

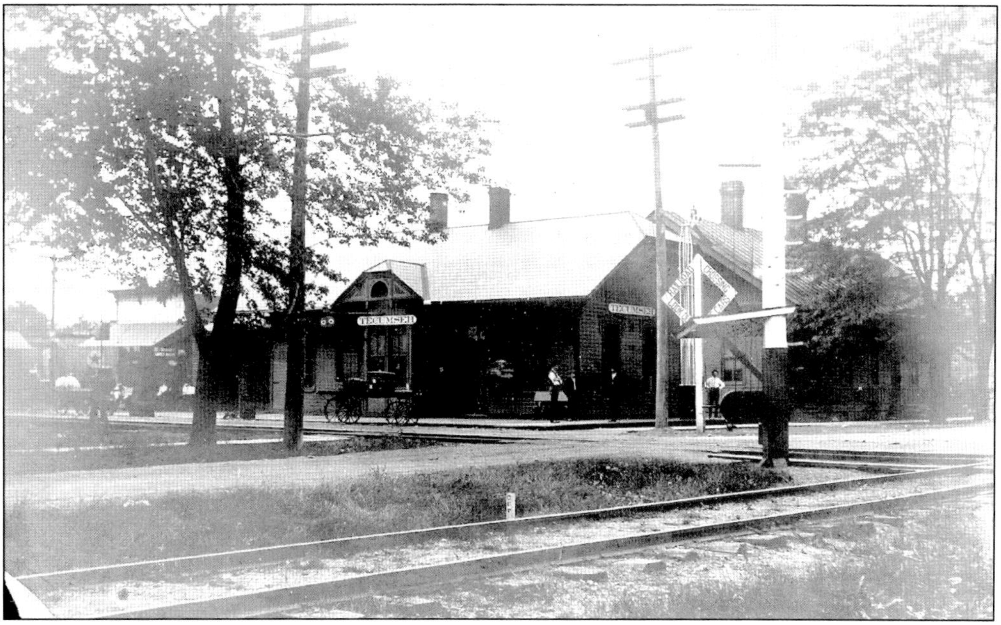

This view is of the Tecumseh Junction Depot looking northeast across Evans Street. The building on the right is the Detroit and Lima Northern Railroad general offices. The depot stood at the intersection of Cummins Street and Evans Street facing south. In 1986, the depot was saved from imminent destruction and moved, at a cost of $60,000, to the southwest corner of Chicago Boulevard and Ottawa Street, where it is now used for retail space.

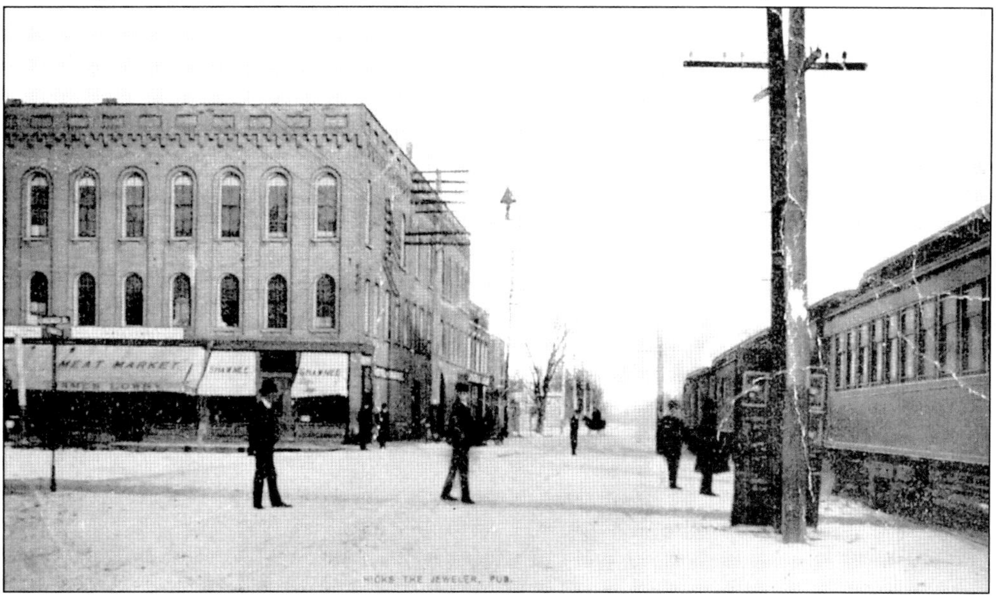

In 1881, the intersection of Chicago Boulevard and Evans Street became a regular station stop on the Michigan Southern even though there was no station located there. The railroad would let passengers board right downtown and purchase tickets later at the stations north or south of town. In 1882, William Gaston sold tickets for the railroad at his meat market, which in 1885 became Gaston's Jewelry store. The station stop on Chicago Boulevard lasted until 1918. (Photograph courtesy of Ashley E. Chase.)

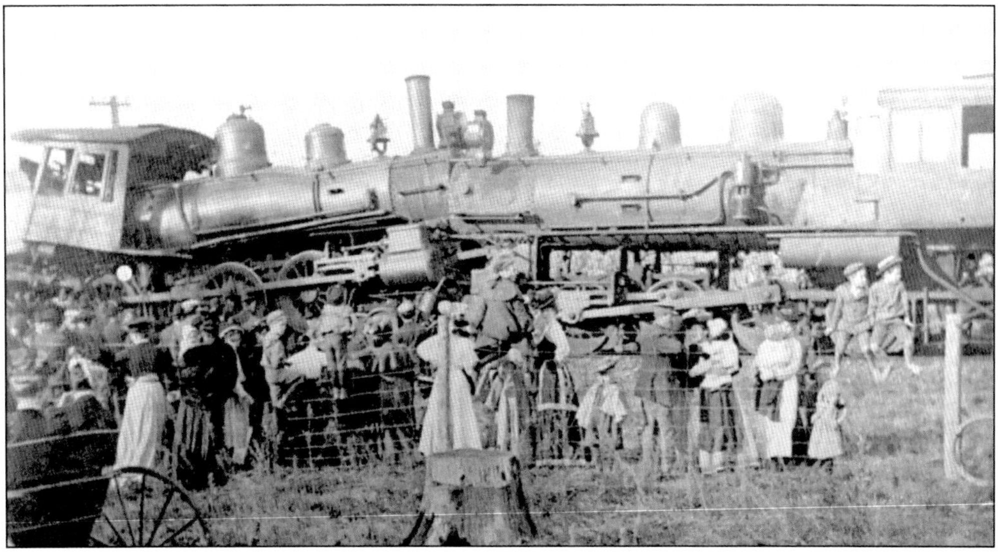

The Lakeshore and Michigan Southern owned the tracks running east and west through Tecumseh. The Detroit, Toledo and Ironton Railroad had rights to travel on them, but the two companies did not always discuss who was scheduled to use the track. On Sunday morning, October 6, 1907, on a small curve in the tracks by Waring Farm close to Britton, two and a half miles east of Tecumseh, this lack of communication lead to quite a spectacle, but not a tragedy. The train on the left is a Detroit, Toledo and Ironton work train, and the one on the right is a Lakeshore and Michigan Southern freight train.

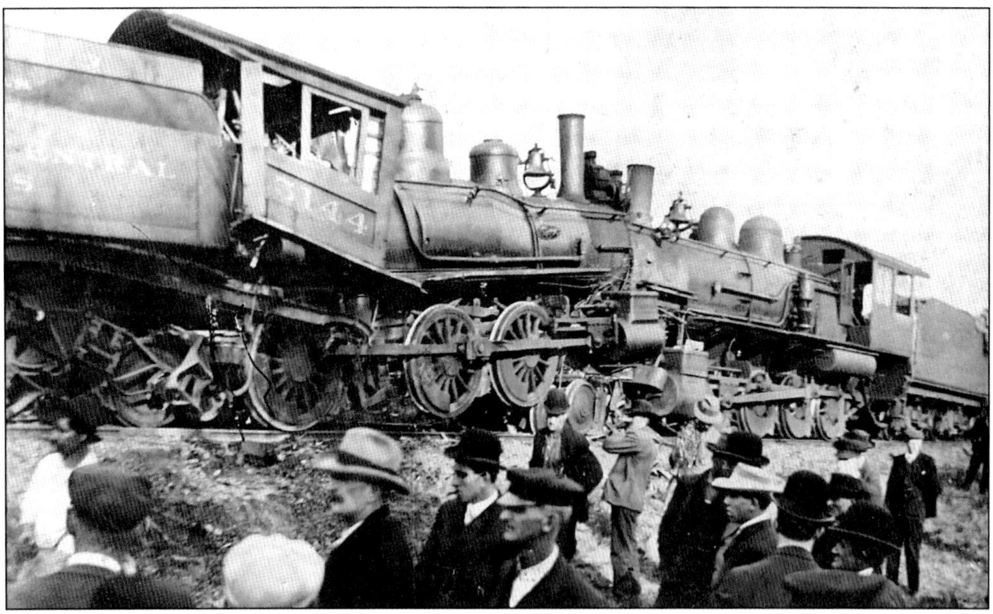

This second picture of the October 6, 1907, wreck is from a slightly different angle. It was reported that as the trains were rounding the corner, the crews each saw the oncoming locomotive. They had just time enough time to set the breaks and leap from the cab. Fortunately there were no injuries. According to notes from J. Newton Satterthwaite, Dan Cleveland is in the "center of photo wearing black bowler hat and puffing a cigar," and Mayne Henderson is "right of Mr. Cleveland, and wearing a cap."

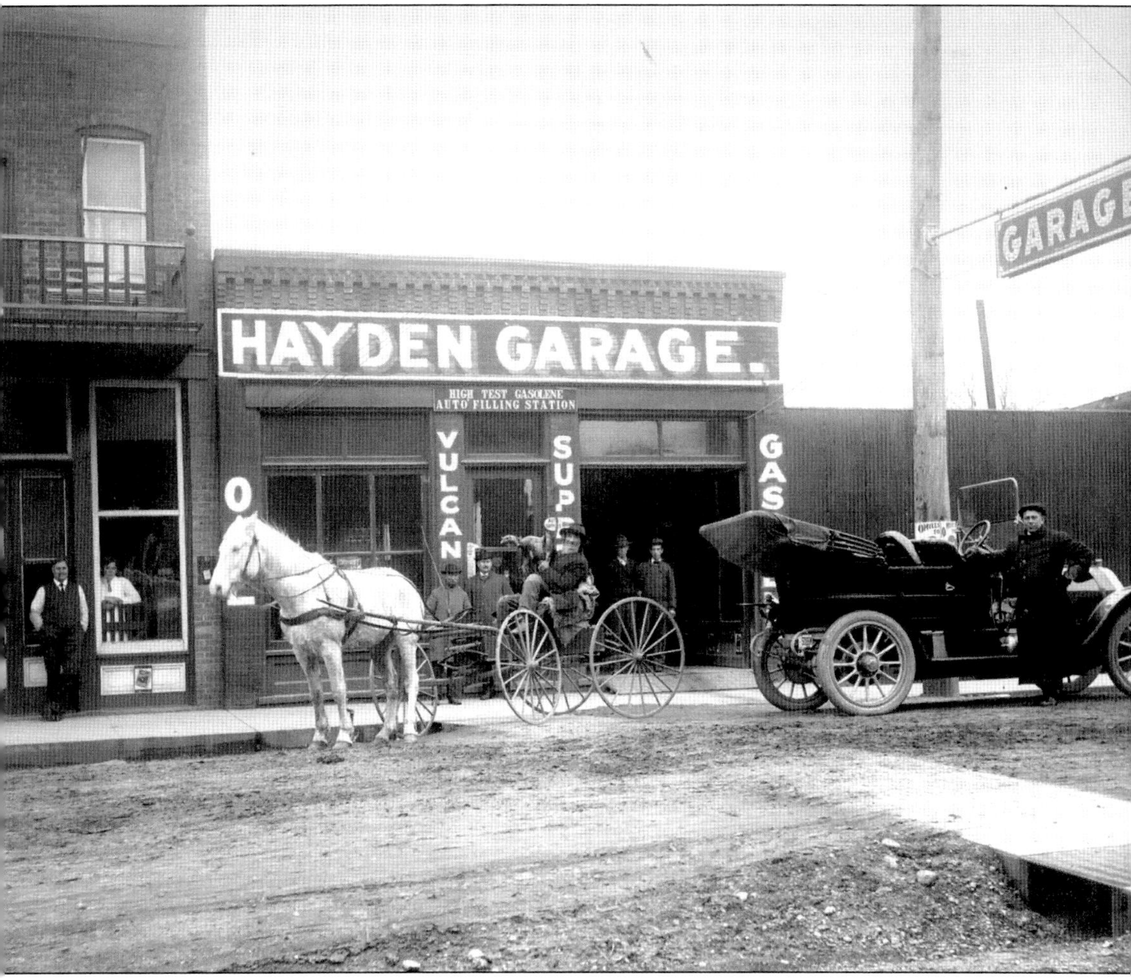

The transition from horse and buggy to horseless carriage was not instantaneous. This picture illustrates that even those who lived during that time had some inkling of the almost comical novelty that a picture of both modes of transportation would become in the not too distant future or had already become by the time this picture was taken. The chicken is clearly an added comedic bonus. Levi Hayden, proprietor of Hayden Garage, is standing next to the automobile.

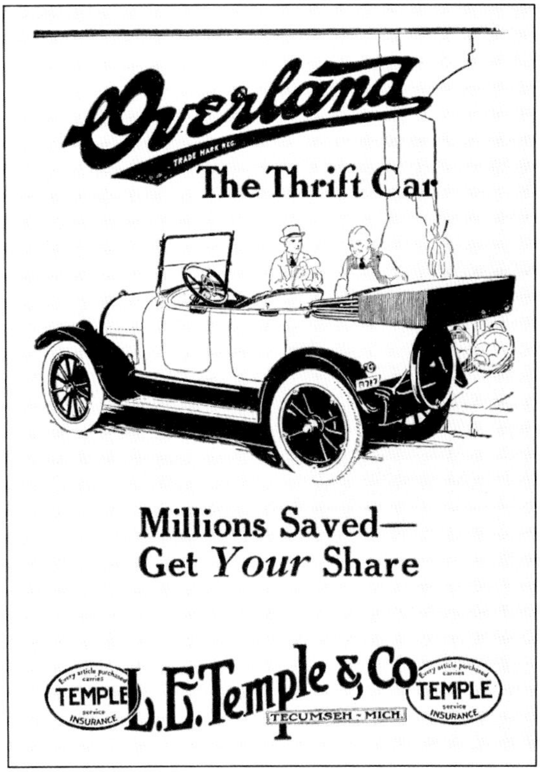

This 1919 advertisement is for Willys-Overland cars, available in Tecumseh from L. E. Temple and Company. Leon E. Temple was the son of Samuel W. Temple, a successful carpenter, businessman, and grocer, and Hattie A. Smith, Samuel's second wife. Leon was a partner in business with his father, but this advertisement suggests that he branched out following his own interests as well. Willys-Overland was a Toledo, Ohio, company and was second in sales to Ford Motor Company in the early 1900s.

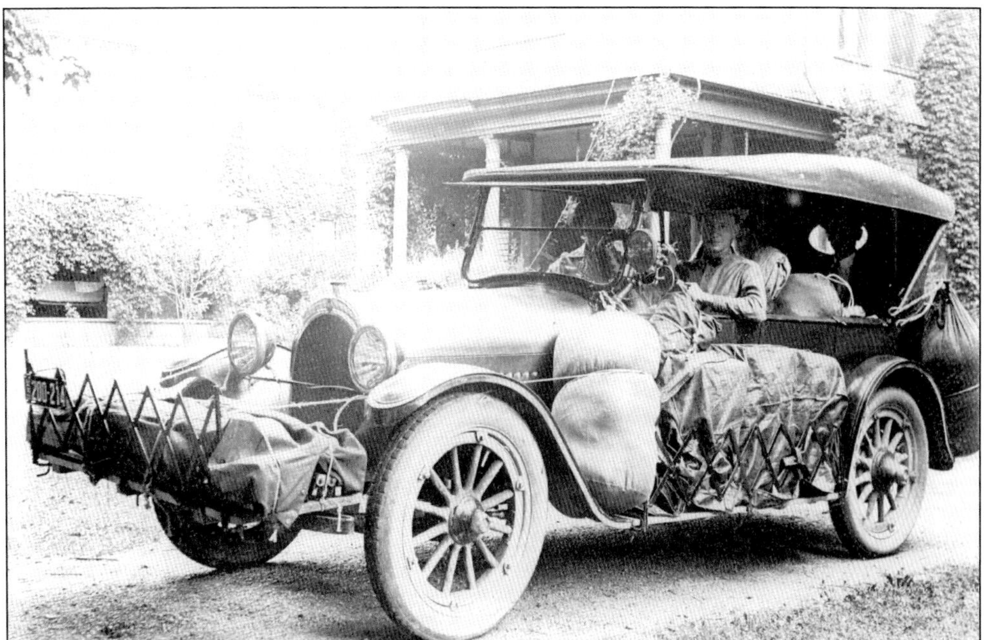

Taken in 1922, this photograph shows Eugene Rosacrans at the wheel of his heavily laden automobile. His father, Fred Rosacrans, proprietor of the Rosacrans Dry Goods store in the Masonic temple building, owned the house in the background.

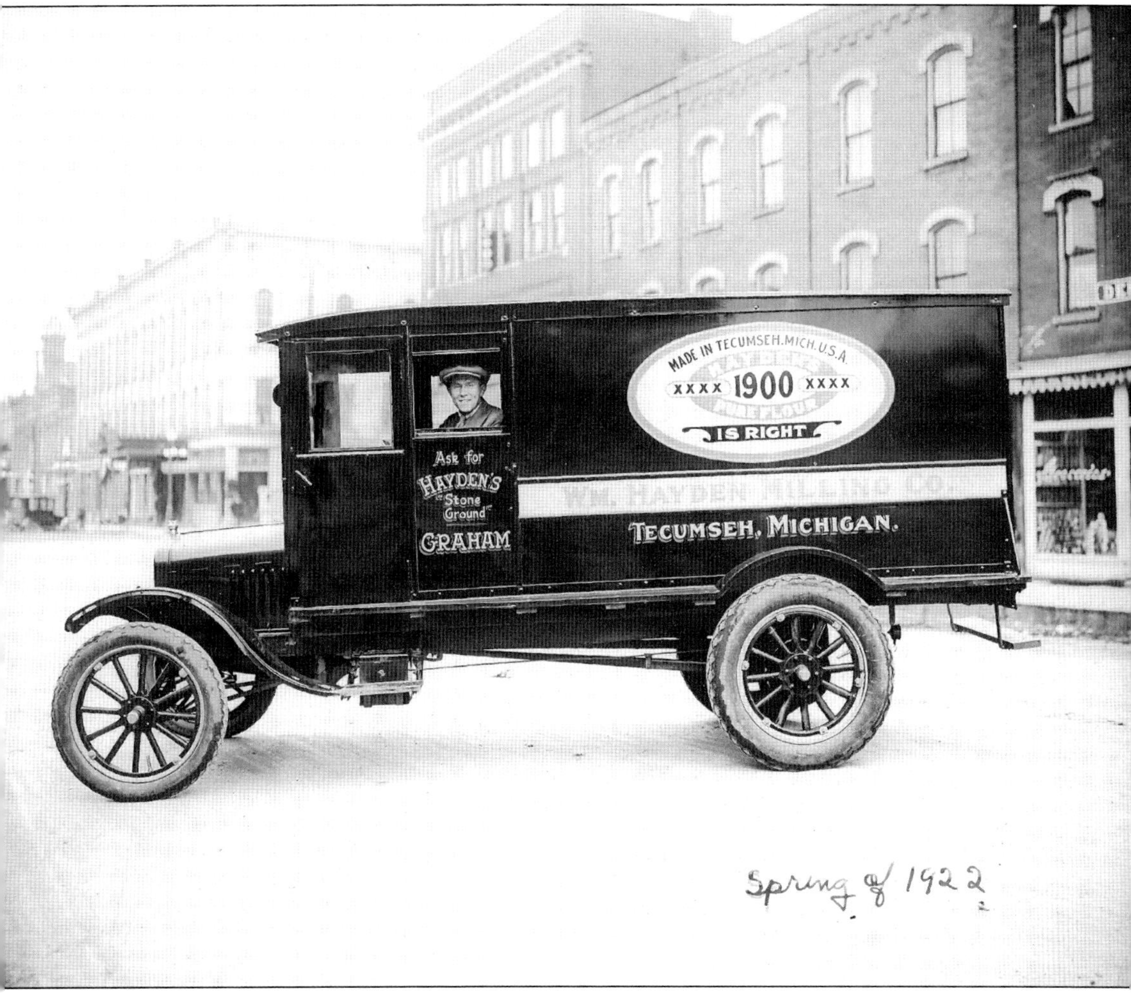

Here Perry Hayden is proudly posing in the new Hayden Mills truck in the spring of 1922. Some notes indicate that this was the first truck to be purchased by the company; however, other photographs suggest that it may have been the first enclosed delivery vehicle. Perry Hayden was William Hayden's grandson and would play a very important role in the history of Tecumseh's second century.

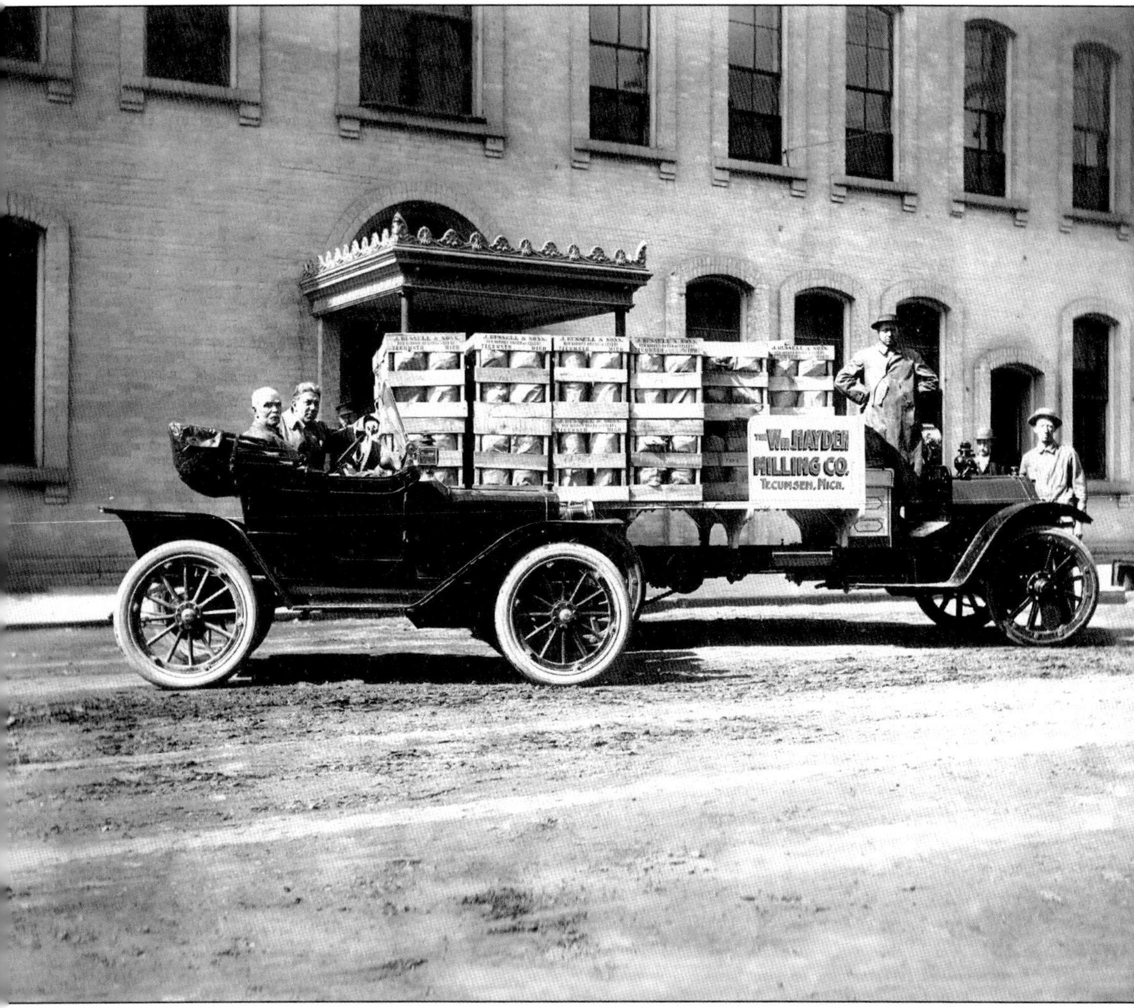

This federal flat bed truck belonged to the Wm. Hayden Milling Company around 1910. The cargo of the truck is of special interest because it is not Hayden flour but J. Russell and Sons Red Ribbon Brand of Celery. A written caption on the back of the picture states that the driver of the car is Levi Hayden "in Mitchell . . . (which he sold)" and that the man standing in the truck is "Hiram Gove, driver of truck for Hayden Mills." Behind the vehicles is the east elevation of the Merchants Block, at that time the Barrett Brothers Hotel and the Tecumseh State Savings Bank. (Photograph courtesy of Lenawee Historical Museum.)

Six

People, Parades, and Portraits

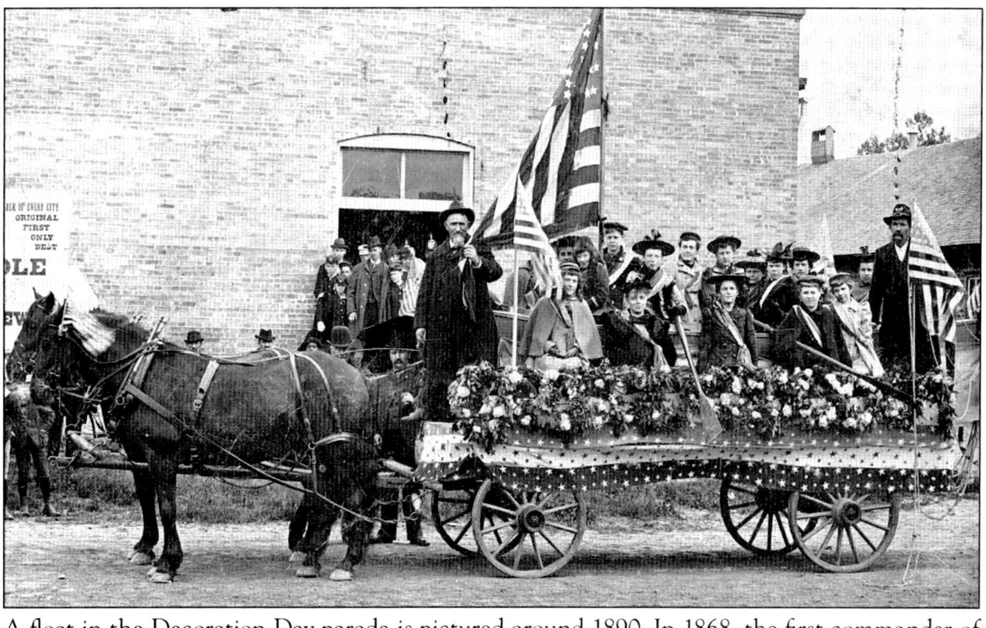

A float in the Decoration Day parade is pictured around 1890. In 1868, the first commander of the Grand Army of the Republic (GAR) established Decoration Day as a day to remember those who had died in the Civil War by putting decorations on their graves, decorating the town, and holding parades and memorial celebrations. Many newspaper articles and photographs attest to Tecumseh's dedication to this day and its veterans. Memorial Day, as it is now known, was made a national holiday in 1971.

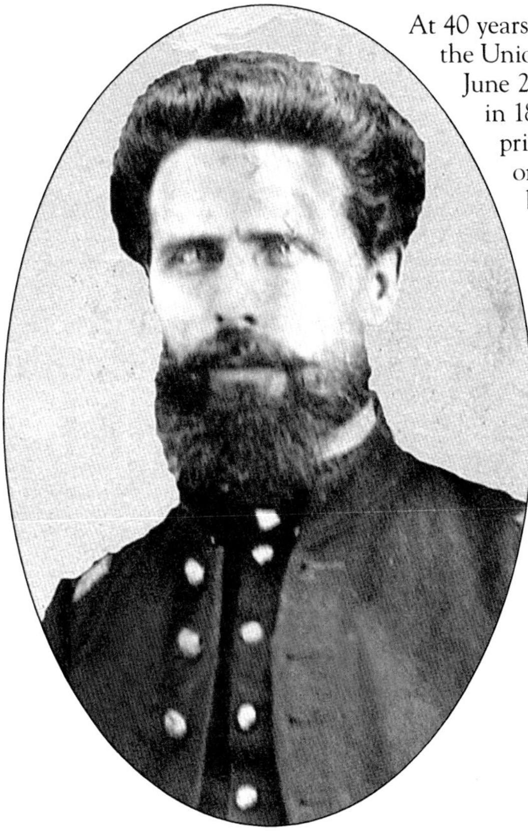

At 40 years of age, Jeptha W. Beers of Tecumseh joined the Union Army, Company G of the 4th Infantry on June 20, 1861. He was promoted to first lieutenant in 1862. Beers was wounded in action and taken prisoner at the battle of Gaines Mills in Virginia on June 27, 1862. Beers died on July 6, 1862, becoming the first Tecumseh soldier to lose his life in the Civil War.

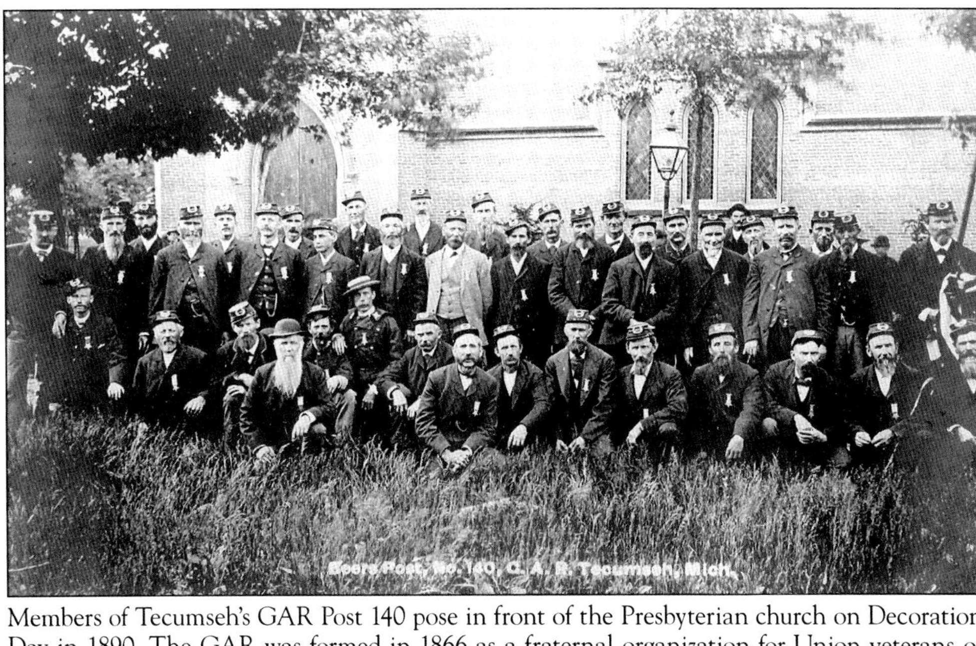

Members of Tecumseh's GAR Post 140 pose in front of the Presbyterian church on Decoration Day in 1890. The GAR was formed in 1866 as a fraternal organization for Union veterans of the Civil War. Tecumseh's post was formed on March 13, 1882, and was named Beers Post after Jeptha W. Beers, the first Tecumseh casualty of the Civil War.

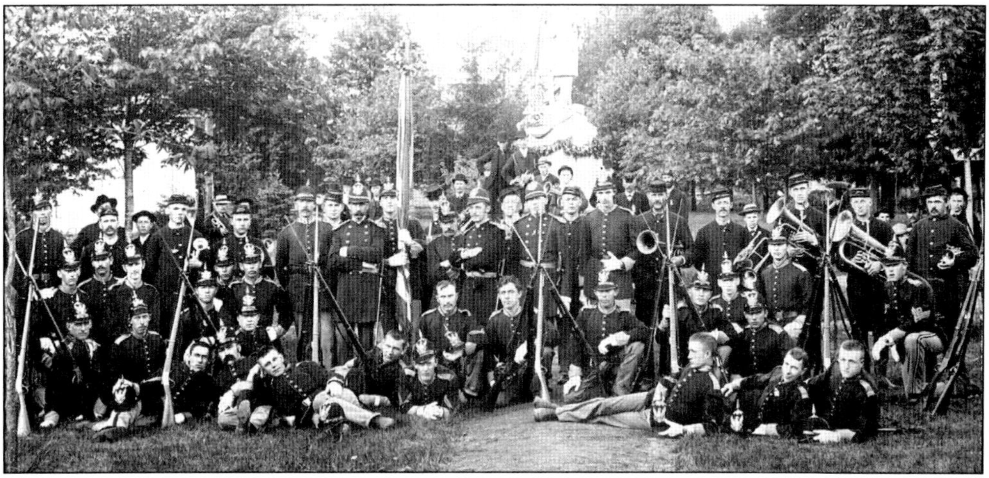

The 31st Regiment, Company C, of the Michigan State Militia gathered for this photograph in front of the Civil War memorial in Military Square on May 30, 1885. The memorial was erected in 1882 as a tribute to Civil War veterans and was moved to Brookside Cemetery in 1928. Company C was the pride of Tecumseh in the late 1800s and was a social and political force in the village.

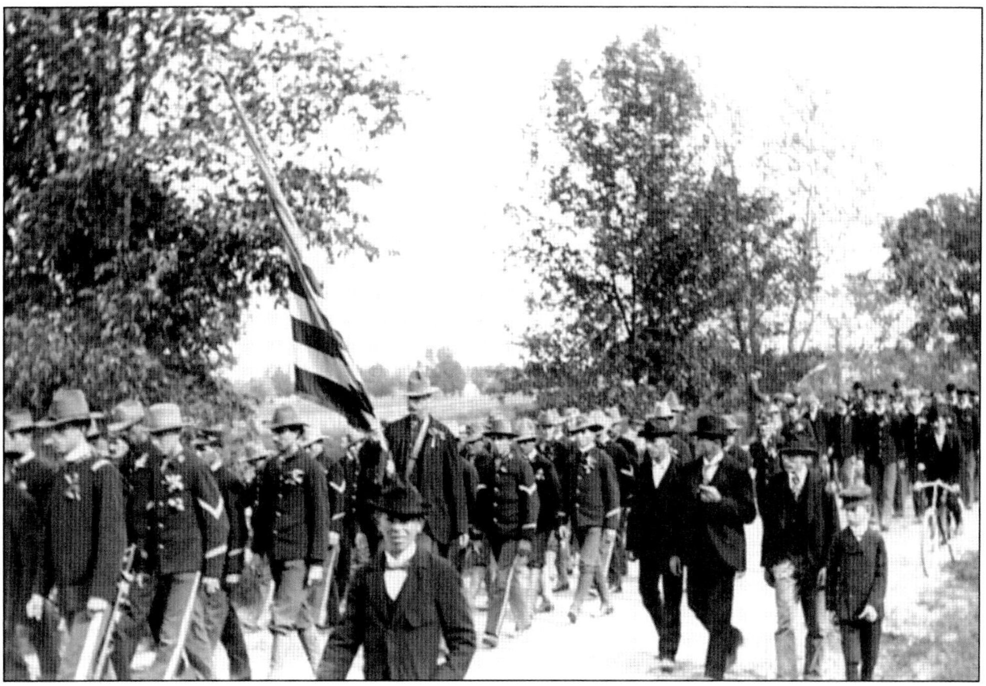

Tecumseh's Spanish American War veterans march in the Decoration Day parade around 1910. In April 1898, the 31st Regiment, Company C, of the Michigan State Militia was called to active duty. Most of their 13-month tour was spent at Camp Chicamagua, Georgia, where two unfortunate soldiers died from disease. Company C spent about two months in Cuba but never saw action.

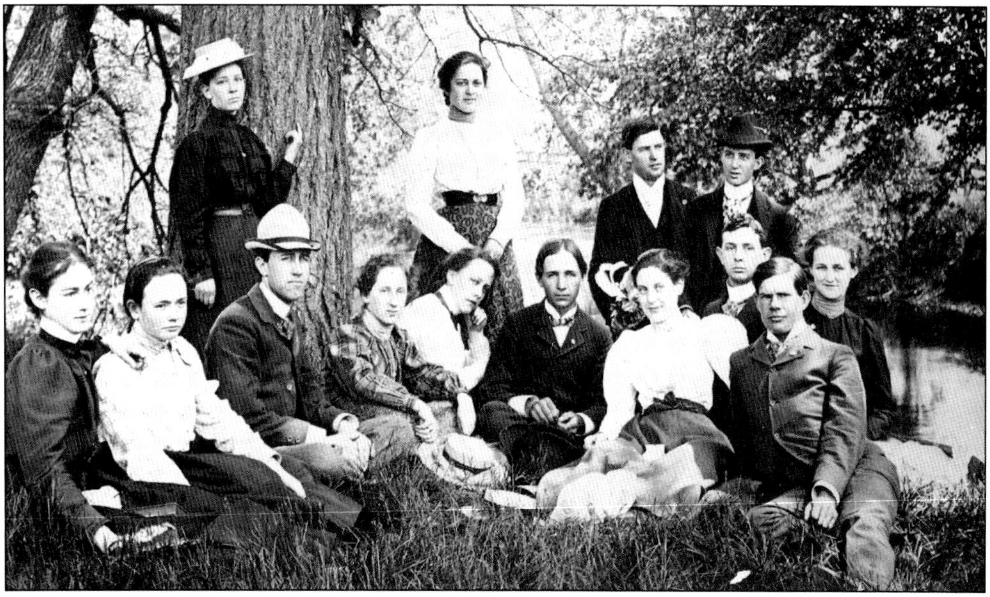

The Tecumseh High School class of 1899 is pictured. The first high school yearbook was issued in 1919, and a number of earlier graduating classes were listed. According to the 1919 yearbook, the class of 1899 included N. Clare Brazee, Bessie Camburn-Russell, Ina Jackson-Barrett, Claude L. Kniffen, Frank M. Morgan, Dora L. Pocklington-Hardman, William J. Taylor, Adah Beebe-Seger, Laura Gooding-Temple, Florence Jenkins-Lockwood, Anna McClure-Mead, William O'Reilly, E. Winnifred Slattery-Sisson, and Halleck E. Wilson.

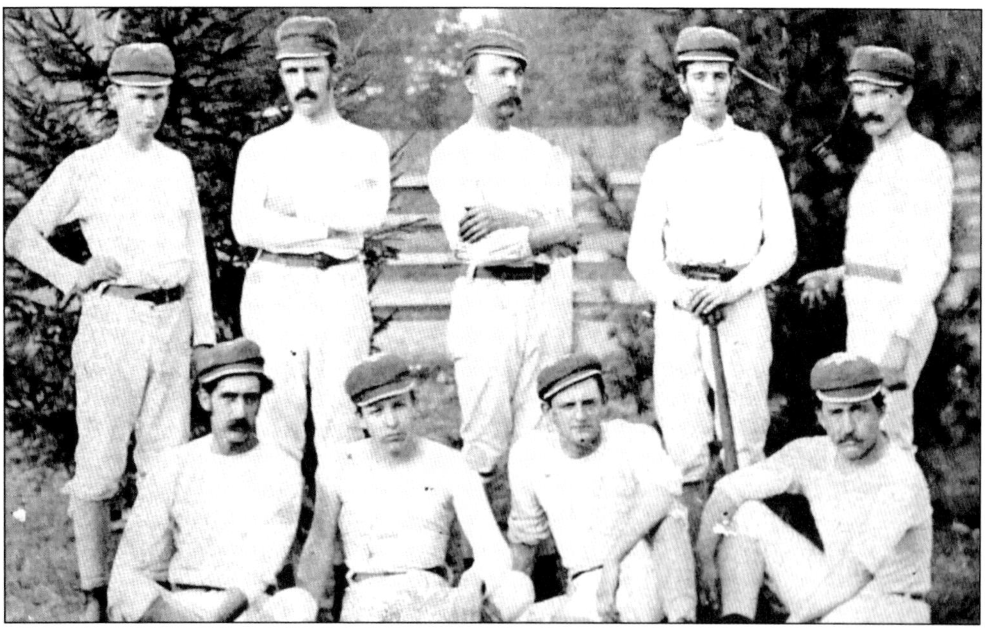

The Tecumseh Blue Stockings, photographed in 1874, was one of the many baseball teams that existed in Tecumseh. Team members pictured are Fred Rosa, Hub Stout, Jim Cummins, Frank Baxter, Will Lee, Gno. Gillen, Chas. B., Chas. Cummins, and Web. Frasir. Teams were sponsored by local businesses and would play each other at Bills Racing Park. Occasionally exhibition games were played with teams from other towns.

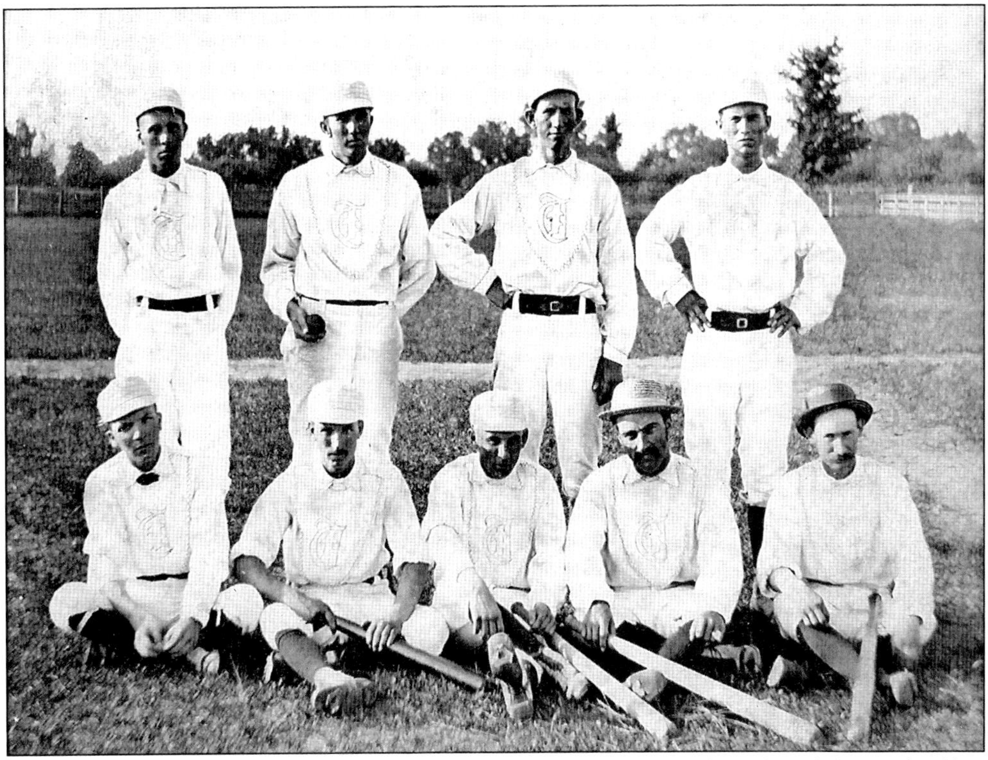

The Tecumseh Baseball Association is photographed in 1879. Pictured are, from left to right, (first row) Harry Snell, Ed McKinney, two unidentified Detroit players, and Fred Rosacrans; (second row) John Anderson, John Freeman, Jim Tracy, and Matt Root. According to Clara Waldron's history of Tecumseh, this is the team that "won a decisive victory over a Detroit nine."

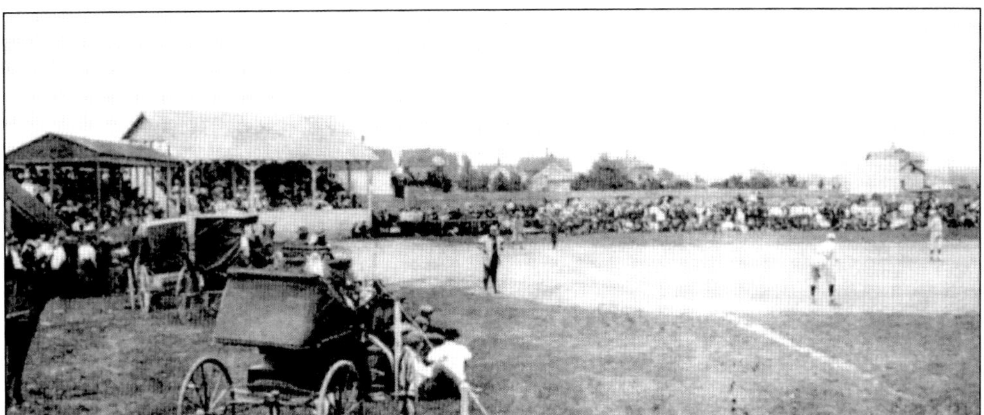

In 1902, the Tecumseh Baseball Association abandoned Bills Racing Park as a venue and made improvements to Athletic Park, located at the south end of Maiden Lane, to better accommodate the game and its fans. In 1907, the Tecumseh Indians Baseball Club joined the Southern Michigan League, which included Battle Creek, Bay City, Flint, Jackson, Kalamazoo, and Tecumseh's archrival, Mount Clemens.

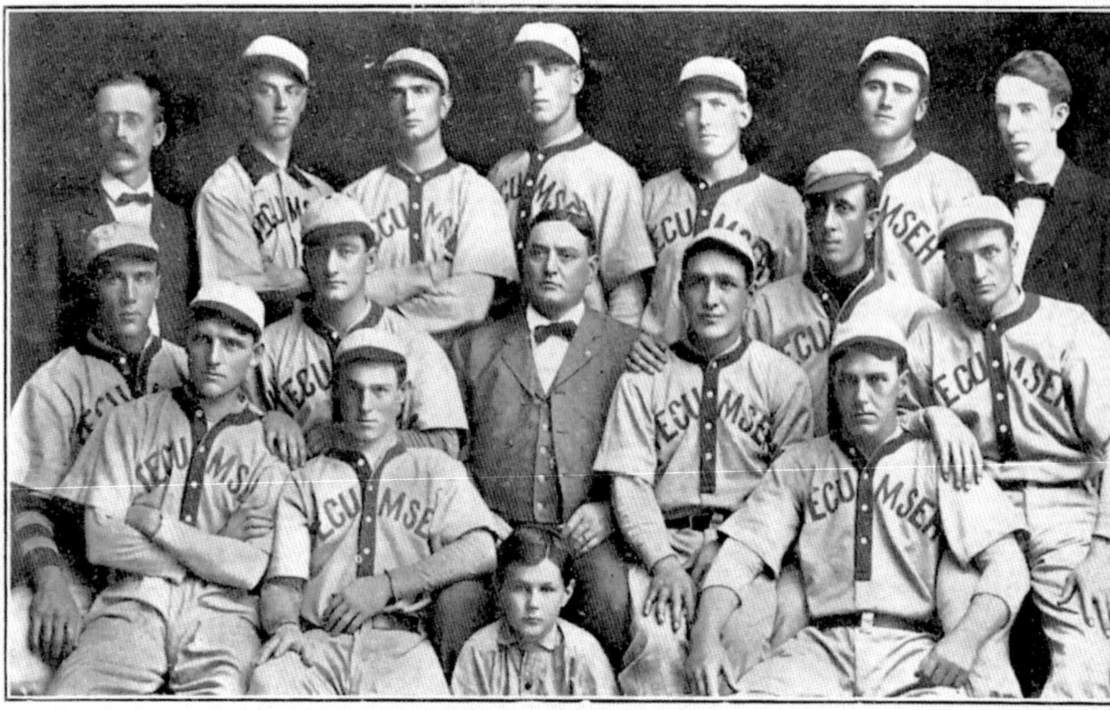

J. H. SMITH, L. FLETCHER, T. RAILING, F MERKLE, C. WAGNER. E. DOTY, H. TEMPLE,
J. SOMERLOT. E. PRESTON, R. A. HEESEN, H. TEAL, "BO" SLEAR,
R. WOLFE, J. BRADLEY. DALE HODGES. J. MITCHELL, W. HILLINGER.

TECUMSEH BASE BALL CLUB, SOUTHERN MICHIGAN LEAGUE CHAMPIONS, 19

The 1907, Tecumseh Indians were the Class D Southern Michigan professional baseball league champions. The players were all big stars in town, but the biggest star of the 1907 team was Fred Merkle (third row, center) from Toledo, Ohio. Also in this photograph are the three main investors of the team, J. H. Smith, president of Tecumseh State Bank; R. A. Heesen, president of the Lilley State Bank; and H. Temple, cashier of the Lilley State Bank. In 1907, the Tecumseh Indians sold Fred Merkle, then 19 years of age, to the New York Giants for $2,500.

This portrait was taken in 1907 of, from left to right, (first row) Eddie Preston, Raynor Brewer, and H. Teal; (second row) Bo Slear and John L. Anderson (or his brother Raynor). These handsome young men were all associated with the Tecumseh Indians baseball team. Bo Slear, H. Teal, and Eddie Preston were team members; both Anderson brothers and Raynor Brewer were involved in team business management or ownership.

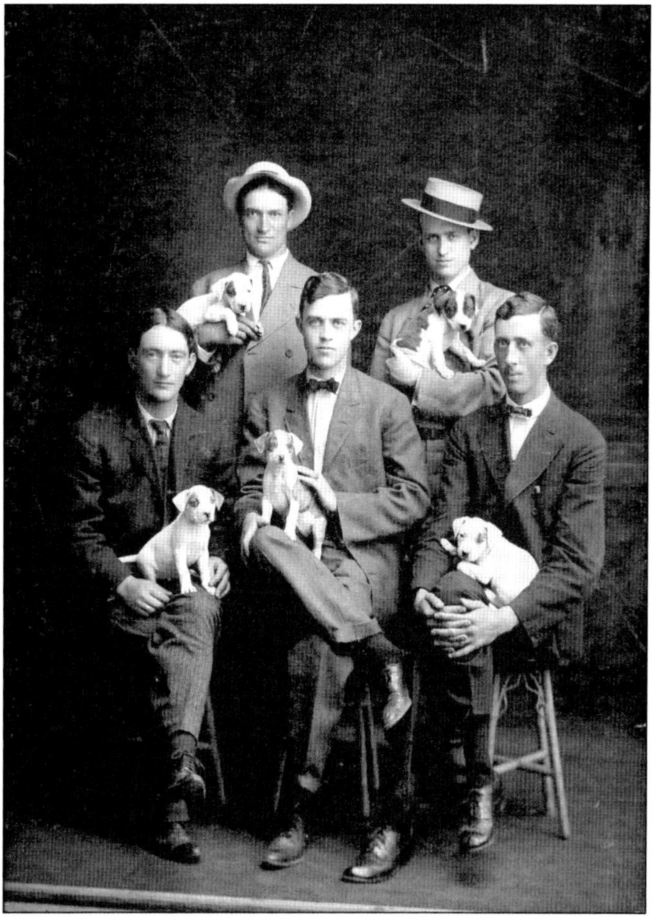

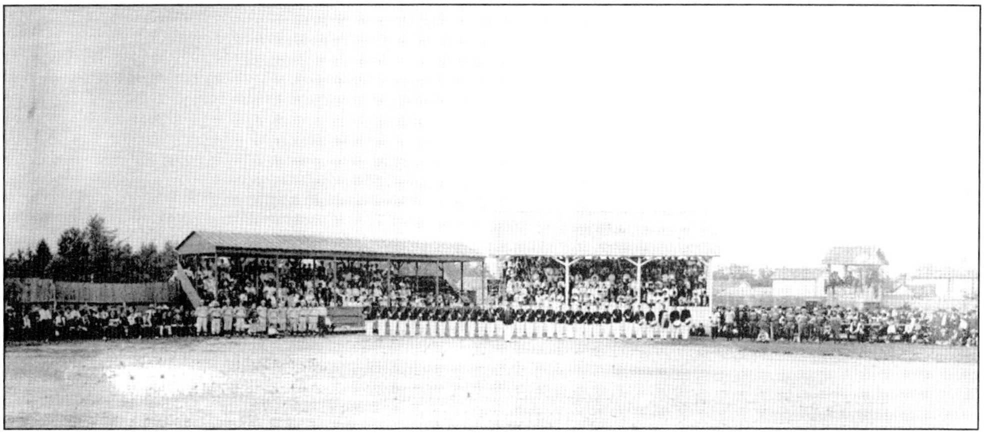

This view was taken before a game at Athletic Park, around 1907. The Tecumseh Indians are on the left, the Adrian Band is in the center, and the team from Angola, Indiana, is on the right. The Indians were not as successful in 1908 as they were in 1907 and not as profitable as the investors had hoped. The players were sold off and the franchise sold away from Tecumseh.

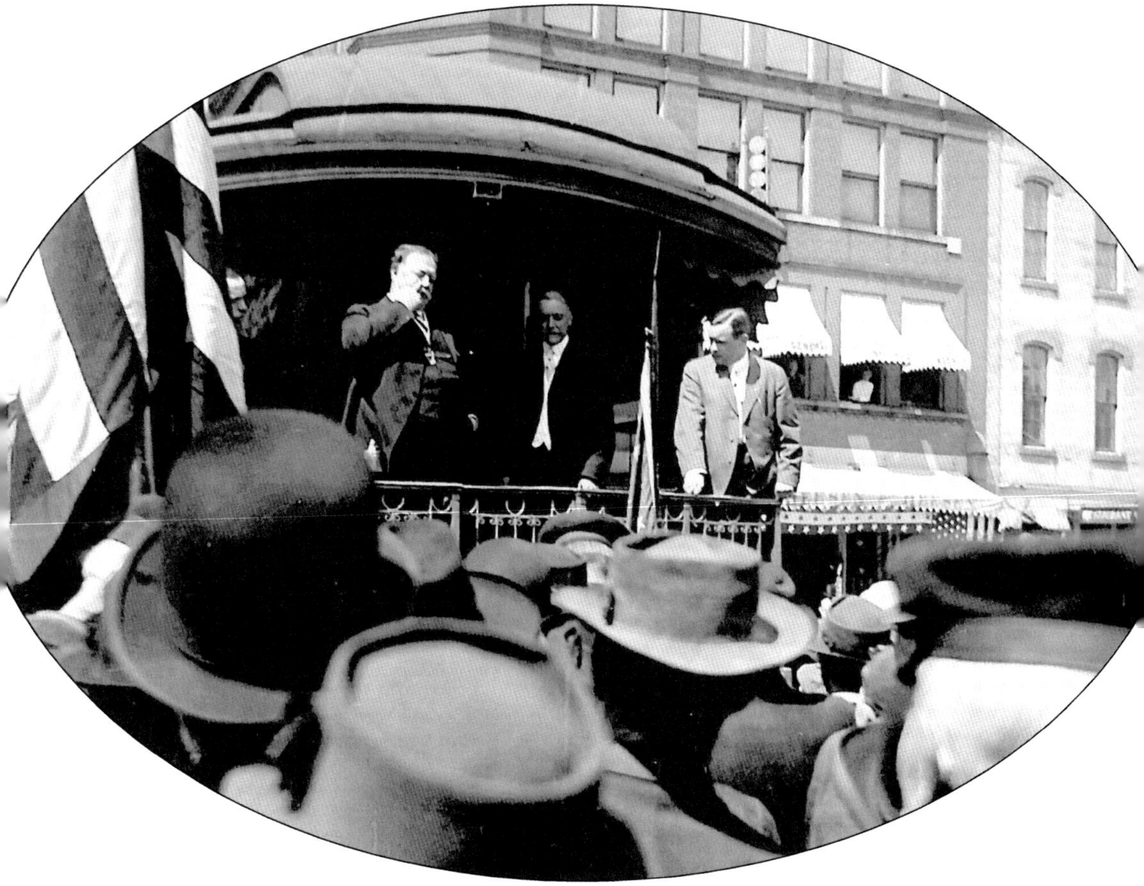

Reportedly President Taft was the most traveled president up to his time, and his travel schedule in 1910 seems to bear this out. Taft's itinerary included a trip to Bryan Mawr to see Helen Taft graduate, followed by a circuit of the Midwest, stopping in Monroe, Michigan, to unveil the Custer Monument, and then on to Jackson to speak with some of the surviving delegates from the first Republican Convention, who still lived in Jackson where the party was founded. He would then return to Yale to see his oldest son, Bob Taft, graduate.

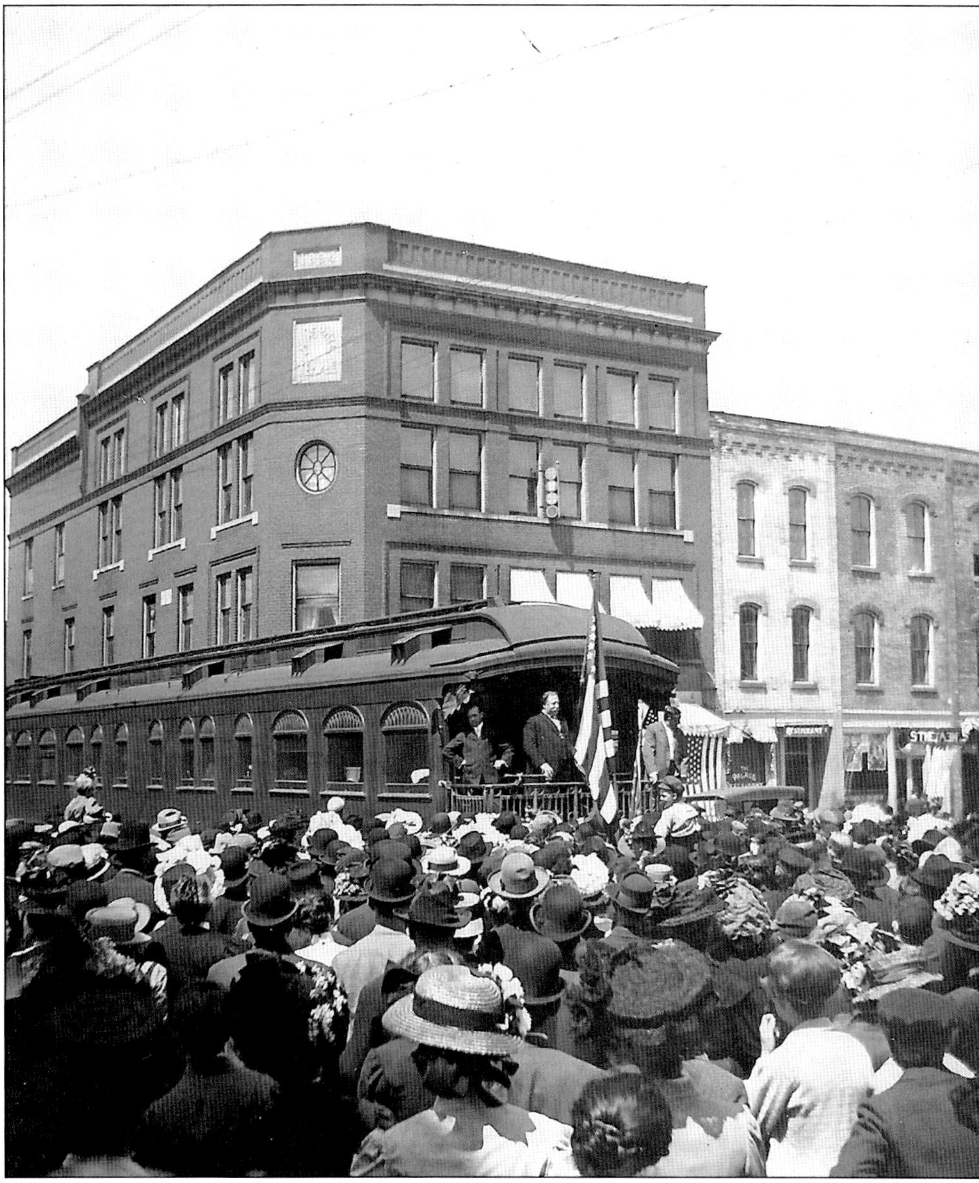

Taft was scheduled to be in Monroe, Michigan, on June 4, 1910, and to leave Jackson for Washington late on the evening of June 5. The trip between Monroe and Jackson passed through Tecumseh, and Taft stopped downtown for all of five minutes. A newspaper article of the time reads, "He came – we saw – The engine conquered for it whizzed the train away before the people were ready . . . President Taft was on the rear platform and was greeted with rousing cheers as he stepped forward for a 5 minute talk. It was brief but enough so we all can say 'We have seen and heard the President.'"

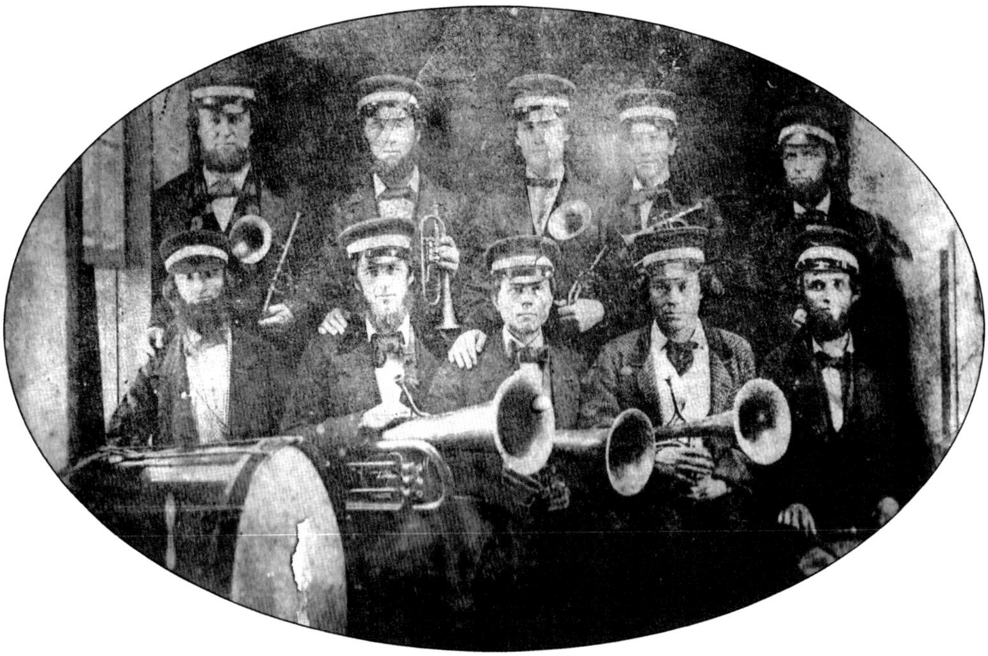

The Tecumseh Band members are, from left to right, (first row) Oscar Adams, Alfred James, ? Beers, Jerome Allan, and George Spafford; (back row) Fred Emerson, David Marshall, and three unidentified members. If these are the Alfred James and Jeptha Beers of prominence in Tecumseh history, that would date this picture sometime in the late 1850s or very early 1860s.

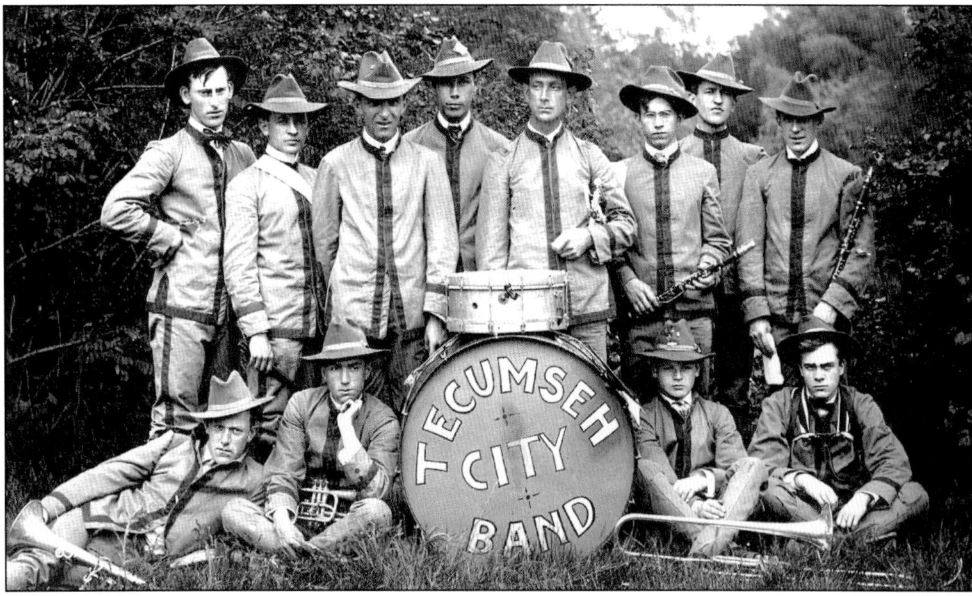

The Tecumseh City Band is photographed in the early 1900s. The band members are, from left to right, (first row) unidentified, Clare Camburn, Albert Skinner, and unidentified; (second row) Don Heesen, Bill Coller, Dell Finch, Clare Gillespie, Charles Skinner and three unidentified people. Clare Camburn later founded the Tecumseh Ladies Band, became the Tecumseh High School band director, and wrote the Tecumseh High School fight song. (Photograph courtesy of Ashley E. Chase.)

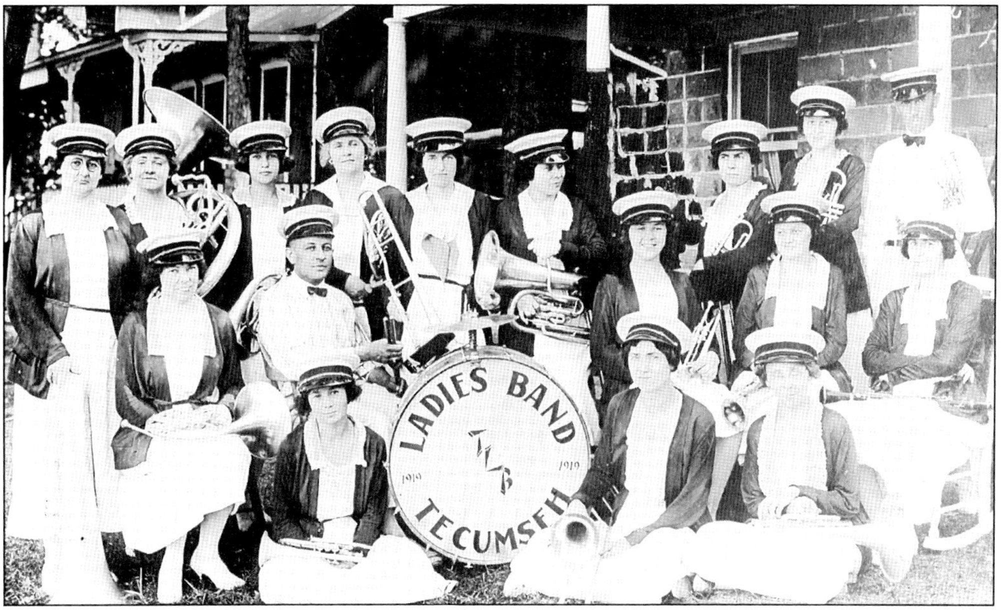

A Tecumseh Ladies Band was formed in 1882, but little is known of this organization. The Ladies Band shown here was founded in 1919 and was said to be the only ladies band in the state. The ladies band played at various concerts and as the pep band for high school events until a high school band was formed. Clare Camburn (center left with bowtie) was the band director and was instrumental in founding the band.

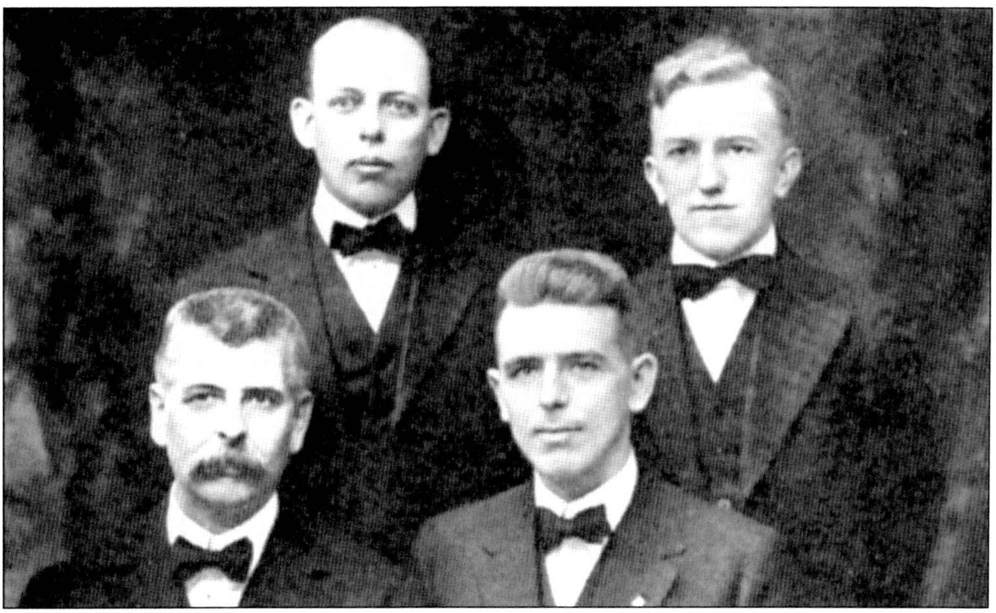
During World War I, a chapter of the Red Cross was formed in Tecumseh. One of the organization's most successful fund-raising efforts was the Red Cross Concert Company, which featured Louise Wood and Ella Hodges on piano and a singing quartette. This group, without piano accompaniment, was known as the Temple Quartette, photographed here in 1919. From left to right are (first row) father and son William S. Dickinson (first tenor) and Fred. C. Dickinson (second tenor); (second row) Floyd E. Juckette (bass) and Harold S. Lowry (baritone).

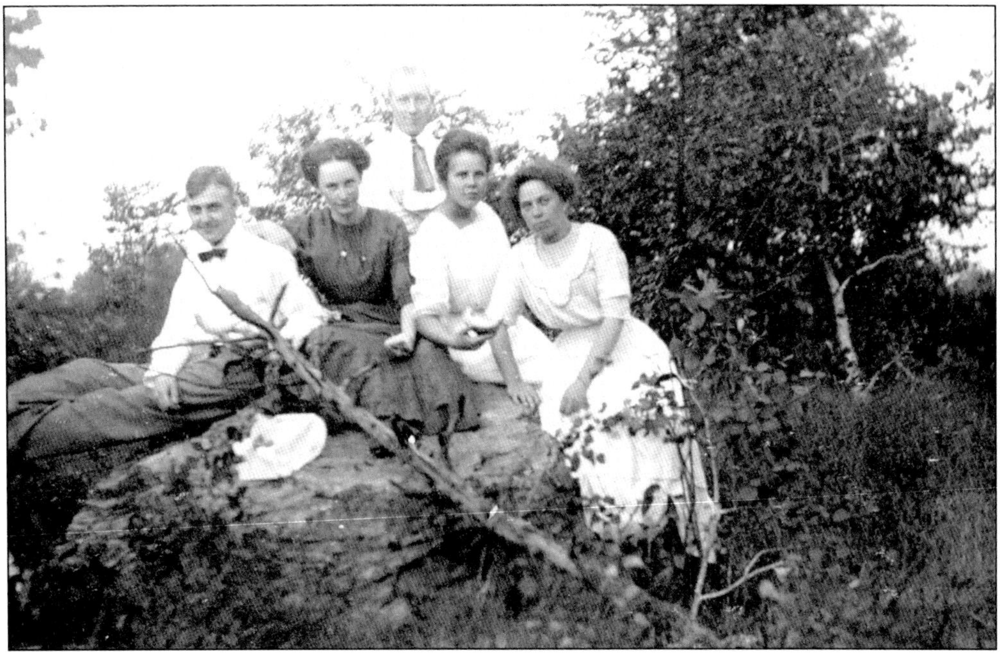

This undated photograph is of, from left to right, George Adamson, Florence Rosacrans-Adamson, an unidentified friend, Ruth K. Rosacrans, and another unidentified friend. In the late 1800s and early 1900s, the Adamson family owned a jewelry and book store in town, while the Rosacrans family owned a dry goods store.

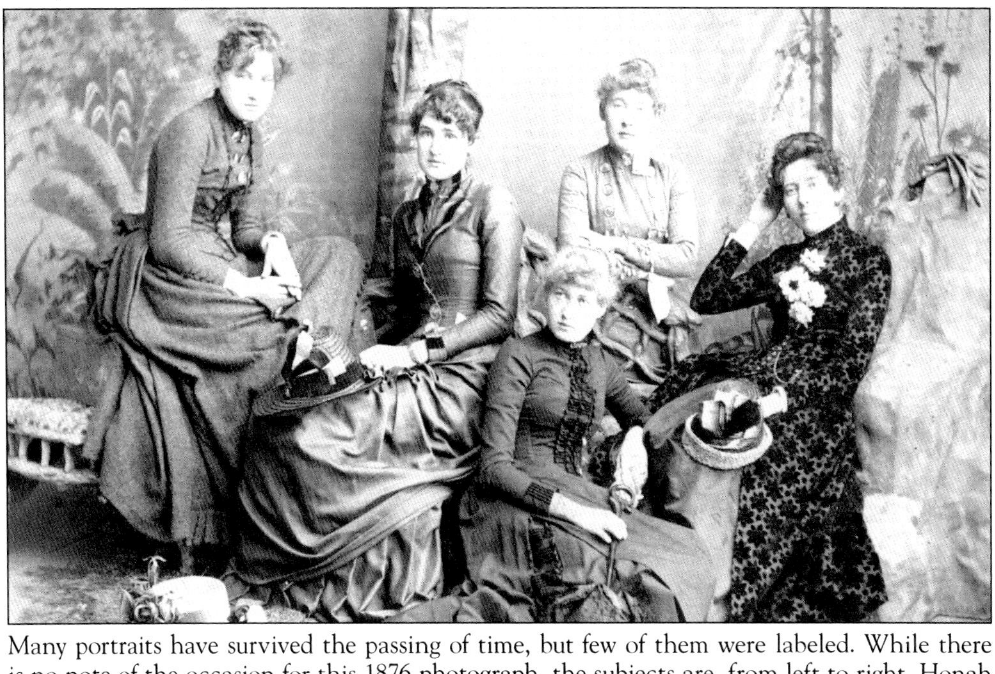

Many portraits have survived the passing of time, but few of them were labeled. While there is no note of the occasion for this 1876 photograph, the subjects are, from left to right, Honah Harsen-Meyer, Jennie Nyland-Tallman, Nell Harsen-Adamson, Nellie Nyland-Richmand, and Hena Harsen-Trann. The Adamson family owned a jewelry store downtown for over 30 years, and the Nyland family owned a successful shoe store.

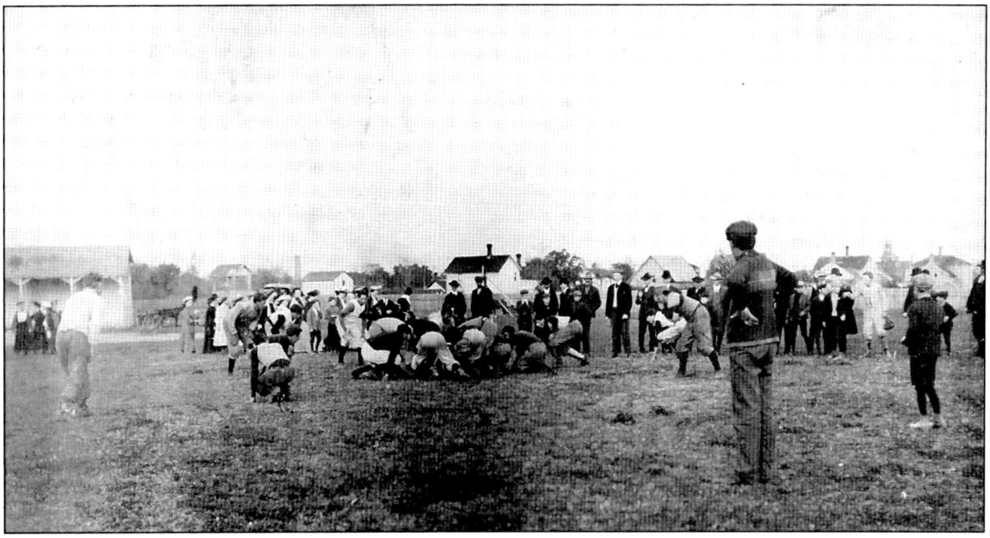

On April 24, 1907, the Lenawee County Athletic Association held its Third Annual Field Day in Tecumseh. The event brought together Lenawee County high schools and a few others outside of the county. Competitions included both team and individual sports and were primarily held at Athletic Park at the south end of Maiden Lane, while some track-and-field events were held at Bills Racing Park across town.

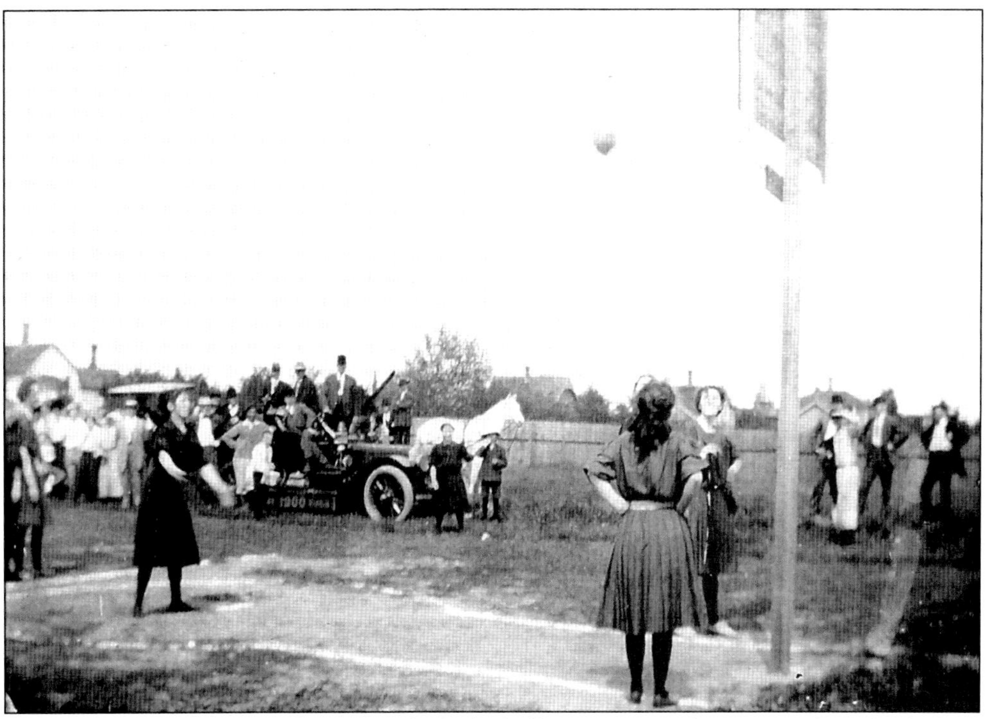

At the 1907 field day, Hudson won girls' basketball over Tecumseh, 10-4. In boys' basketball, Hudson again prevailed over Tecumseh, 15-7. Hudson also defeated Tecumseh at track and tug-of-war, although Fred Dickenson of Tecumseh won the hammer throw, and Rodger Waring of Tecumseh won the running broad jump.

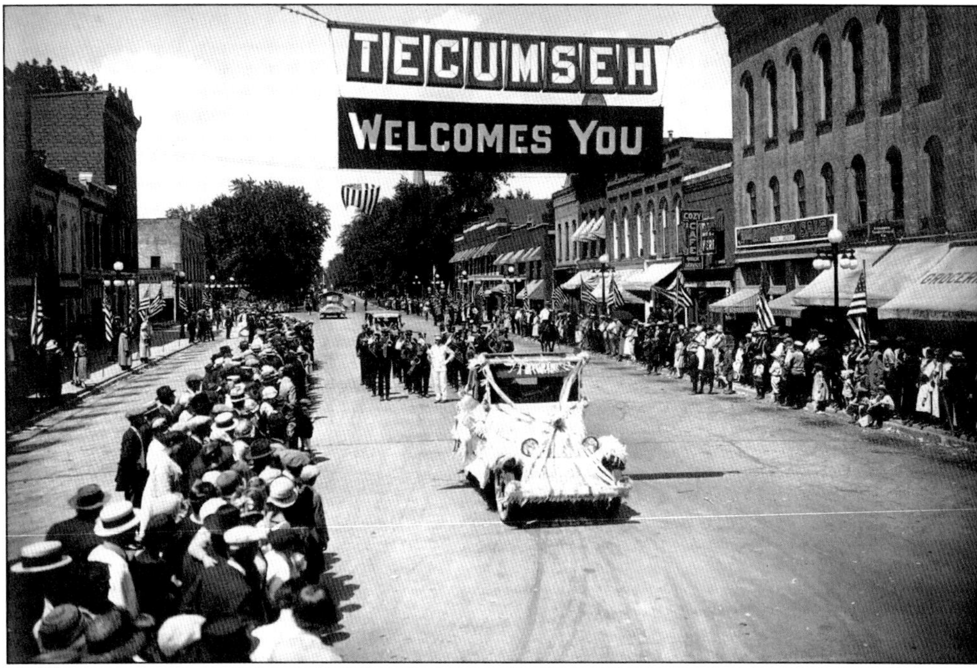

Newspaper reports of the Tecumseh 100th anniversary parade say that over 4,000 residents and guests from all over the country congregated along Chicago Boulevard to witness the opening ceremonies of the celebration, which consisted of a gala parade of floats, bands, decorated automobiles, and other entertainments. (Photograph courtesy of Lenawee Historical Museum.)

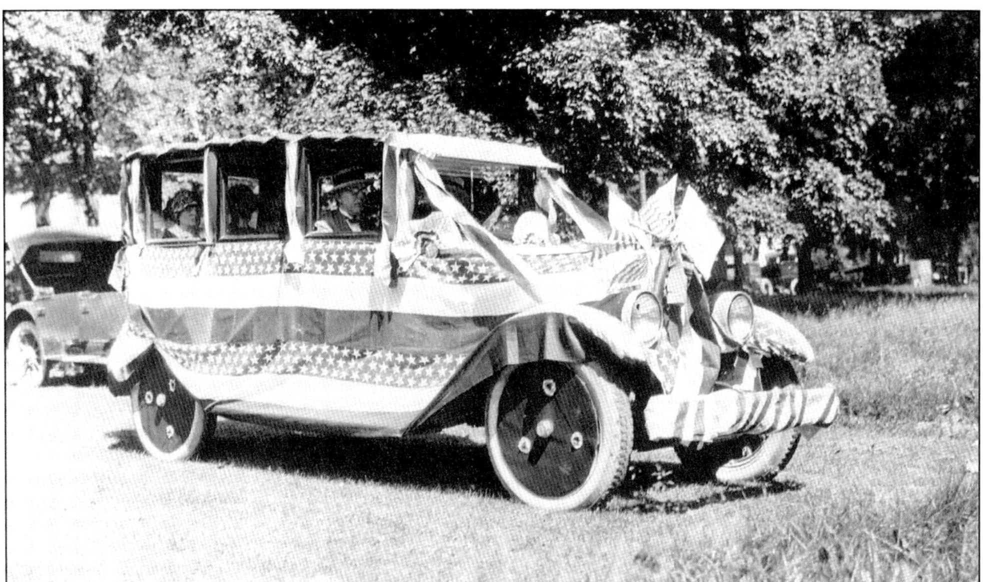

The 100th anniversary parade began at 11:00 a.m., Thursday, July 3, 1924. It was lead by J. H. Smith (executive committee chairman) and Mary F. Smith in a "gaily decorated car," followed by B. J. Pulver (shown here) with the remainder of the executive committee: Clarissa C. Reed, Mary C. Shull, and Mary Ives.

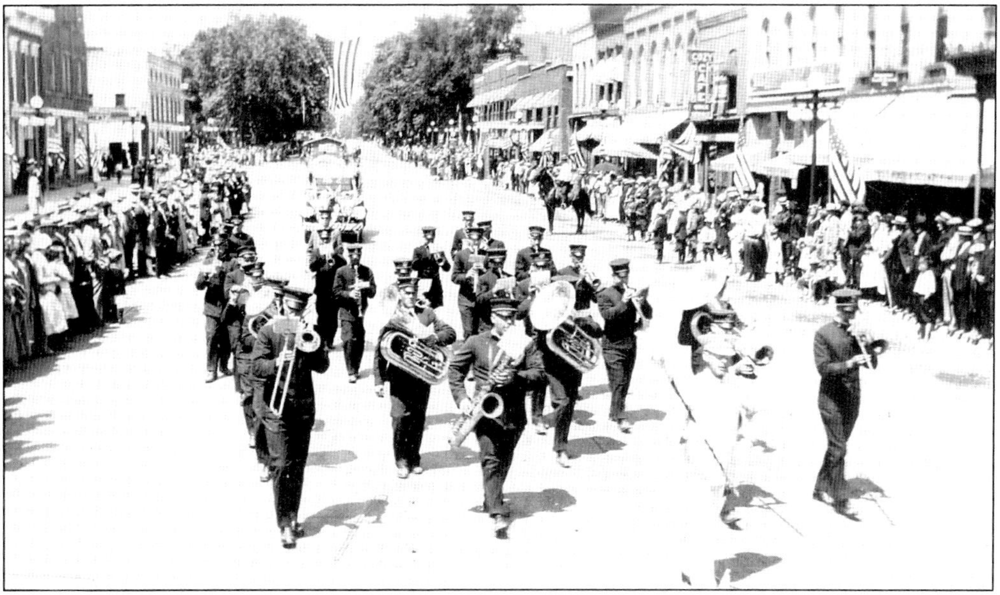

This photograph shows the Tipton Band marching in the 100th anniversary parade. Many nearby communities sent representative groups, bands, and floats to be a part of Tecumseh's celebration, including but not limited to Tipton, Clinton, and Adrian. Fifty-three guest performers from Clinton presented a pageant depicting the visit of Christopher Columbus to Queen Isabella, an event without which the settlement of Tecumseh could never have taken place.

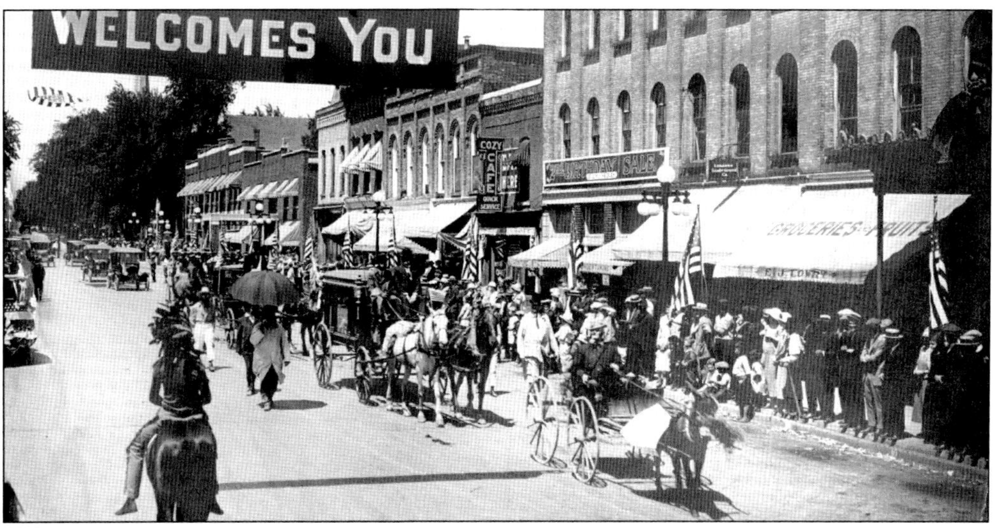

A newspaper of the time states that, "The closing event of the parade was the solemn and pathetic funeral of John Barley Corn who was carried along by his admirers in perfectly correct attire." Since John Barley Corn was symbolic of the barley grain and the beverages made from it, and since 1924 was but a few short years into Prohibition, the authors will let the readers draw their own conclusions regarding the symbolism of the parade's concluding procession.

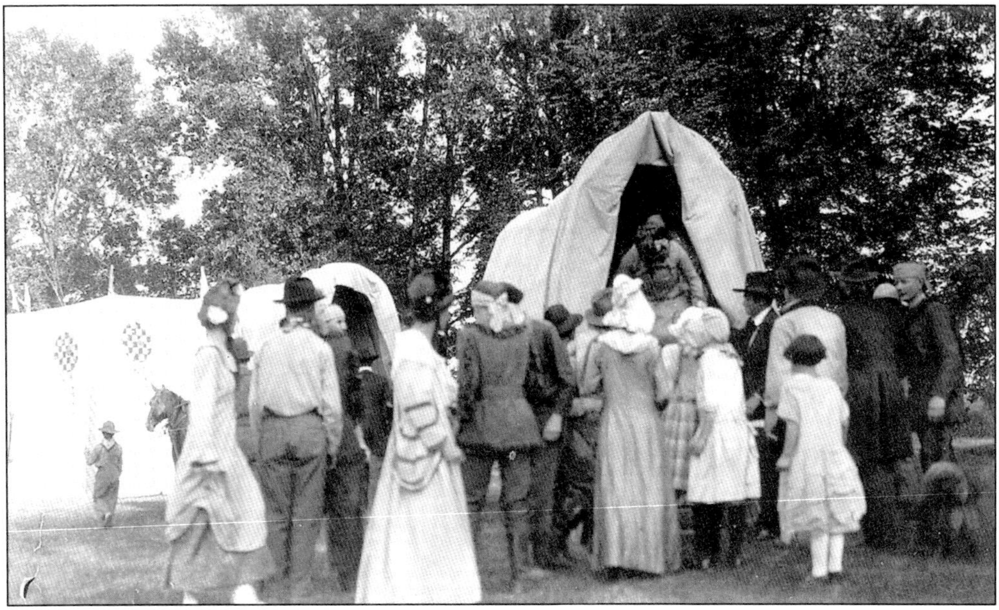

A large part of the 100th anniversary celebration was a pageant in eight acts presenting various patriotic themes, honoring the first residents of the area (the Pottawatomie), and depicted the arrival, challenges, and eventual success of the first settlers in Tecumseh. This photograph shows the first settlers arriving in Tecumseh after their overland trip from Monroe.

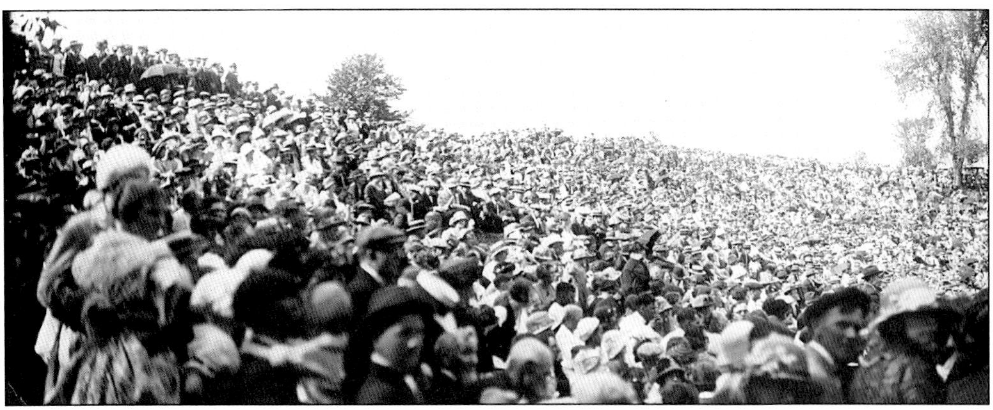

There were three presentations of the pageant, which had a cast of over 1,000 players. It was held in a natural amphitheater near the Hayden Mill. Shown here are some of the 8,000 residents and guests who watched "this remarkable play with perfect comfort," in "perfect proportions in a most beautiful and natural manner."

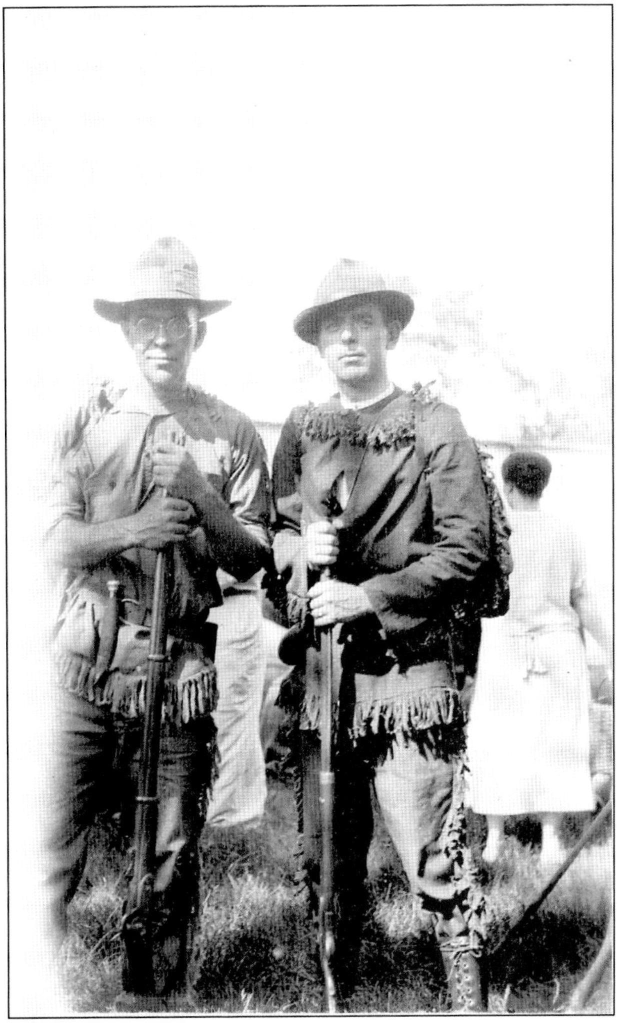

This photograph shows two of the players in the anniversary pageant, W. G. Waldron (left) playing the part of Musgrove Evans and F. C. Dickenson (right) as General Brown. The pageant, written by Mrs. C. H. Williamson and Mrs. Fred Dickenson, received rave reviews and boundless accolades.

BIBLIOGRAPHY

Hendershot, Philip. *Tecumseh the CD, Volume II.* 2003

Proctor, Diane E. *Beyond the Boulevard: Historic Buildings of Tecumseh, Michigan.* Tecumseh: The Tecumseh Area Historical Society, 1996

Waldron, Clara. *One Hundred Years – A Country Town.* Tecumseh: Thomas A. Riordan, 1968.